Fullness of Vision, Fullness of Life

Fullness of Vision, Fullness of Life

The Divided Brain, Improvisation and Leadership in the Church

Jonathan Kimber

scm press

© Jonathan Kimber 2025
Published in 2025 by SCM Press

Editorial office
3rd Floor, Invicta House,
110 Golden Lane,
London EC1Y 0TG, UK
www.scmpress.co.uk

SCM Press is an imprint of Hymns Ancient & Modern Ltd
(a registered charity)

Hymns Ancient & Modern® is a registered trademark of
Hymns Ancient & Modern Ltd
13A Hellesdon Park Road, Norwich,
Norfolk NR6 5DR, UK

All rights reserved. No part of this publication may be reproduced,
stored in a retrieval system, or transmitted,
in any form or by any means, electronic, mechanical,
photocopying or otherwise, without the prior permission of
the publisher, SCM Press.

The Author has asserted their right under the Copyright, Designs and
Patents Act 1988 to be identified as the Author of this Work

Scripture quotations are from the New Revised Standard Version Bible: Anglicized
Edition, copyright © 1989, 1995 National Council of the Churches of Christ in
the United States of America. Used by permission. All rights reserved worldwide.

British Library Cataloguing in Publication data

A catalogue record for this book is available
from the British Library

ISBN: 978-0-334-05914-1

EU GPSR Authorised Representative
LOGOS EUROPE, 9 rue Nicolas Poussin, 17000, LA ROCHELLE, France
E-mail: Contact@logoseurope.eu

Typeset by Regent Typesetting

To three faithful saints whose accompaniment on the path of life and faith has been particularly pivotal for me:
Roy Millar
Richard Kimber and
Robin Smith.

Contents

Foreword ix
Acknowledgements xi

1. Two Ways of Being   1
2. McGilchrist, Attention and Knowledge   13
3. The Clear-cut Left Hemisphere (LH): Simplified Mappings and Positive Purpose   30
4. The Holistic Right Hemisphere (RH)   45
5. Hemisphere Interaction and History   55
6. Further Foundations   81
7. The Bible, Theology and the Hemispheres   95
8. Making Sense of the Strategic Leadership Discourse (Church SLD)   109
9. Improvisation   131
10. Fullness of Vision, Fullness of Life   157

Bibliography and Further Reading   187
Index   191

Foreword

Leadership in churches is almost always difficult as well as immensely fulfilling. We learn this clearly from Scripture and the Christian tradition and if we are honest from our own experience. The difficulties are there for senior lay leaders, for incumbents, for archdeacons and bishops. As leaders we are called to watch over the church of God and to join in the mission of God and to help form disciples and ministers. The calling is one of great privilege and joy but will also stretch us beyond what we thought possible. Who is sufficient for these things?

Careful reflection on leadership is therefore a vital part of the work of every leader. *Fullness of Vision, Fullness of Life* offers a guide to this reflection on the leadership we offer. The book explores one of the (many) tensions in church leadership between offering on the one hand a strategic plan for the life of the community and on the other offering ministry which is life-giving.

This tension can be seen clearly in the local church every time a new round of mission action planning begins. It can be seen in the life of a diocese attempting to find fresh vision. It will be seen in ministry formation in what is taught and caught about leadership. It will be seen in the life of whole denominations in decisions about project funding and accountability and objectives.

Almost 30 years ago, I became Warden of Cranmer Hall in Durham and set out to create a new course on Christian Leadership and Ordained Ministry, bringing into the course many of the insights from my own parish ministry and what this book calls the Church Strategic Leadership Discourse (SLD). I noticed that, as Jonathan describes here, some of the students from certain traditions saw the exercise of this kind of leadership as life-giving and absolutely central to the ministry to which God had called them.

But others from different traditions found the material much more challenging: they saw themselves as called to be priests, not strategic leaders. They found targets and objectives and measurement very alien to that calling: life-sapping rather than life-giving. The challenges the early groups of students offered (including Jonathan) led to a complete revision of my own thinking on leadership and of the courses which emerged – for which I remain deeply thankful.

I've found a similar tension in seeking to develop statements of plans and visions both in the Diocese of Sheffield and the Diocese of Oxford. How can those visions and strategies genuinely be life-giving and serve the mission of God? There continues to be a vigorous debate in the Church of England about the formation of senior leaders. Some believe there is a deficit in forming senior leaders in planning and strategic thinking, and have developed programmes to support this. Others believe, with equal passion, that the main deficit is in forming leaders who are able who are deeply rooted in Scripture and the tradition and are able to be channels of life and grace from these deeper wells.

The Church of England developed a new national vision and strategy for the current decade to be a church which is Jesus Christ-centred and shaped by the Five Marks of Mission. This vision has three priorities and six bold (and measurable) outcomes. There is a vigorous and ongoing debate around the programme of strategic development funding which aims to make these outcomes a reality for the church by 2030.

When does such a vision and strategy bring life, inspiring the people of God to greater creativity and releasing energy for the common good? And when does such a strategy risk becoming oppressive and place too great a burden on clergy and congregations?

Fullness of Vision, Fullness of Life explores all of these very familiar tensions and brings new insights to bear. In particular, Jonathan introduces very clearly and explores the seminal work of Iain McGilchrist and his understanding of the way in which our brains work differently through the right and left hemispheres – each serving a different arm of this tension.

Jonathan encourages his readers to see the tension between vision and life not as an either/or but as a tension to be negotiated and lived through the prioritization of the holistic insights of the right hemisphere and a continual process of wise improvisation and reflection. The book therefore gifts the reader with a new pair of spectacles with which to see the task and challenge of church leadership. *Fullness of Vision, Fullness of Life* is an accessible work of scholarship with very significant practical implications for the life of the church in parishes, dioceses and nationally, and I commend it to you very warmly indeed.

Steven Croft, Bishop of Oxford

Acknowledgements

This book would not have come into being were it not for the wisdom, support and sheer kindness of many people. I am deeply grateful to the wide range of writers whose works have shaped my perception and understanding, not least to those who are quoted or referenced within these pages. Among these, Jeremy Begbie's detailed and inspiring work on the interface between music and theology inspires a central strand of my work, and continues to add depth and vitality to my living. And the impact of Iain McGilchrist's magisterial inter-disciplinary research and thinking, on this book and on my understanding of life and faith, is in proportion to its own scale and clarity of insight.

Martyn Percy was my main supervisor for the doctoral work at King's College London which gave initial shape to the thinking underlying this book. I am especially grateful to Martyn, both for his unwavering reassurance and encouragement to persevere in the early stages of my research, and also for his very brief email in November 2011 (23 months into the doctorate) suggesting that I might like to have a look at a recent book by Iain McGilchrist.

I am grateful to many friends, former colleagues and course participants over my years in the Diocese of Worcester, conversations with whom helped deepen and clarify my understanding: not least Alison Maddocks, Andrew Preece, Emma Sykes, John Fitzmaurice, John Inge, John Preston, Nikki Groarke, Simon Hill and Stuart Currie. Special thanks go to those who read and commented on drafts of my writing at various stages, including Doug Chaplin, Emma Woollaston, my brother Paul Kimber, and my father, Richard Kimber. Among those who read drafts, David Sims deserves special credit for his generosity of time and spirit, integrating truthfulness and deep encouragement.

I am very grateful to all who have worked with me from and via the editorial team at SCM Press: David Shervington, Rachel Edge, Rachel Geddes, Linda Carroll, Meg Davies and Richard Pearson. Again, your combination of kindness and clarity has been just what was needed at all stages.

The process of thinking, researching and writing underlying this book has occupied a significant strand of my life since 2004, with only a few intermissions. Whatever gift it may offer to its readers would simply never have come into existence were it not for the commitment and generosity of my wife and best friend, Lynne, for whose practical help, moral support and belief in the project I am deeply thankful.

I

Two Ways of Being

You look out of your window. A chaffinch is carefully picking up small seeds from the garden path. Its activity requires detailed focus, as the seeds are interspersed among small pebbles. The chaffinch pecks carefully for a couple of seconds, then raises its head and looks around. The alternating pattern is repeated: peck, then scan; peck, then scan. What motivates this behaviour? On the one hand, the bird needs to eat, and so focuses on acquiring the seed for its purposes; on the other hand, the bird needs to not be eaten, and therefore scans the environment for possible predators. Peck, then scan; peck, then scan.

The two components to the behaviour are contrasting and complementary. The first – the peck – involves narrow, focused attention. This focus is linked to action that completes a desired task (getting and eating the seed). The second – the scan – involves a quite different form of attention: a broad awareness, alert, sustained and open. This attention is open to the reality of whatever it finds (be that predator, potential mate, or approaching thunderstorm). Survival of the chaffinch requires *both* modes of attending and acting. It needs to eat. It also needs to avoid being eaten. Both modes are necessary: peck, then scan; peck, then scan. Focus, then openness; narrowness, then breadth.

As well as differing forms of attention, the chaffinch also shows two contrasting ways of relating to what is around it. When pecking, it reaches out in order to acquire something (a seed): to take hold of it, to grasp it for itself. It reaches out in order to obtain or achieve something that it knows it wants. By contrast, when scanning rather than pecking, it is initially simply open to whatever shows itself (predator, mate, more seed). The subsequent response then varies, depending on the nature and intention of whatever came into view.

In each case, the form of attention and the way of relating are interlinked and offer a way of being in the world. In this simple activity of the chaffinch, we encounter two contrasting and complementary ways of being, two different approaches to the world. In one of them, characterized by pecking, the chaffinch has a narrow tunnel of attention, focused on the task of acquiring something the bird already knows that it wants. This is one way of being in the world. It stands in clear distinction from the second approach. This second way of being, seen in the scanning, is not framed as a task to complete, but is a much more open attentiveness to whatever else is there. A response will follow, and it will be a response to whatever is encountered, be that food, friend or foe.

The chaffinch needs to be able to call on both of these ways of being. Both are required for its life to continue.[1] And both are needed and deployed not only by chaffinches, but by the vast majority of animals, not least human beings.

These two approaches to the world will together form one of the central strands in the developing understanding offered by this book. The chaffinch's behaviour offers a simple first taste of these two ways of being. A fuller picture will begin to develop with our second cameo.

A meal with friends

You've been invited, with others, to visit long-standing friends for dinner. After some initial conversation, your hosts usher you through for the meal. As you enter the dining room, a beautifully prepared table comes into view. Napkins, mats and cutlery have been painstakingly arranged with a pleasing symmetry, complemented by a floral arrangement gracing the centre of the table. You smile, and your shoulders relax. You appreciate the care that has obviously been taken, further heightening your anticipation of an enjoyable evening. Fast forward to the end of the gathering, as you leave your hosts and travel home. If the only positive you can find about the occasion is the pleasingly symmetrical initial arrangement of the cutlery, we can assume that the evening did not go well. We hope, instead, that it will have been a rich experience, in which the shared good food offered a great starting point for enjoyable conversation, and for the deepening of friendships old and new.

A meal with friends, and the two ways of being

It may not initially be obvious, but in this shared meal we can discern exactly the same two ways of being that the chaffinch deployed. Rather than a simple alternating rhythm between the two, however, there is much more interweaving and overlap. It's worth slowing down, therefore, and highlighting them separately.

Let's start by considering the narrow-beamed focus involved in pecking, with purposeful action directed towards completing a task. This clarity will have been used, for instance, in setting the date and time for the gathering, and making sure that everyone was invited. It will have been called upon in making decisions about what food to serve, and completing the tasks involved in its preparation. The mindset of precise action and task completion will have helped construct the beautiful table arrangement. And when you and the other guests picked up your cutlery to eat your meal, you will have used that same approach and way of being to collect food from your plate and deposit it in your mouth.

You and others will also have drawn on the broad, vigilant attention of the second way of being through many periods of the evening. For instance, on arrival, you are likely to have scanned (to some extent) each room you entered. In doing so you will have taken in something of its contents and décor (perhaps registering any changes since your last visit). You will also have sensed the tone and energy of the social interaction of the people already in the room. You will have repeated this scanning of the social environment throughout the evening, as conversation has ebbed and flowed, perhaps shifting from small groups chatting standing up, to some times of general conversation around the meal table. There may be another guest with whom you are particularly keen to speak. There could be another guest you would prefer to avoid. You may pick up that someone seems more subdued than normal, and look for an opportunity to come alongside quietly. In several of these possibilities we see a further feature of the second way of being: the desire to connect with others, and to relate with them. This desire for connection and relationship links well with this second mode of attention: it wants to see reality as it is, and engage with it (and with the people in it) as appropriate, rather than take hold of it and manipulate it for its own purposes. We also see a further associated feature: it is this second mode that is more skilled and comfortable at being flexible and responsive (for instance, to people and to the gradual unfolding of events), rather than sticking with a pre-planned, purposeful agenda. Overall, then, these are some of the ways in which the same two broad ways of being that we observed in the chaffinch will have been in action throughout the evening.

A meal with friends – the interaction between the two ways of being

As well as noting the contrast between the two approaches, the relationship between them deserves attention. With the meal scenario, their relating was much more sophisticated than in the chaffinch cameo. One aspect of their interaction is the pattern of their deployment over time. With the chaffinch, this was a simple alternating rhythm, with the two modes taking it in turns, one at a time. With the meal, the pattern was more complex. Here, there was fluid interweaving between the approaches, and they often overlapped, for instance when those present were eating and listening at the same time.

Importantly, the relationship between the two modes also included the first approach serving the purposes of the second way of being. The primary overall aim of the evening was the hosts' desire, shared by the guests, for the deepening of relationship. They hoped to enable an evening in which all present could join in with rich conversation, with grace and laughter, with friendship and togetherness. This aim is much more closely aligned with the second way of being, notably with its desire to relate, connecting with people just as they are at this moment in time. This priority was greatly helped by the actions of the first way of being: setting the date, contributing to the food preparation, completing the precise task of making the symmetrical table arrangement and so on.

Naming the two modes

These two approaches, these two modes or ways of being, together form a central ongoing strand throughout this book. It is high time that we named them.

Clear-cut is the term I will use for the first way of being – the chaffinch focused on pecking seed from the path. (Throughout the book, when I use this word in capitalized form, I am using it as a label for this way of being in the world.) As we will see, near the heart of a Clear-cut approach is the action of separating one thing from another – making 'a clear cut'. When the chaffinch attends to the seeds with narrow focus, it mentally separates those seeds from everything else (such as the nearby pebbles). When your hosts were preparing for the evening, they drew a metaphorical dividing line between those who were invited and those who weren't. They clarified which food they would serve, and that which they wouldn't. Clear-cut questions include, 'Is it one of these, or one of those? Is it seed, or is it gravel?', 'Have all the guests arrived?', 'Yes or no?' Overall, the Clear-cut is characterized by clarity, by purpose and by focus. It likes to get a grip on things. With each situation that it encounters, whatever its nature, it tends to construe it as a problem to solve, or as a task to complete. It then focuses the narrow beam of its purpose onto that task or problem, ideally until a Clear-cut solution or completion has been achieved. At this point, a Clear-cut response of 'Yes!' can be offered to the Clear-cut question 'Have we finished?'

Holistic is my label for the second way of being – the chaffinch looking around, surveying its context. In this mode, attention is open, vigilant and broad. Whereas the Clear-cut focuses on what is done, the Holistic attends especially to the manner in which it is done. Whereas Clear-cut attention has a bias towards things, and especially what is man-made, Holistic attention is drawn to the living and personal. The Holistic is also attuned not just to separate entities (living or inanimate) but also to relationships between them: the quality of those relationships, and also their ebb and flow, or their absence. The Holistic perspective not only includes the visible and explicit, but also registers subtle shifts in aspects that can never be fully articulated (such as facial expression, tone of voice, body language and the energy in the room). It seeks to attend to reality as it is, and then to relate to that which is around it, with openness and curiosity. It prioritizes understanding and connection over impact and control. Holistic attention takes in an overall 'Gestalt' sense, in which the interconnected whole is more than just the sum of its parts.

We noted earlier that the chaffinch needs to be able to access the specialized skills of both ways of being. It needs ready access to a Clear-cut approach in order to be able to eat, and a Holistic approach to avoid being eaten (and indeed to perpetuate the species). As with chaffinches, so with humans: we all need at least some level of facility with both of these approaches. You may already be beginning to recognize activities which draw more on one or the other. You may possibly be noticing something of a preference towards one or the other, whether in yourself or in other people. I hope that, at least in broad outline, you are beginning to recognize each way of being, to gain a sense of it.

These, then, are the Clear-cut and the Holistic approaches to reality, both of which we need. There is more to say about them, individually and in relationship, and questions about them may already be arising for you. We will return shortly to a fuller development of their basis, their interaction and their impact. For now, however, we press pause, registering and holding the ground we've covered. For it is now time to step back and address the broader question of what this book is about. Responding to that question will begin to explain why I have commenced by introducing these two ways of being, the Holistic and the Clear-cut.

What this book is about – the particular and the general

The content of this book

On the one hand, the content of this book is very general. Already we've seen it connecting with the daily habits of chaffinches, and with attractive table decoration. It relates to how we go about engaging in life itself and participating with others as we do so. As a consequence, its relevance is remarkably broad.

And yet, on the other hand, it began its journey in response to something very particular – questions around leadership in the church. This subject, the understanding and practice of church leadership, is a specific focus. In particular, I will be exploring an understanding of church leadership that has arisen since around 1970 and become widespread. This understanding gives an important place to issues of vision and strategy, to plans and measurable objectives. I will refer to this approach as the Church Strategic Leadership Discourse, or Church SLD for short. The second of the book's four sections gives an overview of the background and key features of the SLD. And it is with respect to leadership in the church that this book will flesh out and apply its more general considerations, in its fourth and final section.

The specific area of church leadership, then, is the main domain in which I explore the outworking and impact of what I'm discussing. However, most of this book's content is applicable well beyond that territory. For a start, most of the theory and practice that we encounter in the Church SLD is also widespread in approaches to leadership in many other sectors. (Indeed, many sectors engaged with such an approach rather earlier than the church did, and some of these have since substantially moved on from it.) But that's not all: the perspective will also offer insight well beyond the domain of leadership. However, the area of leadership in the life of the church will form the specific territory on which most of the book's examples will be worked out. This is primarily because it was through my engagement with leadership in the church that I first encountered the perspectives I will introduce.

The story behind the book's beginnings

Matters of church leadership first began to engage my attention during my theological college training as a Church of England vicar (1999–2002), and in the early years of my parish ministry. I served in Northampton as a curate from 2002 to 2005, then as a vicar (or equivalent) of a large suburban parish, on the other side of the town, from 2005 to 2015. I had previously graduated in mathematics, and worked for seven years in commercial computing, during which time I had begun to develop an interest in leadership more generally. Following my parish ministry, I served as Director of Ministry and Discipleship for the Diocese of Worcester, from 2015 to 2023. A crystallizing experience for me happened at an early stage of my time as a vicar: my 2007 engagement in a diocesan course, entitled 'Godly Leadership', spread over a calendar year. The course approach was centred on the creation of a parish vision, from which we should create or discern measurable objectives, then plans, leading to action. I was especially struck by two aspects of my overall experience of the course.

The first thing that struck me was how the cohort members responded to the course material in very different ways. One group seemed to find the approach advocated straightforwardly helpful, and to welcome 'the whole package' as a promising way forwards. A second group were typified by Ben,[2] a 'mid-career' vicar: sensible, competent and committed to the handful of rural parishes he served. As he and I left the final session together to drive home, his first words were: 'What a relief that's over! Now I can get back to being a parish priest.' It's not that Ben was stuck in the past. Rather, the material, as presented, simply hadn't proved convincing to him. The third group sat somewhere in between the other two. They weren't convinced by the whole package, and yet they could see value in some of the practices. I got the sense they would hold the overall approach lightly, but would still incorporate, in a fairly intuitive way, a selection of the recommendations into their ministry. I found myself intrigued to observe these three broad shapes of reaction.

The second striking feature was that this approach was commended by means of assertion. We were told that this was what we should do, but I remember no depth of explanation as to why. In particular, there was little (if any) attempt to connect the practicalities under discussion with the broad realm of Christian theology. This was epitomized in a memorable exchange with one of the course speakers. A self-supporting minister in the Church of England, his 'day job' was as chief executive of a very large public-sector organization. From early in the course, we were encouraged to look forward to his visit within the final residential, and to the inspiration we were likely to receive from his input. After sharing some broad introductory material, he opened up the session for discussion. Keen to make the most of his presence, and to hear rather more of the depth of his wisdom, I asked what felt like an obvious question: 'When it comes to leadership, what do you think the church can learn from the world of business, and what can the world of business learn from the church?' His response: 'I haven't really thought about that.'

I found myself intrigued by these two phenomena: the diversity of participants' responses, and the lack of substantial engagement between the material presented and the Christian tradition. My curiosity had been snared – and so I came to embark on a doctorate to explore these issues. My hope was that I might at least contribute to enabling some depth of conversation between the two 'sides' apparent on the course. The first step was to immerse myself in the literature. I began to absorb seemingly countless books on 'How to be a vicar', written since about 1970. Trends and patterns were discernible, but hard to describe. It wasn't obvious how to connect the newer approaches with any depth of theology. Genuine traction and conversation seemed elusive. I felt I was swimming in treacle, with my head only just above the surface.

It was two years into my research (late 2011) that my supervisor[3] emailed to suggest I might like to look at the recently published *The Master and His Emissary*, by the philosopher and neuroscientist Iain McGilchrist.[4] It very quickly became clear that McGilchrist's work offered a perspective that helped me both describe and make sense of the developments in which I had been immersed. It shone fresh light on both the newer trends, and the divergent reactions to them. Moreover, McGilchrist's perspective also offered clues as to how all that was good within the newer approaches might constructively be integrated with what had gone before, leading to deeper and richer ministerial leadership.

It was clear that McGilchrist's neuroscientific insights were relevant to what I was observing in the realm of church leadership. His work became my primary conversation partner in developing and completing my doctoral thesis. It was also very obvious, however, that the illumination offered by McGilchrist's perspective extended well beyond the realm of leadership, whether in the church or elsewhere. Indeed, it brings insight and opens possibilities in almost every area of our participation in life, both as individuals and with others. And so we return to the fact that this book is both very general in its relevance, and also very particular in where it primarily shows some working out of that relevance. As a consequence, I can helpfully describe in several different ways, from different angles, what this book will offer.

What this book seeks to offer

First, this book shines a neuroscientific light on life in general, and on church life in particular. It offers an introduction to one major understanding of neuroscience, and fleshes out how this understanding can help bring more richness and joy to our lives. It also includes exploration of the considerable resonance between this neuroscience and Christian theology.

From a different angle, this book puts a case for the need to rebalance dialogue around leadership. As we will see, there are very understandable reasons why, in many discussions of leadership practice, Clear-cut voices have often seemed most convincing. Not only does this book illuminate why this is the case. It also spells out why rebalancing the dialogue – or indeed having a dialogue in the first place – is so important. A rebalanced dialogue about leadership (and about life) continues to give careful attention to a Clear-cut perspective, but will often involve increasing the value accorded to a Holistic point of view.

Overall, what this book offers is an understanding, and a way of seeing. The perspective it describes is relevant to all of life – and I focus especially on how it relates to life in the church. This way of seeing does not prescribe a method to follow, or offer a solution (and some may find this frustrating). It does, however, draw attention to significant patterns: some that are life-giving, and others to avoid. (I also refer to a range of work by other writers, inspired by a similar perspective, several of whom have developed templates to guide practical application.[5]) This book pays attention not just to what we do in the life of the church (and elsewhere), but also to the manner in which we do it. Moreover, the nature of the attention that we pay itself turns out to be of foundational importance.

The book's title begins with the phrase 'fullness of vision'. By this I mean both something general, and also something specific. In general terms, fullness of vision is about richness, depth and perspective. It's about a spaciousness of perception, that offers room for both clarity and complexity, and doesn't seek to shut down or foreshorten.

As well as this general meaning, I also intend a specific sense of the term 'fullness of vision'. Such fullness of vision comes from learning to integrate well the Clear-cut and the Holistic approaches. We will explore the patterns that enable such healthy integration. I personally want to grow in fullness of vision, whether I am attending to the present, the past or what the future might hold. And I want to grow in my capacity to offer fullness of vision as I interact with individual people, with groups and organizations and with all that I encounter.

Fullness of vision is followed by fullness of life – within the book's title, and often in experience. Importantly, while my own growing fullness of vision will frequently enable greater fullness of life for me, I will not be the only beneficiary. Rather, the life-giving impact will extend to all with whom I engage.

The previous paragraphs are true when considering the human and natural realm. And they carry even more truth when our fullness of vision incorporates God within its perspective. Additionally, all of this is true at an individual level, and even more true at a communal level. The more that any group can inhabit and offer fullness of vision in how its members engage with life, the more its attending and relating (within the group, and beyond its boundaries) are likely to share in the fullness of life and love that continually flow from God.

Concluding comments

What this book will explore, then, are insights and patterns that contribute towards such fullness of vision, and such fullness of life. Before setting off to do so, four comments are worth making.

First, when I write about leadership in 'the church', I am referring first and foremost to the Church of England. Although my initial Christian upbringing was in the Presbyterian Church in Northern Ireland, it is in the Church of England that I have worshipped and served since my early twenties, and within which I am ordained. Much of the Church SLD writing to which I refer arises from a Church of England context, and some of the research is exclusively focused within the C of E. This is the church domain which I know best.

The reach of the SLD, however, extends well beyond the Church of England. Its origins arguably lie in the USA, and key influences along the way have come from (and extended to) a range of denominations. I have not researched the extent of Church SLD influence within different denominations, and so I won't comment beyond the Church of England.

Nevertheless, I hope that readers from a wide range of backgrounds will find plenty in this book relevant to their circumstances, and can make appropriate adjustments as necessary – whether in the life of the church or elsewhere.

Second, leadership is not just about clergy. I am recommending a form of leadership that welcomes and incorporates the varied gifts, skills and experience of many. One characteristic of such leadership is that it prioritizes involving others in shaping the life of the community. Clergy do often have an important role in shaping the leadership approach, but the content of this book is relevant to all involved in the life of the church.

Third, the chapters ahead draw substantially on neuroscience – but not on all of it. For now, let me register that the important considerations and questions of neurodiversity lie beyond the scope of this book.[6]

Fourth, I confess I have something of a love–hate relationship with the word 'leadership'. Leadership is very much a 'contested concept'[7]: different people have very different understandings of what it should involve. Much harm can be done by some versions of (what some consider to be) 'good leadership', however well-intentioned. In brief for now, if you are not overly keen on the idea of leadership, and especially if you don't think of yourself as a leader (for whatever reason), I would encourage you to read on. (And please also keep reading if you are an enthusiast for leadership, however you currently understand it.) The concept of leadership highlights important territory for our consideration, and I don't want to let go of it. But part of the point of this book is to raise awareness of what we currently think and assume about leadership, and to explore alternative ways in which it might helpfully operate. In order to begin to do so, we turn first to explore the neuroscientific perspective of Iain McGilchrist.

Notes

1 The idea for this cameo arose from the RSA ANIMATE video 'The Divided Brain', which summarizes in less than 12 minutes much of what this first section of the book is about. See RSA, 2011, 'RSA ANIMATE: The Divided Brain', *YouTube*, 21 October, www.youtube.com/watch?v=dFs9WO2B8uI, accessed 30.01.2025.

2 Not his real name.

3 The Very Revd Professor Martyn Percy, at that time Principal of Ripon College, Cuddesdon.

4 Iain McGilchrist, 2009, *The Master and His Emissary: The Divided Brain and the Making of the Western World*, New Haven, CT: Yale University Press.

5 I do so primarily in Chapter 10.

6 For some of McGilchrist's perspective pertaining to this area, see his chapter 'What Schizophrenia and Autism Can Tell Us' in Iain McGilchrist, 2021, *The Matter With Things*, London: Perspective Press, pp. 305–70.

7 For a brief introduction to contested concepts, see Keith Grint, 2005, *Leadership: Limits and Possibilities*, Basingstoke: Palgrave Macmillan, pp. 17–19.

2

McGilchrist, Attention and Knowledge

By the end of Chapter 5, we should have a good grasp of the core principles of Iain McGilchrist's neuroscientific perspective. These four chapters will introduce us to some brain science, but not too much – the only technical term it's important to remember is 'hemisphere', of which the brain has two. These are commonly termed the 'left hemisphere' and the 'right hemisphere', which I will frequently abbreviate to LH and RH respectively. Before turning to McGilchrist and his work, it makes sense to begin with a short introduction to the brain, its hemispheres, and some sense of how we know about them.

Initial introduction to brain hemispheres

As early as the third century BC, people have been interested in the difference between the two hemispheres of the human brain, for it has long been clear that the brain is not symmetrical.[1] Some of the differences are relatively easy to observe (in appropriate circumstances):

- The right hemisphere is consistently found to be larger than the left one: longer, wider and heavier.
- The two hemispheres have different numbers of neurons; the individual neuron cells are of different sizes; and there is a different amount of connectivity between cells and brain areas. (It is the right hemisphere that has more cells connecting *across* brain regions.)

Additionally, the two hemispheres have different degrees of sensitivity to specific hormones, and to particular medical drugs. They also primarily respond to different neurotransmitters.

Chemical and physical hemisphere differences such as these are relatively accessible. This is much less the case with questions of hemisphere function and disposition: what does each hemisphere do, and in what manner does it go about doing it? We now turn to an overview of how knowledge and understanding has been gained in this whole area. This will give us a feel both for some of the issues involved in interpreting hemisphere research, and also for the complexity of the brain itself.

How we know what we know

Many of us will have seen a diagram of the brain, with different regions clearly labelled.[2] Perhaps contrasting colours highlight the regions, and dark lines separate them. There is value in such a diagram, so long as we remember that it is a considerable simplification. The brain as a whole is substantially integrated. It incorporates an amazingly complex array of interconnections, operating dynamically as a whole. Activity in one region of the brain (perhaps connected with recognizing the word 'snake' on a page) will trigger one or more types of activity in other regions of the brain (for instance, involving memories). The response in these subsequent regions may in some way enhance or develop the initial response, or trigger further action elsewhere. Alternatively, the response may act to reduce or inhibit the initial reaction (maybe relating to recent deliberate practice at reducing anxiety when encountering snakes). If the initial event is complex – emotionally charged, or requiring careful thought – then it may well be challenging to make sense of what is going on within the brain.

In the face of such complexity, researchers proceed by drawing on several different sources of information. Some of these rely on research involving people who have, sadly, suffered in one way or another. One such source is people with brain lesions, where one part of the brain is no longer present or functioning, due to illness or injury. Another involves a procedure for temporarily anaesthetizing one hemisphere while the other remains active.[3] Or again, an electromagnet can be used to temporarily depress (or enhance) brain activity in either a whole hemisphere, or a specific part of one. A similar effect was gained in the past by the one-sided application of electroconvulsive therapy (ECT). This would lead to about 15 minutes during which one hemisphere was rendered inactive, within which time the subject could be asked to carry out specific tasks.

In the 1950s and 1960s, a revolutionary new technique to control severe epilepsy was developed. In this, the *corpus callosum* (which connects the two hemispheres of the brain) was divided, leading to patients with so-called 'split brains'.[4] The primary purpose of this procedure was to enable the patients to lead relatively normal lives. A secondary benefit is the research insight that ensued — for which one example must suffice: if an image is shown only to the left eye of such a patient, she or he will not be able to say what they have seen. The image seen by the left eye is sent only to the right side of the brain and, for most people, the right hemisphere on its own cannot control the act of speaking. However, although the person cannot name the object, they are able to use their left hand (controlled by the right side of the brain) to point to another similar object. This procedure made clear that it's not the recognition of the object that has been disabled, but purely the ability to speak its name.

Finally, information also comes from EEG recordings, and from a range of neuroimaging techniques.[5] The basic principle with these techniques is that, while any area of the brain is active, it requires an increased blood supply. Neuroimaging can indicate where blood supply is greatest. This suggests that such techniques will yield precise and clear information. The area does indeed hold great promise, but understanding its results calls for some subtlety. A central reason is that brain imaging will highlight primarily the peaks of activity. One writer uses the analogy of a high rate of fuel consumption in a car.[6] Guzzling the gas may happen because it's a high-performance sports car, or because it's a very old inefficient runabout, or because it's a normal, good car, driving with its handbrake on. Increased consumption is an interesting pointer, but doesn't tell us everything. Correspondingly, peaks of activity in the brain tend to indicate where there is most effort — but what follows needs careful interpretation. As our skill level for an activity increases, the regions of the brain that are involved are likely to stay the same, but the effort and thus the 'activation' is likely to decrease, and so these regions may no longer show up in neuroimaging. What's more, with current methods, it may not always be possible to distinguish between inhibition in brain activity — that which is suppressing another part of the brain — and activation.[7]

The list of challenges continues. Significant differences in neuroimaging results can be triggered by: small differences in the presentation of a task; adjustments to its novelty or complexity; the gender of the subject; not only whether they are left- or right-handed, but how strong their handedness is;[8] race; age; and, at root, individual differences. What's more, the same brain of the same person can give different results on different occasions, for instance linked to a different context, or following a different previous task.

The extent of the list of challenges might tempt one to give up on the search for understanding. Instead, good practice is to cross-reference evidence from different sources, avoiding where possible reliance on one technique alone. On the one hand, then, this area is a rather less precise science than one might assume. However, and despite the challenges, the cumulative impact of all the evidence does still indicate consistent differences between the hemispheres.

It is to the examination of these differences that we shall shortly turn. But first, let me introduce our major conversation partner, Iain McGilchrist.

Iain McGilchrist, and brain hemisphere research

Biographical introduction

When Iain McGilchrist began his medical training in the early 1980s, not only was he about ten years older than his fellow students, but his main focus for the previous decade had been in the humanities: after an Oxford degree in English literature, a prestigious seven-year Fellowship at All Souls College let him pursue interests in areas including philosophy, psychology and the history of ideas. Throughout this time, McGilchrist became intrigued by the relationship between the mind and the body, and increasingly convinced of its importance. This led to his decision to retrain as a doctor.

Having done so, he combined specialisms in psychiatry (he is a Fellow of the Royal College of Psychiatrists, and was a Clinical Director at the Bethlem Royal and Maudsley Hospital, London) and neuroimaging (in which area he has been a Research Fellow at Johns Hopkins University, Maryland, USA). Around the early 1990s, when McGilchrist entered the field of brain hemisphere research, his friends and colleagues advised him that to focus on this area would be career suicide. Interest in brain hemispheres was beginning to go out of fashion, for a very understandable reason. For decades, the primary research question had been about which brain functions were located in which hemisphere. Increasingly sophisticated equipment had yielded an increasingly predictable answer: for almost any function, both hemispheres were involved. McGilchrist, however, was entering the field with a different primary question.

McGilchrist's primary question

The question that McGilchrist wanted to answer was this: 'Why is it that our brains are divided into two substantially separated hemispheres?' You might expect that, the larger the brain, the more substantial will be the connection between the hemispheres. In fact, the opposite has happened: as brains have grown larger, the connecting tissue (the *corpus callosum*) has become proportionally smaller.[9] Moreover, the asymmetry between the hemispheres has also increased. The larger the brain, the smaller the connecting tissue, and the greater the difference between the hemispheres. What value, then, is added by the substantial separation of the brain into two asymmetrical hemispheres?

After around 20 years of research, McGilchrist published his first major book (of which more shortly), which addressed this striking question. His answer, in brief, is that this separation within the brain is how animals solve a central conundrum: how can I eat, and simultaneously avoid being eaten. If we are to eat without being eaten, we need ready access to two very different ways of being in the world – as we have already noted in the previous chapter.

At this point we make a key move in the developing argument of this book. The key move is this: the two ways of being (that we met at the start of the first chapter) correspond to two contrasting approaches enabled by the two hemispheres of the brain. The reason that the brain is divided into two contrasting hemispheres is so that we can have ready access to these two different ways of being. What I have introduced as a Clear-cut approach corresponds to the left hemisphere (LH). The Holistic way of being arises from the right hemisphere (RH). These two ways of being are offered, respectively, by the two hemispheres of the brain, which are 'separate enough to function independently, but connected enough to work in concert with one another' (McGilchrist, *The Matter With Things*, p. 20). A central point is that what we need is not flexibility along a spectrum, but access to two discrete contrasting approaches. The reason we have two hemispheres is because of the clear evolutionary advantages of keeping substantially separate these two ways of being, enabling us to eat, and also to avoid being eaten.

It is, then, the Clear-cut mode that correlates to the left hemisphere (LH), and the Holistic approach that arises from the right hemisphere (RH). It may be worth taking a moment, at this early stage, to consolidate in your memory which way round this correlation works. The LH specialises in Linear Logic – and the CLear-cut can be characterized by straight lines separating this from that. Indeed a capital L has the shape and feel of Clear-cut LH clarity. By contrast, a capital R, with its rounded upper part, has more resonance with the curved line feel of the relational Holistic approach. Or again, the upper part of the R encloses a hole – as with the Holistic. Alternatively, some might find it helpful to think of the abbreviation HRH as standing for Holistic Right Hemisphere. Don't worry if you get confused as to which is which. I will repeatedly use both conventions together – Clear-cut LH, and Holistic RH.

There is, then, something very important about keeping separate these contrasting, asymmetrical brain hemispheres. The separation, however, is not total. Another key strand of McGilchrist's thesis focuses on the relationship between the two hemispheres. The research sheds remarkable light on the nature and dynamics of healthy relating between the hemispheres. (Our initial cameos of the chaffinch, and of the meal with friends, have begun to illustrate some positive dynamics between hemispheres.) The same research also makes clear why healthy hemisphere relating can easily become skewed. There are understandable reasons why the hemispheres can, as it were, shift from life-giving cooperation to a stance that includes competition and antagonism. Indeed, there can be some initial attractiveness to what then ensues – but its longer-term consequences are not good (and 'longer-term' may not take very long at all).

These paragraphs begin to introduce the theme of McGilchrist's first major book, *The Master and His Emissary: The Divided Brain and the Making of the Western World* (2009).[10] The book overall brings together his medical and cultural interests, and puts forward a thesis of remarkable breadth and intent. It is a rich and rewarding read, and also a substantial one.[11] (Indeed, my encounter with this book since 2011 has turned out to be one of the most significant elements in my life so far.) What I have mentioned so far introduces the first half of *The Master and His Emissary*. Within this, McGilchrist summarizes research on the hemispheres of an individual brain.[12]

With the second half of his book, McGilchrist takes an audacious turn around another conceptual corner, in two bold steps. He has already established what healthy hemisphere relating looks like, and how it easily goes wrong, at the level of an individual human. His first bold step is from the individual level to the communal or cultural level. Just as we might sense a greater or lesser degree of healthy hemisphere cooperation in an individual, so there might be evidence of corresponding patterns in the life of a group of people. Of course, the bigger the group, the broader the generalization. Nevertheless, some such patterns might genuinely be discernible.

His second bold step, then, is to take that concept on an audacious canter through Western cultural history – and this is the project of the second half of his book. Here, he looks out for the signature characteristics of the hemispheres, and of their relating, and suggests key patterns and trends in that light. (I offer a highly condensed summary of his findings as part of Chapter 5.) The two halves of his book, therefore, make sense of its subtitle: *The Divided Brain and the Making of the Western World*.

So how does all this relate to the scope and purpose of this current book? Well, the Strategic Leadership Discourse (SLD) has arisen within the Western world, and can best be understood in the light of its broader context. We will find that the neuroscientific insights of McGilchrist help to illuminate the Church SLD at three levels: some of the factors that may have contributed to shaping it; why people respond to it in such a range of ways (as illustrated by my diocesan leadership course experience); and, not least, what might be good ways forward from here.

The first few chapters of this book, then, lay a foundation by giving a sufficiently thorough introduction to the neuroscience. We will gain a solid grounding in appreciating the approaches of each hemisphere separately, and we will then explore the vital question of how the hemispheres relate. When, we then go on to approach the Church SLD, we will find that our neuroscientific foundation offers a fresh and enlightening perspective, making its features stand out in sharper relief.

Turning back to McGilchrist, he has subsequently written another major work, *The Matter With Things* (2021).[13] This builds on the foundations laid by its predecessor, with an even broader scope and ambition (and nearly three times the length). It is primarily in Chapter 6 that I introduce some of the new themes from this later work.

We turn now towards a fuller explanation of McGilchrist's neuroscientific perspective, framed according to the purposes of this book. Our first step in doing so is to explore why how we pay attention (a major focus of McGilchrist's approach) carries such significance.

The far-reaching significance of attention[14]

My attention changes the world I experience

The way in which we pay attention makes a foundational difference to our engagement with the world. Paying attention is not simply yet another brain function, on a par with learning the seven times tables. Rather, the attention with which we approach the world significantly impacts the type of world which we then find ourselves experiencing. The sense of the world which 'comes into being' for us, moment by moment, depends in part on the nature of the attention that we are paying. The manner of our attention, although frequently unnoticed by us, is never neutral. This point can initially seem subtle, and hard to grasp. It is also important, so let's illustrate with an example.

Imagine a diverse group of people all looking at the same mountain: a mountain climber, a hydro-electric engineer, an artist, and an indigenous tribal member who views the summit as the dwelling-place of the gods. These four will all attend to the same mountain in notably different ways. The four forms of attention will yield correspondingly different experiences for those involved. For instance, the engineer is likely to view the mountain primarily as a rock-mass with potential for internal channels – in which case that is how she will experience it. For the artist, it may take form as a striking juxtaposition of shapes, colours and textures. McGilchrist puts it like this: 'Attention changes what kind of a thing comes into being for us.'[15] This is highly significant. How I experience the world (and how I experience the church) will vary considerably depending on the nature of the attention with which I approach it in the first place. And that's not all.

My attention changes the world others experience

Imagine me meeting in turn with several different people: a close friend; the subject in a scientific experiment; a prisoner; my wife; an elderly relative with restricted mobility. It is not only that the variations in my attention would affect my experience of each of these people. The attention I brought to each of these would affect their experience of themselves to at least some degree. Attention is not neutral, and it impacts others, not only the one paying the attention.

For instance, if a good friend sits with you in a way that is fully present and attentive, you will normally be very aware of this, and experience it positively. In one sense, they may not seem to be 'doing anything'. And yet, you receive from their attention a sense of spaciousness, of respect, of value. You know you have been seen, in a deep sense. You may well have experienced this as life-giving.

A very important underlying theme of this book, then, is that how we dispose our attention 'is a moral act: it has consequences'.[16] The nature of our attention itself has impact, for better or for worse. The attention we bring to any context is not neutral.

The paying of attention and McGilchrist's hemisphere hypothesis

We started this book with the chaffinch, alternating between two ways of being as it pecked its seeds, and then scanned its environment. There is a clear contrast between the attention the chaffinch offers when in its Clear-cut LH mode, and in its Holistic RH. To unpack further the hemisphere correlation of attention, I'll use the terminology of where and how we are centred.[17]

At any given moment, I suggest, we will be centred primarily in either the Holistic RH, or the Clear-cut LH. We will be rooted in a mode more similar to the chaffinch pecking (Clear-cut LH), or more like the chaffinch looking around (Holistic RH). Going back to our mountain scenario, perhaps the engineer approaches the mountain centred in Clear-cut LH mode. She may look at the mountain as a potential factor in a problem to be solved: how can we design and implement a hydro-electric scheme here? And perhaps the artist approaches it centred in Holistic RH mode, seeking to be present to it in its entirety, with an openness of attention, waiting to see what artistic impulses emerge from the relational encounter.

The mode in which we are centred sets the tone for our engagement. It's not that the other way of being is necessarily ruled out. Nevertheless, our metaphorical centre of gravity will primarily be in one hemisphere or the other. Either we will be centred in the Holistic approach's openness to connection and relationship, or with the narrower purposeful focus of the LH Clear-cut, seeking to make a difference by solving a problem or completing a task.

If you experienced positively your good friend's attention, receiving warmth and connection from it, you can be confident she was centred in her relational Holistic RH. Exaggerating for clarity, if, instead, you felt viewed more as an object (perhaps as a means to an end, as a cog in a machine), and not really seen as a person, then she may well have been centred in her Clear-cut LH.

The work of the Jewish philosopher Martin Buber is remarkably relevant here.[18] In brief, Buber described two ways of relating. One is *I–it* relating: I relate to the other as an 'it', whether that other is a human being, some food, or a chess piece. The other way of relating is what he termed *I–thou*.[19]

A first principle, then, is this: we should always aim to be centred in the Holistic RH. This is especially important in any situation involving people, in line with Buber's perspective: treating another human being as an 'it' is not recommended. As we'll see and explore, some careful thinking is needed here, teasing out exactly what we are saying. There will be appropriate ways in which we do at times stand back and take an 'objective' view of a situation, including its people. And we will develop an understanding of how we can hold such a perspective well, from a context of remaining centred in the Holistic RH.

Alongside that first principle must be held the second: we should always draw generously on the great strengths of the Clear-cut LH – to a degree appropriate to the specific situation. If my dentist is drilling a hole in my tooth, I hope she will draw considerably on the task-focused narrow spotlight of Clear-cut LH attention. At the same time, I want her to remain centred in the Holistic RH. I want her substantial focus not to exclude peripheral awareness and vigilance. If, for instance, I stop breathing, I hope she will notice. Being centred in the RH can be combined with the channelling of large amounts of LH focus.[20] This question of how we best integrate the contrasting capacities of the two hemispheres will form an important strand of our developing understanding in the chapters ahead.

The primary theme of this section, then, has been the foundational significance of how we pay attention. How I look out at the world will shape what sort of a world I experience. Moreover, how I attend to the world around me will impact on those within it – for better or for worse. There is one further subject to consider in this chapter, which has similar foundational significance.

Knowing and knowledge

The one further subject to address can be summarized, in English, by the single word 'knowledge'.[21] In many cultures and languages, however, what we may think of as 'knowledge' is not one subject, but two. French, German, Italian and Latin (for instance) all recognize a significant difference between what I will refer to as 'personal knowing' on the one hand and, on the other, 'fact-focused knowing' – so much so that they refer to them by different words.[22] It is striking that the dividing line, in all these languages, falls in a similar place.

As with the foundational question of attention, so with knowledge: the Clear-cut LH and the Holistic RH each engage very differently. And, as you may already have guessed, for each of these languages, one word describes the sort of knowing that relates to the Holistic RH approach, and the other the knowing of the Clear-cut LH. For instance, in French, *savoir* is about the knowledge of facts, whereas *connaître* is about knowing a person, or being familiar with a thing or a place.

Deepening our appreciation of these two distinct 'forms of knowledge' will prove invaluable as we continue to develop our sense of the strongly contrasting approaches of the two hemispheres.

Personal knowing

Let's first attend to what I'll call 'personal knowing' (related to the Holistic RH, the French *connaître* and the German *kennen*). For instance, when I say that 'I know' my friend, Susan, what do I mean by this? What is the nature of this knowing, and how do I gain it? Let me highlight some primary features:

First, personal knowing comes from direct personal encounter. If I've never met Susan, I can't claim to know her. Second, I can describe something of my knowledge of Susan, but I cannot fully articulate it. The knowledge itself exceeds my description of it. Despite this, my knowledge of Susan is genuine. That said, I wouldn't claim to know her completely. Personal knowing (on a human level) is indeed never complete – and that is not a problem. There will always be more to learn, even of people I already know very well. Questions of degree are always relevant with this personal knowing.

Next, Susan is not exactly the same as how she was when we first met, 30 years ago. My knowledge of her can cope comfortably with such change and flux. Personal knowing is not based on a list of separate, fixed facts, but depends on an integrated sense of 'the whole of Susan'. Coherence and continuity can be identified and embraced, even in the face of substantial change.

Taking all of this together, I cannot simply transfer my personal knowing of Susan to George, who has never met her. I can give him some sense of who she is, by describing her qualities, and by showing him a photograph of her – especially of her face. But for George to gain personal knowledge of Susan, he will need to encounter her himself. If he does so, his knowledge of her will not be identical to mine, but there will be considerable overlap.

In order to participate in relationship with anybody, we will need to draw substantially on the Holistic way of being offered by the RH (resonating with Buber's *I–thou* relating). It is Holistic attention that will be open to encounter them as they are, and flexible to respond accordingly. The Holistic RH desires relationship and connection. (If Susan were only to respond to me in a purely Clear-cut LH way, that would not be most helpful in developing friendship.) Moreover, it is the Holistic RH that notices, values and desires the growth of such personal knowing, and the underlying experience of participating in shared relational connection. Overall, there is thus a very strong correlation between this form of knowing and the Holistic RH.

Fact-focused knowing

The second form of knowing correlates with the Clear-cut LH (and with the French *savoir*, and the German *wissen*). It contrasts with all the main features we have highlighted regarding personal knowing.

For a start, this knowing does not require personal encounter, but engagement with 'facts'. By 'facts' we mean things that are certain, and not a matter of personal opinion: for instance, the capital cities of Europe, the timing of church services in a town, or the rules of snooker. Next, I will never fully know another person, but I can fully know some facts. I can know a fact completely. Third, in contrast to the reality of change in other people, we expect our facts to be fixed – at least at any given point in time. For instance, the score will change many times throughout a game of snooker. However, at any point in time, that score is clear, unambiguous and fixed. It's never nuanced, subtle or a matter of interpretation.

As we've seen, knowledge of a person involves integrating multiple aspects into a sense of the person as a whole. Fact-based knowing is different. There may or may not even *be* a sense of the whole. But if there is, it is simply composed of all the discrete, fixed, factual components. Nothing extra is added when they are brought together. The combination of all these characteristics means that, unlike personal knowing, Clear-cut fact-focused knowing can straightforwardly be transmitted to another person. In principle, it can be made fully explicit. One person can write it down, and somebody else can pick it up, read it, learn it and absorb it. Personal knowing correlated with Buber's concept of *I–thou* relating. This fact-focused knowing correlates with *I–it* relating.

Which form of knowledge to use?

Holistic knowledge is particularly called upon in relational knowing of another person. Not surprisingly, it is also very relevant when getting to know a group of people (a family, a club, a church, a business). Holistic knowing engages not only with each individual, but also with the quality of relationships within the group, and the tone or atmosphere of their interactions. In this realm, what is done is not the only consideration, but also the manner in which those things are done. Interestingly, when engaging with music, nature and art (among other things), it is Holistic personal knowing that comes to the fore. In these realms, facts can be helpful, but are insufficient. Personal encounter, engaging actively and receptively, is essential, and leads to a sense of familiarity.

Clear-cut left hemisphere knowing is applicable in a wide range of areas. It comes into its own most fully when engaging with things that are not alive. Here there is often less flux and greater fixedness. Many aspects of the physical sciences (with some notable exceptions) make great use of Clear-cut knowledge, and depend on its characteristic of repeatable certainty. This form of knowledge is also prevalent within many human constructions, be they buildings, plans or computer systems. All of this tallies with the left hemisphere's affinity with machines. Machines can be (more or less) fully known in a Clear-cut LH sense, because they have been put together from their constituent parts, and because the manner in which they function should not vary over time.

Some aspects of reality, then, lie primarily in the domain of right hemisphere knowing, and some primarily in that of the left. But there are also many aspects of life for which both personal and fact-focused knowledge are relevant. For instance, there will be factual aspects of the nature and life of any group of people. Knowing these facts can be very helpful – and can contribute to our personal knowing of the group.

These two 'forms' of knowing are so intermingled in our daily lives that we may rarely register the considerable contrast between them. At several points in the chapters ahead, however, we will see the relevance of recognizing the distinction between them.

Conclusion on knowing and knowledge

The two brain hemispheres each engage, then, with a valuable, but substantially different, 'form of knowledge'. For the LH, the priority is knowledge that is clear, certain and fixed. It wants to deal with 'facts' that can be straightforwardly and explicitly conveyed to others. The personal knowing prioritized by the RH is often harder, or impossible, to articulate. It is therefore often harder to 'grasp': 'getting a feel for it' is a more realistic ambition. It is often fluid, and rarely complete, but, from the perspective of the RH, these characteristics are not problematic, but simply the way things are.

When the two hemispheres turn their attention to the world, there is a similar contrast between what they each notice or overlook, and why, to what end and with what purpose. It is to such considerations, beginning with a deeper understanding of the Clear-cut LH, that we now turn.

Questions for reflection

1 Can you call to mind an occasion when the quality of attention someone offered you was particularly helpful and life-giving? What difference did that make for you?
2 Are there any patterns in the form of attention you tend to offer in different situations?
3 What strikes you about the distinction between personal knowing and fact-focused knowing?

Chapter 2 thumbnail summary – McGilchrist, attention and knowledge

1 *Brain research*

- The individual human brain is asymmetrical in many ways.
- Brain hemisphere research has long focused on which function happens in which hemisphere.

2 *Iain McGilchrist*

- Iain McGilchrist's primary question is different: why is the brain divided into two hemispheres?
- His short answer: this is how we solve the conundrum of needing to eat, but avoid being eaten.
- We need ready access to two distinct forms of attention. Each hemisphere offers one of those forms. The two forms are those we met in Chapter 1.
- The left hemisphere (LH) offers Clear-cut narrow focus towards task completion and problem solution.
- The right hemisphere (RH) offers Holistic breadth and openness, towards understanding and relational connection.

3 *Attention*

- How we pay attention shapes the world that *we* experience, and also impacts on the experience of others.
- Paying attention is thus not neutral, but is a moral act.
- Two of the principles arising from McGilchrist's work are these:
  We should always aim to be centred in the Holistic RH.
  We should always draw on the strengths of the Clear-cut LH as needed for each situation.

4 *Knowledge*

- Personal knowing is different from fact-focused knowing.
- Personal knowing relates to the Holistic RH, and arises from encounter. It can't be made fully explicit, or transferred to a third party.

- Fact-focused knowing relates to the Clear-cut LH. It works well with subject matter that is clear, certain and fixed.
- We need both, in varying degrees, in different situations.

Notes

1 This section is informed by Iain McGilchrist, 2009, *The Master and His Emissary: The Divided Brain and the Making of the Western World*, New Haven, CT: Yale University Press (hereafter *Master*), pp. 32–3.

2 This section is informed by *Master*, pp. 34–7.

3 This is most commonly carried out prior to certain forms of neurosurgery.

4 The *corpus callosum* is one of the two parts of the brain I will mention, other than the hemispheres.

5 These include functional magnetic resonance imaging (fMRI), single photon emission computed tomography (SPECT) and positron emission tomography (PET).

6 B. E. Wexler, 1988, 'Regional Brain Dysfunction in Depression' in M. Kinsbourne (ed.), *Cerebral Hemisphere Function in Depression*, Washington DC: American Psychiatric Press, pp. 65–78, pp. 68–71, quoted in *Master*, footnote 21, p. 467.

7 Analogous to the difference between having your foot on the brake or on the accelerator.

8 Let me address here the often-asked question of how talk of left and right brain hemispheres relates to people who are left-handed. If we call the most common arrangement of brain hemispheres 'the standard pattern', McGilchrist summarizes the situation as follow: of the 11% of the population who are broadly left-handed, about 75% appear to follow broadly the standard pattern. Of the remainder (less than 3% of the overall population), some have a simple inversion of the hemispheres. For such people, from the point of view of the argument that follows, all that is needed is to swap the references to left and right brain hemispheres. There is then a third group, which includes some left-handers, as well as some people with a range of other conditions, who have unconventional ways of brain lateralization. This may bring some special benefits, and/or lead to particular disadvantages. McGilchrist recommends, as a superlative explanation of this issue, the book C. McManus, 2002, *Right Hand, Left Hand: The Origins of Asymmetry in Brains, Bodies, Atoms and Cultures*, Cambridge MA: Harvard University Press.

9 What's more, the evidence suggests that a significant proportion of the 'traffic' across the corpus callosum is designed to inhibit the other hemisphere, rather than to stimulate it.

10 His one previous book, on the subject of literary criticism, was written in his late twenties. It didn't sell many copies then – but any such copies are now much sought after.

11 The 462 pages of fairly dense text are supplemented by over 1,800 footnotes, which take a further 50 pages of small print.

12 There are three dimensions of the brain – loosely 'left/right', 'up/down' and 'front/back'. McGilchrist concentrates very much on the 'left/right' axis, but also mentions the other two dimensions in some detailed discussions (*Master*, pp. 9–10). Such details lie beyond the parameters of this book, however, which attends purely to the left/right axis. Relatedly, it is worth highlighting that the terms 'left brain' and 'right brain' have been used in a range of ways in different contexts, such as 'pop psychology' and some therapeutic training. Readers who have formed an understanding of 'left brain' and 'right brain' from previous engagements should expect some difference between such framing and McGilchrist's proposals regarding the two hemispheres. In particular, the phrases 'left brain' or 'right brain' are sometimes defined elsewhere as incorporating considerations from the 'up/down' or 'front/back' dimension.

13 Iain McGilchrist, 2021, *The Matter With Things*, London: Perspectiva Press (hereafter *Things*).

14 McGilchrist, *Master*, pp. 28–9.

15 McGilchrist, *Master*, p. 28.

16 McGilchrist, *Things*, p. 17.

17 I first encountered this terminology in the work of Bonnie Badenoch, a therapist who combines McGilchrist's insights with perspectives from relational neurobiology. See www.nurturingtheheart.com, accessed 21.05.2025.

18 Martin Buber, 1970, *I and Thou*, 3rd edn, trans. Walter Kaufmann, Edinburgh: T&T Clark.

19 He was writing in German, and his term 'Ich–Du' is traditionally translated I–thou, rather than I–you.

20 I'm grateful to David Sims for highlighting the importance of this point, leading to this example.

21 This section is informed especially by McGilchrist, *Master*, pp. 94–9.

22 In French, *connaître* and *savoir*; in German, *kennen* and *wissen*; in Italian, *conoscere* and *sapere*; and in Latin *cognoscere* and *sapere* (McGilchrist, *Master*, p. 96).

3

The Clear-cut Left Hemisphere (LH): Simplified Mappings and Positive Purpose

Simplified maps of reality

The need for a map

As I write, an outline plan for today sits in the top drawer of my desk. I prepared it last night, surveying possible priorities for today, and jotting seven tasks on an A6 piece of paper. The process of preparing it helped me clarify both what I do want to do today, and also what I will not attempt to progress.

I find it helpful to have such a plan (and will refer to it throughout the day). It helps me focus on what I have chosen to do. Without it, some of my background attention is taken up with wondering if I've missed something crucial. My simple day plan is an example of a central signature practice of the Clear-cut LH: constructing a simplified map of reality. The fact is that life is complex and multidimensional. Many situations feature intertwined strands of relationships, history, tensions and possibilities. In the face of such complexity, we can feel overwhelmed and bewildered. As McGilchrist puts it: 'We need to be able to be open to whatever there is, and yet, at the same time, to provide a "map", a version of the world which is simpler, clearer and therefore more useful.'[1]

Having a 'map' can help us get our bearings. It can reduce the sense of overwhelm. For we simply cannot pay attention to all of the detail, all of the time. We do not have the capacity always to engage with each aspect of every passing moment. A 'map' can help direct our attention. By deliberately ignoring large chunks of important information, it can free us to be more engaged with the world around us.

With respect to the above quote from McGilchrist, it is the Holistic RH way of being that helps us to be 'open to whatever there is'. Complementing this, it is the Clear-cut LH that constructs and offers a simpler, clearer version of the world. Such a 'map' – a simplified map of reality – contains what seem to be the most significant facts, and omits everything else. This describes well my plan for the day. It deliberately ignores much detail, but highlights seven important tasks (according to my judgement last night).

Simply having the plan, however, is not a magic wand. On the one hand, I could write it, then ignore it. On the other, an unexpected opportunity could arise that deserves to be prioritized above everything on my list. In such a scenario, sticking slavishly to my plan would not be wise. Overall, if I pay appropriate attention to it, my plan for the day can be a great servant, but makes a poor master. This is a theme with which we will become familiar.

Other examples and uses of simplified maps

A simplified map indicating the way things are, or the current state of play, can be very helpful for initial orientation. The central office reception area of the Diocese of Worcester contains a large map of the diocese. This map prioritizes displaying a few things clearly. It includes perhaps ten of the largest centres of population, several prominent roads and natural features (the Malvern Hills, the River Severn), and the boundaries of the six deaneries of the diocese. Had this map been present when I first moved to Worcester, it would have been very useful for me, unfamiliar as I was with the area. It would have offered a first step towards familiarity, and a useful framework around which I could build further understanding. Before long, however, I would have needed to expand my knowledge beyond what the map shows: the ten largest population centres aren't the only places worth knowing.

Another use for simplified maps is when making a decision. Perhaps you want to decide on a holiday destination for the summer. Or perhaps it's time to move to a new job, and you are discerning what sort of role might be best. In either case, one way of beginning the process is to articulate a range of possibilities, and see what you think and feel about them. It's worth noting that your final decision may or may not have featured as one of the initial options. Nevertheless, considering a 'menu of possibilities' can be a helpful way to get started towards a decision. Such a menu of possibilities is another form of simplified map.

Or, a simplified map can helpfully indicate how we envisage events unfolding over time. My plan for the day offers one simple example. Other examples could include a teacher's curriculum plan for the year, or a five-year career plan for a school leaver or graduate. Clearly, the theme of mapping anticipated future events forms an important part of project planning, sometimes in a fairly formal way. This theme of planning will recur at several stages through the book.

A special form of planning-related simplified map is the protocol (or procedure, or checklist). Here, clear steps are articulated when dealing with a certain event. Many variations are possible: the level of detail; the level of expertise assumed; the rigidity or flexibility of the protocol; the amount of initiative or discretion left to the person or people responding to the situation. Simplified maps of this form can be incredibly helpful – and have a wide range of potential downsides.

The construction of such simplified maps, then, are a key part of the Clear-cut LH approach, and we will engage with many examples throughout this book. To help us do so well, it's worth registering at this stage a few main aspects of their construction.

Constructing the map

Constructedness

The first aspect is to underline that such maps are indeed constructed. They are not naturally occurring phenomena: rather, we construct them. What's more, for any given context, there will be more than one possible way of shaping a simplified map. Of these possibilities, some maps will prove more helpful – or more misleading – than others. When faced with an existing simplified map, it can therefore be worth exploring whether an even more relevant mapping may be possible. This could be as a replacement, or for a complementary additional perspective. Given that they are constructed, how exactly are they formed?

What's in and what's out of the map?

In order for the map to be a simplified map, some features need to be included, and others excluded. Simplification can only be achieved if some things are left out. There is a clear division between what is in and what is out. Those things included in a map generally share some common features.

For a start, the map will include features we see as especially useful or important. They will be relevant to our needs and purposes. The pile of seeds will have featured in the chaffinch's simplified map, because it is a source of food to keep it alive. Conversely, excluded from the map will be things we see as minor details, or irrelevant.

Things included also tend to come from the realm of Clear-cut LH fact-focused knowledge. The contents are likely to be conveyed as clear, certain and fixed. Different parts of the whole may well be mentioned, but the relationship between them is less likely to feature. We would expect the focus to be more on quantity than quality. Having said which, there may be reference to some more Holistic RH features. A church noticeboard, for instance, might describe different services as 'reverent' or 'relaxed' (or indeed both). Any such qualitative features will tend to be represented as definite and unchanging. In many cases, there will be no indication of flux, fluidity or variation. What is conveyed will normally either focus on one point in time, or be presented as a sequence of distinct steps.

It is entirely understandable that the contents of a simplified map are likely to be primarily Clear-cut. It is, however, worth underlining the very considerable significance of this: Holistic RH aspects will often not feature at all in a simplified mapping. The simplified map itself will frequently be skewed towards the Clear-cut.

Grouping things into categories

Once the map's contents have been determined, they will often then be divided into groups, adding a greater sense of clarity and structure. For instance, a church noticeboard might have a heading of 'Services' and list its regular worship times, then similarly for a heading of 'Midweek groups'.

Such grouping into categories makes it easy to count things and people. Quoting the total numbers can give a very helpful sense of scale. For instance, a diocese might state on its website how many people or things it has in different categories: the population of the diocese; the number of churches; the number of regular worshippers; the number of ministers (divided into subcategories) and so forth.

Categories themselves come in very different forms. Some categories are very straightforward – this building (often) either is or isn't a church building; this person (in most cases) either is or isn't an ordained minister. Other forms of category are less intrinsic by nature. By this I mean that there will be more than one legitimate way of determining what belongs to such a category. To give one example, a diocese might want to categorize its churches as small, medium and large. But different dioceses might well choose different thresholds, and/or criteria, for distinguishing between these categories. To be a large church, do you need 100 regular worshippers, or 250, or 500, or 5,000? Such constructed categories can be helpful – and remembering the fact that they are constructed can prove important.

The key move – separation

One Clear-cut LH 'move' is repeatedly deployed in the construction of a simplified map. That move is the act of separating or dividing, making a 'clear cut' between some things and other things. There is, first, the separation of what is in the map from what is not included. There is then often the division of its contents into distinct categories, separating things into groups according to their similarities. These two acts of separation are the most obvious, but there are also often others.

This can be seen most distinctly when considering how a person might feature in a simplified map. One possibility is that they are described purely in terms of their role, or perhaps a list of their role-related responsibilities (organist; finance director; responsibility for engaging with young families; and overseeing junior church volunteers). Another possibility is that they are simply one component of a larger number: for instance, one of the '120 licensed and authorized lay ministers' in the diocese. In either case, the person concerned has been separated from their relationships, their history and their personal character. They are taken out from their context – abstracted from it, becoming 'conceptualised rather than experienced'.[2] They have been divided from most of what makes them unique.

Separation and division thus feature in several ways in the construction of a simplified map. Indeed, McGilchrist describes the act of separation, of dividing one thing from another, as arguably the central 'governing principle'[3] of the left hemisphere's Clear-cut disposition. It was the centrality of this action that led me to choose the term 'Clear-cut' as the main description for the LH way of being in the world.

How we can relate to LH simplified maps

How do we treat such simplified maps once they have been constructed? As we've said, there are a range of ways in which they can serve us well: by helping introduce us to a new area, subject or situation; by offering metaphorical scaffolding as we learn a new field; by offering some options for decision-making, or early indications of possible future outcomes. A Clear-cut LH mapping can be an effective servant in any of these ways.

A Clear-cut LH, operating on its own, having constructed a simplified map of a situation, will then go on to relate primarily to the simplified map. This is understandable. The LH has gone to the effort of grasping what it sees as important about the situation, and re-presenting that information in a way that is clear and certain. McGilchrist, therefore, frequently refers to such a simplified mapping as a 're-presentation' of the reality it seeks to summarize. Extraneous detail has been omitted. It is not surprising that the Clear-cut LH then treats the map as if it is an adequate substitute for the reality. It is no wonder that, for the Clear-cut LH, the 're-presentation comes to take the place of the thing itself'.[4]

The simplified map, the re-presentation of the situation, is something we can grasp and work with for our purposes. Used well, this map can indeed help the whole person, using both brain hemispheres, engage more fully and constructively with the situation. In Chapter 5, we will explore the dynamics of this in more detail. For now, there is one important point to note: as well as looking at the simplified map, we also need to look beyond it, to reality itself. Failure to do so leads to us treating the map as if it were itself reality. Failure to distinguish between the reality and the map is one of the key ways in which we can (all too easily) begin to go astray.

Purpose, change and control

A strong sense of purposefulness lies near the heart of the LH's sense of self.[5] The LH's *raison d'être* is to be an agent of change, to be instrumental in making a difference. This powerful sense of purpose is interlinked with the type of attention that it gives to any situation. Thus any given scenario will typically be viewed primarily as a problem to solve (for instance, how can I reduce my hunger?), or as a situation to improve.

The question of what 'counts' as change from an LH perspective is an important one. For change to 'count', it needs to be tangible in terms of Clear-cut fact-focused knowledge. It is unlikely to be satisfied with comments like, 'It just feels a bit better now'. Considering again a Clear-cut LH simplified map – which is broadly how it sees the world – for the left hemisphere to 'know' that it has made a difference, the map of reality at the end needs to be different from how it was at the beginning.

What might this mean in practice? It might mean that something new has been added to the map – perhaps a new service or midweek group at a church. Or perhaps that a target threshold has been crossed. Thinking of a diocese, it might mean that a certain percentage of church congregations have risen from small to medium, or medium to large. There are also a wide range of possible shifts which the LH might not recognize. For instance, deepening the relationships and learning in midweek groups, or sensing that children in school assemblies are normally listening more attentively.

Importantly, the LH seeks change that it itself has pre-identified. From the start, it normally identifies a specific end, towards which it channels its narrow beam of attention, energy and effort – ideally until that end has been achieved. For some forms of change, such an approach is necessary, or at least helpful. This is not true in all cases, however. For now, let me register that much worthwhile change happens without the end being known from the beginning (although sometimes a broad sense of direction is in evidence). Such change can be described as emergent. It typically unfolds more gradually, one step at a time, and often involves the input and participation of many.

Rather than emergent change, Clear-cut LH strength and preference is around making a difference in ways that are pre-planned. Whatever the timescale involved, the concerns of the LH centre around control. Such a desire for control makes sense – in the context of LH working assumptions. In particular, the LH assumes that getting from A to B is best done by analysis of the best route, then taking the necessary steps. All can be broken down into logical, linear, component chunks. And the chunks can be delivered straightforwardly through the direct application of effort and energy. The LH therefore seeks to control the planning and execution, and also to identify anything that might contribute to the cause, and harness it for that end. The Clear-cut approach seeks to identify what works, and to roll that out, replicating its effectiveness as widely as possible.

It is the LH that is principally concerned with utility, with taking hold of whatever might prove useful to our purposes. Indeed, reference to grasping is connected with LH activation, as is reference to tools.[6] It is notable the number of phrases which relate to control, and refer to our hands.[7] For instance, we talk of 'getting a handle' on something, 'putting our finger' on it, 'getting a grip' on something, or 'grasping' what's going on. Indeed, the word 'manipulate' combines the sense of using our hands, and changing things in line with our agenda.

When the LH has pre-identified its desired change, this leads to a Clear-cut judgement on whether that change has been achieved. The result is binary: either the task has been completed, or it hasn't; either the problem has been solved, or it remains outstanding. This binary clarity is related to the tenacity of the LH. This tenacity, or 'stickiness', is a quality that can prove either a great strength, or a considerable weakness, depending on the context. With respect to the strength of this quality, if a problem needs solving, the LH can contribute remarkable determination in persevering through to completion. Think, perhaps, of a dog chasing a ball. The downside is a pronounced LH tendency to stick to its existing point of view, even in the face of mounting evidence that its understanding is faulty.

Further, there is a notable difference between the hemispheres when it comes to self-awareness. The RH is much more realistic, and much more clear-sighted about itself, its relationships with others, and its capabilities. By contrast, the LH is much more optimistic, but often to an unrealistic degree. In particular, the LH is frequently out of touch with its shortcomings, seeing itself as always being successful, always being a winner, tending to deny anything that might contradict this view. The theme of unrealistic over-optimism is also seen in the denial of limitation:

> A patient with a completely paralysed (left) limb may pointedly refuse to accept that there is anything wrong with it, and will come up with the most preposterous explanations for why they are not actually able to move it on request.[8]

In some contexts, cause and effect can be predicted with great accuracy. Here a Clear-cut approach has a lot to offer. However, Clear-cut assumptions on their own fall well short when it comes to many more personal and interpersonal contexts – not least to much of church life. For instance, it is impossible to control another person's sense of feeling welcome, or having a sense of God's presence and reality. It is impossible to control the growth of friendship, or of faith. Indeed, many of the most important aspects of life simply cannot be controlled.

In such a context, different considerations apply (as we will go on to explore). In such a context, in fact, LH effort can prove highly counter-productive, however well-intentioned. There may still be space for some LH contribution: for careful thought, appropriate planning and well-judged initiative. Each of these, however, can be taken too far. And what is most needed will sometimes include no pre-planning or control.

The Clear-cut LH may sense that its best efforts have not yielded the sort of fruit that it wanted – for instance, in terms of depth of friendship or growth in faith. It may realize that it has not caused a sense of life. When this happens, its tactic can be to try to generate what it sees as 'the attributes of a living thing: novelty, excitement, stimulation'.[9] Novelty, excitement and stimulation can be worthwhile, and do sometimes flow from life – but they are not life itself. We cannot cause life by replicating some of its fruit.

Models, connections, consistency and a cameo

LH use of models

The LH has a strong affinity with general models. It looks for patterns that work in one context, and might reasonably be expected to work in another. Such a model might represent an algorithm for completing a mathematical operation (for instance, to find the average, add the two numbers and divide by two). The model might be a plan for a Roman fort, deployed throughout its expanding empire. Or it might be a routine for a corner shop to follow at closing time each night. Such models are themselves examples of simplified maps of reality.

Internal LH connections and consistency

There are strong connections between different aspects of the world of the Clear-cut LH. Its predisposition is to view each new situation as a problem requiring a solution, or at least some improvement. The LH then looks out for what it expects to be instrumentally useful towards such a solution, possibly drawing on a model with which it is already familiar. From this perspective it shapes a simplified map, discarding what seems like irrelevant detail in order to focus on a smaller number of likely main factors. Those features that make it on to the map will be based on fact-focused knowledge.

For now, it is worth highlighting the substantial inner consistency of the world of the LH. The LH constructs a version of the world (via its simplified maps) within which consistency is a highly valued principle. Strikingly and importantly, the LH world is primarily consistent with itself. This is essentially an internal consistency: if one starts with LH assumptions, and with the simplified maps it has made, the conclusions that it draws are very reasonable.

Not all of reality, however, conforms with LH assumptions on predictability. And LH simplified maps do not always include all that is relevant. To illustrate the considerable importance of such factors, I offer next an imaginary cameo, set this time in the realm of international development.

A QALY cameo

Healthcare economists have developed a system to compare the relative impact of different health interventions. The concept that facilitates this approach is the QALY: the Quality Adjusted Life Year. Within this approach, a health intervention (such as an operation, or prescription of medication) that is expected to give one person one extra year of life in full health is registered as adding 1 QALY. Adding one extra year of life without sight, but otherwise in good health, is registered as adding 0.4 QALYs, while an extra year of life in a coma is given a lower value. Not surprisingly, not every blind person appreciates the fact that their life is portrayed as 'counting for' just 40% of that of a sighted person. Nevertheless, the aim of the system is to offer a framework within which difficult decisions about funding priorities can be made as rationally as possible. Such QALY-based decisions can be used by public health services, and also by NGOs seeking to maximize the impact of charitable donations.

The aim of making rational funding decisions seems a good one, and we can see why the notion of a QALY could be attractive. However, let's explore what it might lead to. Imagine, for instance, a medical NGO, and work in a developing country. The trustees want to maximize the benefit they can bring, and therefore decide to adopt a QALY framework to shape their decision-making. After exploring some options, they choose a primary strategy of offering cataract operations: each operation is short and inexpensive and so this approach enables much good (measured in QALYs) from a given amount of charitable donation. The donors can therefore be assured that they have given strategically (which itself encourages more funds), and the patients receive the very great gift of restored sight. This all sounds good.

If we adjust our attention outwards, however, we begin to see that this approach could also have some less desirable side-effects. Consider, for instance, what might be its likely impact on the local labour market for nurses. The attractions of working at the donor-funded cataract clinic could just mean that the nearest government-run health facility, already in a precarious position, finds it even harder to recruit or retain medical staff. Even if the government clinic does manage to stay open with fewer nurses, the cumulative negative impact on people in the region, other than those with cataracts, could easily be substantial. Notice that *some* of that negative impact could feasibly be measured in QALYs – as local people have to wait extra months or years for life-improving treatment. The total of that unintended negative impact could be significant – potentially even outweighing all the positive benefit of the cataract operations. What's more, the QALY metric is simply unable to take account of the impact on a whole range of further considerations: for instance, the impact on the morale of nurses, sufferers and carers; the distance people have to walk for treatment; the length of waiting lists. It could easily be, however, that the NGO chooses only to take account of the direct positive impact of the cataract operations. If so, it will remain oblivious to such broader considerations, will continue to have positive news to communicate, and will continue to reassure its donors that they are being strategic and effective in their targeted giving.[10]

This cameo is imagined, but broadly imaginable. Within it, several aspects of the practice of the NGO illustrate some of the characteristics of a left hemisphere approach: the desire for clarity and certainty; using a general model (which is a formalized 'simplified map of reality'), seen as universally applicable; a focus on a narrow aspect of the situation, to the exclusion of broader context; a strong desire to make a difference. This cameo, then, offers one illustration both of the attractiveness of a simplified map, and of the importance of looking beyond the map to the reality – to the terrain itself.

Strengths, limitations and strategically reduced vision

Strengths

The LH possesses considerable strength. Its capacity to analyse, to distinguish and to systematize is quite remarkable. Over the centuries, the Clear-cut hand of the LH can be seen in countless developments across numerous civilizations. The majority of humanity's greatest achievements would have been impossible without its contributions. As we have noted, the LH is at its best in domains which are themselves as Clear-cut as possible. These are contexts in which linear logic is most relevant, and in which cause and effect are highly predictable. For instance, the LH has great affinity with the world of machines in general, and of computers in particular. In such a domain it is accurate, efficient and potentially very fast indeed. In these and many other contexts, the signature LH move of constructing a simplified map of reality can be very helpful. It can help with initial orientation, with clear communication, and in steps towards decision-making.

Limitations

The more clearly we understand the limitations of the LH, the more fully we can employ and appreciate its great strengths. McGilchrist highlights three limitations in particular.[11]

First, the Clear-cut LH frequently misreads the nature of what it's attending to. It is at its best engaging with human constructions, but much weaker when it encounters the Holistic domain, not least all that is living or personal. Importantly, therefore, the Clear-cut LH does not notice, understand or appreciate important aspects of the nature of being human, of Christian faith, or of the church. Second, the LH tendency, having created a simplified map, tends to mistake its map for reality itself. Failing to distinguish between the map and the terrain can lead to all sorts of negative consequences (as the QALY cameo illustrates). This limitation is again very relevant when the Clear-cut LH maps the nature and purpose of the church. The third primary limitation, relatedly, is to assume that its linear explanations of 'how things work' are relevant in all contexts.

We have also noted some further weaknesses, or potential weaknesses. One is the 'stickiness' with which the LH clings to its existing view or explanation, even in the face of evidence to the contrary. A second is its desire to be in control, which can be counter-productive. Last, and of great significance to inter-hemisphere relations (of which more in Chapter 5), the Clear-cut LH struggles to realize that it has limitations.

Strategically reduced vision

This book is entitled *Fullness of Vision, Fullness of Life*. Neither hemisphere can offer on its own either fullness of vision or fullness of life. Each hemisphere, however, has an important role to play, and those roles are complementary.

The gift of the Clear-cut LH is to offer a form of attention to the world that, rather than prioritizing fullness, deliberately seeks focus. It is by narrowing its field of attention that the LH contributes best. It is by a deliberate contraction of its vision, setting aside detail and distraction, that the Clear-cut LH proceeds. This approach enables its simplified mapping, its distinctions and separations, and its targeted and tenacious pursuit of projects through to completion.

What the Clear-cut LH offers, then, is strategically reduced vision – which, counterintuitively, can be a very positive contribution towards an overall fullness. The richest moments of life do not lie within the gift of the LH on its own. However, when the Clear-cut LH uses its strengths to the full, and offers their fruit to the broader wisdom of the Holistic RH, its contribution towards fullness of life can be considerable. It is to a fuller understanding of that Holistic right hemisphere that we turn next.

Questions for reflection

1. Can you think of simplified maps that you have found helpful? Where might you make more use of such a map?
2. When has a simplified map had negative consequences, for you or for others? What can you learn from this?
3. Which of the limitations of the Clear-cut LH particularly rang true to your experience?
4. Which of its strengths would you like to engage more deliberately?

Chapter 3 thumbnail summary – The Clear-cut Left Hemisphere (LH)

1 *Simplified maps*

- A central practice of the Clear-cut LH is to create a simplified map of a situation. This can enable focus and clarity, and avoid overwhelm and distraction.
- Such maps primarily include Clear-cut fact-focused information, which is typically grouped into distinct categories.
- In constructing such a map, the central governing principle of the LH is repeatedly at play: the act of separating or dividing one thing from another. This includes the map separating its contents from their context and uniqueness.

2 *Sense of purpose*

- The Clear-cut LH has a strong and focused sense of purpose. It likes to solve problems, and make a difference. For change to 'count' for the LH, something Clear-cut needs to have shifted.
- The priority of the LH is thus centred around control: harnessing what might be useful in order to make things happen. Not to be actively making a difference can feel like unthinkable failure.

3 *Strengths*

- The LH is at its best in contexts in which cause and effect are highly predictable, and linear logic prevails. Here it can be accurate and very efficient.

4 *Limitations*

Primary:
- Misreading the nature of what it's attending to – assuming it is simpler than it is.
- Having created a simplified map, tending to relate to the map, rather than the reality.
- Assuming that everything 'works' in a predictable linear manner.

Additional:
- Its 'stickiness': having adopted a plan or perspective, it struggles to relinquish it.
- Its desire to be in control, and to feel certain.
- It struggles to see that its approach is not always best.

5 Fullness of vision?

- The Clear-cut LH on its own offers strategically reduced vision. This strategy is effective when its focus and tenacity are deployed in conjunction with the Holistic RH, contributing to fullness of vision, and to fullness of life.

Notes

1 Iain McGilchrist, 2009, *The Master and His Emissary: The Divided Brain and the Making of the Western World*, New Haven, CT: Yale University Press, p. 30 (hereafter *Master*).

2 McGilchrist, *Master*, p. 154.

3 McGilchrist, *Master*, p. 137.

4 McGilchrist, *Master*, p. 154.

5 Some readers may balk at this use of personal language in relation to a single hemisphere. There is indeed an important underlying question at stake. In brief, the question is essentially linguistic. The choice is between mechanical and personal language: do we consider the 'way of being' that is enabled by a single hemisphere to be more like a machine, or more like a human being? McGilchrist opts for the latter, for reasons I find convincing.

6 It is striking that this is the case even in left-handers (as they would normally use the right hemisphere to manipulate tools with their left hand).

7 This is also true for languages other than English.

8 McGilchrist, *Master*, p. 84.

9 McGilchrist, *Master*, p. 199.

10 A hypothetical scenario on these lines was described by developmental economist Natalie Quinn in the BBC Radio 4 program *Effective Altruism*, first broadcast 13 May 2018.

11 Iain McGilchrist, 2021, *The Matter With Things*, London: Perspectiva Press, p. 408.

4

The Holistic Right Hemisphere (RH)

The concerns of the Holistic RH stand in considerable contrast to those of the Clear-cut LH. Rather than a primary desire to map and change, the RH seeks understanding and connection. Relating, to people, places and things, is an important RH priority, enabling a sense of belonging. Contributing to all of this is the RH's remarkable capacity for integrating multiple parts into a coherent sense of the whole. This integration includes joining together theory and experience, past and present, memory, concepts and sensory input.

Overall, the RH way of being has a very different feel to the Clear-cut consistency of the LH. RH concerns can easily feel less tangible than those of the LH. And let's register the fact that, especially in contemporary Western culture, 'less tangible' attributes can easily be assumed to be 'less important', or indeed 'unimportant'. A key part of the message of this book is that such an interpretation is utterly misguided. The sensitivity, care, connection and integration offered by the RH are deeply valuable, and essential for human flourishing.

The neuroscientist Antonio Damasio tells a moving tale about one of his patients, 'Elliot', that illustrates the foundational importance of the role of the Holistic RH. It is one of many striking, and sad, tales from brain hemisphere research that relate to people who have lost significant parts of their RH functioning. A right hemispheric tumour and consequent removal of damaged parts of 'Elliot's' brain led to him losing 'his intuitive and emotional understanding'.[1] What happened is that his life 'ground to a standstill, because every decision had to be calculated from first principles – as if by a machine, from "outside"'. He had lost, along with parts of his RH, any integrated sense of desire, purpose and meaning. While contemporary society often treats the emotional and intuitive realm as peripheral, 'without it we are foolish, however much we may know, and we are only alive in a diminished sense of the word'.[2] To develop our understanding of the Holistic way of being, we turn now to consider in turn a number of aspects of the disposition of the brain's right hemisphere.

Aspects of a Holistic RH way of being

Breadth, flexibility and the new[3]

Our opening encounter with the Holistic RH was when the chaffinch looked up from the task of eating, in order to take stock of what was going on. One of the major overall purposes of the brain is to offer us awareness of what is around us. Our capacities of alertness, vigilance and sustained attention are key contributors to this, and are all mainly dependent on the RH. The breadth of RH attention is a significant feature.

Whereas the Clear-cut LH tends to lock its attention on to its current narrow focus, the Holistic RH is much more able to be flexible. Such flexibility might be seen in openness to consider different interpretations of what's going on, or in adjusting priorities because of altered circumstances.

Importantly, it is nearly always through the RH that we gain awareness of something new. This is partly because such awareness is often via the periphery of our vision, to which the Holistic RH alone attends. It is also because of the RH's posture of broad, vigilant openness, which makes it much more likely to notice what is different. Interestingly, the RH is predominantly involved not only in processing novel experience, but also in learning fresh skills or information. Once the information or skills have become familiar, they then move to become the concern of the LH.

Flexibility of thought, and unpredictable situations[4]

In situations where accurate prediction is possible, the Clear-cut LH is much stronger and more efficient than the Holistic RH. In less predictable situations, the LH struggles. Here, even if it can't produce the right answer, it may still put forward a solution anyway, and will resist letting go of its proposal. The RH, in contrast, is unfazed by uncertainty, or by not being able to offer an explanation.

When flexibility of thought is required, however, it is the RH that is much more effective and efficient. Three factors contribute to this. First, the Holistic RH can hold open several possible solutions or interpretations at once, deliberately resisting premature closure in order to discover the best alternative. Second, the RH actively plays the role of devil's advocate, on the lookout for any indications that the current approach is not the best. One major writer, Ramachandran, describes this as being the RH's strength as an 'anomaly detector'.[5] Third, having spotted anomalies, it is the RH that is much more adept at shifting its frame of reference to adopt a new perspective. Overall, the consistent flexibility of the RH is in marked contrast to the 'stickiness' of the LH.

The integrated whole[6]

The narrow attention of the LH tends to focus on details, and on parts of what's going on. Moreover, it will tend to view those parts as separate from each other. In contrast, the Holistic RH scans the overall picture, with rather less attention to detail. In its scanning, it offers a broad, exploratory perception. It looks out for patterns in what is before it. It has a more durable working memory than the LH, which is a significant asset. Relatedly, it is able to synthesize a wide range of different types of information – right across the range of the different human senses, and from memory. Overall, the LH pays attention primarily not to the whole, but to the parts, whereas the RH sees the bigger picture, both literally and metaphorically.

As Damasio's account of 'Elliot' illustrates, such integration is foundationally significant to human living in the world. One review of patients whose right hemispheres had been removed noted that the impact was especially tangible 'in the higher and more complex integrations involving insight, emotional control, initiative, constructive indication, and imagination'.[7]

Context, depth and symbols[8]

The Holistic RH views things and people in their context. Context, which includes relationships, is seen as an important aspect of the thing itself, rather than an irrelevant detail. Thus, for the RH, you can't really know me without having some understanding of the main people, places and themes in my life.

The RH (but not the LH) can make sense of contextual clues, such as deducing that it is springtime by the state of the trees, rather than because we've been told it's April. It may be surprising quite how much everyday communication relies on contextual communication. People whose RH has been damaged are stuck with literal understandings of conversation, and thus often miss nuance and implication that others may correctly interpret without even noticing.

Much of the sense of clarity that the LH offers is achieved precisely by extracting objects from their normal surroundings. This reduction of the 'field of view' does enable clarity of focus, which can be helpful. However, such clarity is like the two-dimensional plane of a microscope slide, where what is viewed has been shorn of its context and connectedness. The RH restores context. Rather than the two dimensions of a microscope slide, the RH offers much greater depth of field, restoring three-dimensional context and interconnectedness (or perhaps four-dimensional, including a time perspective).

It's also worth registering the very different ways in which the hemispheres engage with symbols. Symbols come in two varieties. An excellent example of one type is the red traffic light. Here there is an explicit, unambiguous correlation between the symbol and its meaning: for example, the colour red and the requirement to stop. It is the Clear-cut LH that processes symbols such as this. An example of the other variety of symbol is the rose. Here the symbol operates in a richer, multi-layered way, sometimes with centuries of historical background. It has depth and context. For example, roses carry connotations in both Christian (including links to the Virgin Mary: hence the 'rosary') and Islamic cultures. The English Wars of the Roses led to the new Tudor symbol of a red and white rose, and the emblem of a rose has adorned the kit of the English rugby team since 1871. It is not possible to make fully explicit what the symbol of the rose 'means' – but its meaning, to at least some people, is significant and important. This realm of symbolism is significantly different from that of the traffic light. Whether this realm is viewed as elusive and incomprehensible, or as rich and deep, it is the domain not of the Clear-cut LH, but of the Holistic RH.

Individuals and categories[9]

The RH, then, attends to specific, unique, often familiar, individual things and people, each with their particular context. In contrast, when the LH attends to an individual (thing or person), it often sees them primarily as a member of a particular category (for instance, a medium-sized church, or a church treasurer). Indeed, the simplification that leads to the LH's virtual map is achieved by dropping the unique detail of the individual, including their context, and replacing it simply by the category of which they are a member. From the perspective of the LH, therefore, any two members of the same category can be treated as equivalent, and effectively interchangeable.

Both hemispheres do make use of categories, but they approach them differently. For the Clear-cut LH, categories are defined, using explicit characteristics or rules. The Holistic RH, instead, recognizes members of the same category by an implicit family resemblance, and thus more by description than by definition (when I look at the whole of this object in front of me, it looks very like a table).

The emotional realm and the human face[10]

The overall evidence is clear and consistent: the Holistic RH is superior both at expressing emotion, and at understanding the emotions of others. It is better connected to the parts of the brain and body that process most emotions. It is also faster and more accurate in engaging with expression of emotion, whether verbally or non-verbally. Importantly, the seat of the *inhibition* of emotion is also located in the RH: this hemisphere's affinity with emotions does not mean that it is simply tossed to and fro at their mercy.[11]

Several main exceptions to this RH emotional superiority are worth noting. These include *anger*, which is 'robustly connected' with the LH,[12] as are irritability and elation.[13] The LH is also the primary hemisphere for 'anxious apprehension'. This typically arises from 'fear of uncertainty and lack of control',[14] which are themselves linked strongly with LH concerns. A further main exception is worth noting. It seems that the 'conscious representation of emotion: willed, or forced, emotional expressions' are controlled by the LH, which, relatedly, may also have an affinity with 'more superficial, social emotions'.[15]

The human face plays a particularly important role in the expression of emotion. It is, again, the RH that is considerably more skilled at noticing and interpreting such expression, along with those conveyed by gesture and tone of voice.[16]

It is worth pausing to register the special significance of the human face in the realm of relationships. For a start, it is the face above all that enables the unique identification of individuals. The ability to recognize faces is so familiar to us that we may not realize quite what an achievement it is. Not only do we register relatively small differences between broadly similar faces, but we also cope unthinkingly with the considerable range of expressions that any given face may adopt. Various forms of RH damage lead to an inability to recognize faces.

The face is also a key area for the expression of emotion. Permit me to share some fascinating detail on this subject. Remarkably, it is the left-hand side of the face (the left hemiface), controlled by the RH, which is more emotionally expressive than its counterpart (for humans, and for some other primates, including chimpanzees). This feature appears to be confirmed by the 'strong universal tendency to cradle infants with their faces to the left'. This enables both child and parent to see each other's more expressive left hemiface. Intriguingly, in a study of 103 mother and child sculptures dating from the two millennia before Christ, 99 of them featured leftward cradling. The same bias is exhibited by chimpanzees and gorillas.[17]

Later in the book, we will return to the significance of the human face in improvisation, leadership and Christian living.

Moving more broadly, it is the RH that ascribes emotional value to what we experience. Without a functioning RH, our experience of life is drained of emotion, and becomes much thinner and poorer in consequence. A review of adults whose RH had been surgically removed describes them as having 'shallow affect' and 'rigidity'. 'Together with emotional experience most of their personality vanishes as well.'[18]

The emotional range of the RH is more inclusive, encompassing so-called 'negative' emotions, but possibly also acting as the principal source of pleasurable experience. The emotional range of the LH is more limited, but, as noted, includes anger, irritability, anxious apprehension and elation.

The RH is primarily the one interested in other people, as well as being more self-aware. It is also more favourably disposed towards others, and is crucially involved in our ability to put ourselves 'in others' shoes'. Empathy, belonging and connection all primarily flow from and depend on the capacity of the RH.

There is, then, strong evidence around RH superiority for emotional expression and interpretation (noting some important exceptions). I want to conclude this section by reiterating the fundamentally important role played by such emotional facility. To engage with the world at all well, we profoundly depend on 'the ability to *understand* and *interact* with other living beings'.[19] The Holistic RH is central to this ability.

Time, flow and narrative[20]

The steady passing of time, its flux and flow, is a major part of our unfolding experience of living. It is primarily the sustained attention offered by the Holistic RH that grounds us in this river of time. 'Virtually all aspects of the appreciation of time, in the sense of something lived through, with a past, present and future, are dependent on the right hemisphere ... The sense of past or future is severely impaired in right-hemisphere damage.'[21] The LH's tendency is to break time up, separating it into individual 'slices'. From this perspective, time is viewed as a sequence of discrete static points. When the focus is on a static point in time, the LH has an advantage. However, the LH appears to register something as permanent only if it is unchanging. The RH, in contrast, is much stronger at attending to ongoing and evolving flow over time, and also to fluid motion.

These factors are very relevant when it comes to our engagement with narrative, with stories of life unfolding in time. It is the Holistic RH that is able to sustain the attention, and develop the memories and context necessary to make sense of narrative, and to experience it as meaningful. The LH operating alone has a very different perspective: purely a sequence of unrelated, decontextualized, momentary events.

One example must suffice: an early twentieth-century neurologist had as a patient a musketeer, Robert, with right-hemisphere shrapnel damage. When asked to describe a film, Robert reported 'a large number of correctly observed individual scenes without any grasp of the overall plot structure'. He had 'literally lost the plot'.[22]

Ancient Greece developed two contrasting perspectives on time. *Chronos* is the term used to describe the regular passing of steady time – as in the uniform divisions of chronometer and chronology. This is the terrain in which the Clear-cut LH engages with time. Unlike the LH, the Holistic RH also engages with a sense of *kairos* time. This carries connotations of the right time, an opportune time, or the appointed time.[23] A brief personal example may help illustrate the contrast. I have more than once bought a book, started reading it, and found it utterly incomprehensible. Then, a few years later, I have 'randomly' taken it off the shelf, started reading, and found it utterly gripping and pertinent. The *kairos* time in my life had arrived for this book.

Combining all these considerations with ones of context, the Holistic RH enables a sense of dwelling in time, organically connected in relationships with people, places and things, all part of an ongoing flux and flow. The engagement of the Clear-cut LH is much more like skating over the surface of time, rather than dwelling deeply within it.[24] Indeed, for the Clear-cut LH, time often feels like something with which to do battle, rather than a precious gift.

Conclusion

Where the Clear-cut LH draws dividing lines between contrasting types of thing, the Holistic RH holds them or draws them together. Where the Clear-cut separates, the Holistic unites and integrates.

Where the LH's stance towards the world 'is one of reaching out to grasp, and therefore to *use*, it, the RH's appears to be one of reaching out – just that'.[25]

Where the LH offers a strategically reduced form of vision, invaluable for many tasks in the world, the RH offers a form of vision both broad and deep. RH vision looks not only at 'things', but at their relationships and connections, and at the whole. Moreover, the manner of vision is different. LH tenacious tunnel vision is complemented by RH open breadth, lightly held.

Neither perspective on its own can give us fullness of vision. We need the specialized skills of both hemispheres, along with their distinctive modes of attention. Given the degree of contrast between them, can they really be expected to cooperate? It is to the exploration of such questions that we turn in the next chapter.

Questions for reflection

1 Which of these Holistic RH qualities particularly struck you? In what way?
2 Which of the qualities do you value most? Are there any that seem to you unnecessary?
3 Do you feel you are gaining a sense of the contrasting approaches of the two hemispheres? (If not, I would encourage you to look back and remind yourself of the key features in each case.)

Chapter 4 thumbnail summary – The Holistic Right Hemisphere (RH)

Holistic RH concerns centre around understanding things as they are, connection to other living beings, and offering an integrated sense of the whole. RH considerations can seem less definite than those of the LH, and thus less important. Strong evidence, however, shows that loss of RH function leads to a disintegration of meaning, motivation and personal engagement with life.

Some specific areas of contrast include:

1 The RH has a broader perspective, and alertness to what is new.
2 The LH is strong where accurate prediction is possible. Where it is not, the RH is much more comfortable. The RH can hold open many possible interpretations, rather than jump to premature conclusions. The RH is a strong devil's advocate, and more easily switches to a new understanding when appropriate.
3 The RH receives a wide spectrum of information, and is very good at integrating into a coherent whole.
4 The RH attends to context, to relationships, to depth of meaning and to the symbolic realm.
5 The RH is more attentive to individuals. RH use of categories is based on general description, rather than rule-based definition.
6 The RH has strong affinity with the emotional realm, and thus with social connection and meaning-making. Some exceptions: anger, anxious apprehension, irritability and elation are linked with the LH. The RH has a strong affinity with reading faces.
7 It is the RH that senses time as an integrated flow, rather than as isolated momentary 'slices'.

Notes

1 Antonio Damasio, 1994, *Descartes' Error: Emotion, Reason and the Human Brain*, New York: Putnam, quoted in Iain McGilchrist, 2021, *The Matter With Things*, London: Perspectiva Press, p. 224. For McGilchrist's critique of Damasio's interpretation of Elliot's experience, see Iain McGilchrist, 2009, *The Master and His Emissary: The Divided Brain and the Making of the Western World*, New Haven, CT: Yale University Press, pp. 185–6.

2 McGilchrist, *Things*, p. 224.
3 McGilchrist, *Master*, pp. 37–40.
4 McGilchrist, *Master*, pp. 37–42.
5 McGilchrist, *Master*, p. 52.
6 McGilchrist, *Master*, pp. 42–3, 46–9.
7 McGilchrist, *Things*, p. 213.
8 McGilchrist, *Master*, pp. 49–51, 77–9.
9 McGilchrist, *Master*, pp. 51–3.
10 McGilchrist, *Master*, pp. 57–64.
11 McGilchrist, *Things*, pp. 223–4.
12 McGilchrist, *Master*, p. 61.
13 McGilchrist, *Things*, p. 197.
14 McGilchrist, *Master*, p. 64.
15 McGilchrist, *Master*, p. 62.

16 The partial exception is that the LH picks up the more blunt emotional signals conveyed around the mouth area. See McGilchrist, *Master*, p. 59.

17 McGilchrist, *Master*, p. 61.

18 B. M. Velichkovsky, O. A Krotkova, M. G. Sharaev et al., 2017, 'In Search of the "I": Neuropsychology of Lateralized Thinking Meets Dynamic Causal Modelling', *Psychology in Russia: State of the Art*, 10(3), pp. 7–27, quoted in McGilchrist, *Things*, p. 212.

19 McGilchrist, *Things*, p. 224 (italics in the original).
20 McGilchrist, *Master*, pp. 72–7.
21 McGilchrist, *Master*, p. 76.
22 McGilchrist, *Things*, p. 211.

23 The concept of *kairos* is a regular feature in the New Testament – the term is used 86 times.

24 McGilchrist, *Things*, p. 887.
25 McGilchrist, *Master*, p. 127 (italics in the original).

5

Hemisphere Interaction and History

Introduction

McGilchrist's title *The Master and His Emissary* refers to a fable about a wise master who was selflessly devoted to the people of his small kingdom. One of his cleverest and most trusted emissaries began to interpret his master's moderation as weakness, and so lost respect for him. This led to the emissary usurping his master's role, and then himself becoming a tyrant – resulting in the kingdom collapsing in ruins.[1] McGilchrist intends this as a parable of what can easily happen with the brain hemispheres. The RH is represented by the master, and the LH by the emissary. The clarity and linear logic of the LH, combined with its sense of certainty, can easily seem superior to the breadth and subtlety of the RH. The story of the master and the emissary suggests, however, that the emissary becoming dominant may not lead to the citizens living happily ever after.

Having attended to each of the hemispheres separately, we now turn to questions of their relationship. How should they ideally relate? And if their relationship goes awry, how does it tend to do so?

McGilchrist finds that many of his audiences want to hear that the hemispheres can be described in terms of one of two familiar patterns. One such pattern is a simple dichotomy between good and bad – for instance that the right hemisphere is good, and the left hemisphere is bad. But that is not the case: we need the specialized strengths that each one offers. The alternative wish of an audience is that two things would be equally desirable, in a pleasingly symmetrical balance. But this is not really the case either. There is very little that is symmetrical about the two hemispheres. For instance, the right hemisphere knows the importance of the left, but the left does not understand the importance of the right.

This chapter, then, neither tells a tale of a good hemisphere and bad hemisphere, nor one of two straightforwardly 'equal' hemispheres.

The reality is not that simple. However, the principles and patterns of the reality are not that complex, either. To begin to explore them, we return to the cameo of the meal with friends, this time featuring a minor variation.

Good hemisphere interaction: an example

Meal with a twist

You and the other guests have gathered in the host's lounge. You've been enjoying catching up with friends, and meeting some new people. The clock is ticking towards 7pm, the time at which food was to be served. Just as the host is about to usher the guests through to sit down and eat, one guest asks another, Geoff, how he is. Geoff shares that his elderly mother had a GP appointment that afternoon, and the doctor seemed very concerned by some of his mother's symptoms. Geoff is clearly apprehensive, and is grateful for the chance to unburden himself in the company of caring friends. The host realizes that it's now 7.05, Geoff's flow of words is showing no signs of pausing, and the dinner is already late. The other guests are unaware of the risk of the lasagne being burnt, and are listening with care and attention. A few moments later, still with no pause in the flow of Geoff's outpouring, the host catches the eye of a good friend, Carol, and very subtly inclines his head towards the dining room. A micro-nod in response assures him that the message was received. While still listening to Geoff, the host ever so gently gestures to the guests to begin to move through, without saying a word, and Carol leads the way. Geoff keeps chatting as he walks through, everyone sits down, and the meal has not been burnt.

Meal example – what was going on?

The primary pattern for good hemisphere relating

This cameo describes a situation that could have gone wrong, but ended up going well. What, then, was the nature of the brain hemisphere interplay that contributed to this positive encounter? To begin to answer this question, let's remind ourselves of two important principles from Chapter 2. We first encountered them when exploring the impact of how we pay attention.

The first principle is that we should always aim to be centred in the Holistic RH, not least in any situation involving people. Being centred in the RH helps us treat people as people (rather than as objects). It also keeps us open to the reality of what's actually going on, rather than focusing primarily on our simplified map.

Alongside this, the second principle is that we should always draw generously on the great strengths of the Clear-cut LH – to a degree appropriate to each specific situation. The LH has skills that are beyond the RH. Discerning how best to deploy these well is always wise.

So how do we hold these two principles together? What does that look like in practice? We can describe good hemisphere relating in terms of a common pattern. The short form of the pattern is: right, left, right. This pattern begins and ends in the RH, and draws on the LH in the middle (without losing its RH centring). What does this right, left, right involve?

First, the initial right indicates the broad openness of the RH surveying a situation. The RH notices some sort of development or issue that deserves closer analysis. The RH knows that analysis is not its strong point, so calls in help from the LH. Second, the LH analyses the situation, using simplified maps and linear logic. It then passes the fruit of its analysis back to the RH. This may include a recommendation, or some options.

The third step sees the action return to the RH, along with the fruit of the LH analysis. Within this third step we can distinguish two distinct phases, which I'll label preserve and transform. The first phase is about greater understanding. This begins with the RH receiving the Clear-cut analysis provided by the LH. The RH then sifts the analysis, aiming to preserve all that is relevant to this context. (Some of the analysis may not be relevant: because it is based on a simplified map, and potentially on inaccurate assumptions about the nature of the context.) The result of this phase is an enriched and strengthened understanding of the situation. In the second phase, the RH will have the casting vote regarding what is needed, tailoring its action to the specifics of this situation (rather than to a simplified map). The RH discerns how best to shape appropriate next steps, if necessary transforming the LH recommendations to some degree before taking action.

And so we end up with a slightly longer form of the primary pattern of good hemisphere relating: right, left, right – preserve and transform. This pattern preserves our two principles. We remain centred in the RH throughout. Additionally, we draw on the strengths of the LH, to a degree appropriate to the situation.

The primary pattern in action

Returning to our meal cameo, let's see how that pattern worked out in practice. Around 7 o'clock we can imagine the host's RH picking up Geoff's distress – and also realizing the potential tension with the planned timetable (food at 7). First, it was because the host was centred in his RH that he registered not only that Geoff had begun talking freely, but also the manner in which he was talking – with deep feeling and concern, about his beloved mother. Because he was centred in the RH, the pattern of what unfolded began, appropriately, with 'right'. Had the host, instead, been centred in his LH, he would have noticed that Geoff had begun talking freely, but without registering the significance of what he was saying. He could easily have interrupted, bluntly but cheerily, 'OK, everybody: it's lovely to see you all. Come on through – dinner is served!' Alternatively, he might have become irritable or angry at Geoff's disruption of the evening timetable. The principle of remaining centred in the RH is important, not least in enabling the pattern to begin in the right place – with 'right'.

Next, the RH sensed tension between the timetable and Geoff's needs, and knew that some form of intervention might be appropriate. It wanted to understand more before coming to a decision. The RH knows the limitations of its own abilities, and its need of the LH. Remaining centred in the RH, the host called on their LH for analytical assistance: the second step – left. And so, at 7.05, the host's RH might have said to their LH, 'How much longer can we delay without burning the food? And are there any other options?'

In this cameo, the analysis was straightforward, leading to a single Clear-cut answer, which was passed back to the RH. The LH reply: 'Five minutes max. No other options.' The pattern continues: right, left, and now it's time for the third step: right again.

This third step, then, had two phases. The first, preserve, was straightforward: we need to find a way of eating as soon as possible. The second phase is to transform the good fruit of the analysis. Appropriate transformation both preserves that fruit, and also presents, transforms and sometimes elevates it in a way most fitting for the situation. In this case, the transformation was purely about the manner in which the host proceeded. His subtle and silent use of gesture, first with Carol and then with the whole gathering, proved spot on. The host's centring in the RH was again both crucial and fruitful: the use of gesture and being less implicit indicate RH territory more than LH.

Overall, what could have been an awkward few minutes (potentially leading to an awkward evening) was navigated well. The host remaining centred in the RH proved an important foundation, both at the beginning of this period and in its conclusion. Moreover, the good ending relied both on the LH's swift analysis, and on the RH's discerning wisely how that should be preserved and transformed. These principles and this pattern enabled the two hemispheres to cooperate effectively, drawing on the strengths of both, for the benefit of all involved.

Other possibilities for the third step – preserve and transform

In the meal variation described above, the LH analysis led to a single, clear recommendation: to avoid burnt food, serve the dinner within five minutes. In this scenario, the RH discerned that it was right to enact that immediately: LH analysis was preserved in its entirety. There is a range of other possibilities.

Sometimes, the RH accepts and proceeds on some aspects of the analysis, but not others. Sometimes the analysis is accepted, but not the recommendations. Sometimes the analysis and recommendations may be provisionally accepted, but not the timing of what is proposed. Perhaps further discussion with different people is called for first, or simply waiting to see how events unfold.

Further rationale for the need for RH preserve and transform

We might, however, be wondering whether things need to be this complex. Might not a simpler pattern – right, left, act – be sufficient, or even preferable? Within such a pattern, the RH would discern the need for analysis; the LH would deploy its analytical strength and come up with a recommendation; and then we would get on and do it. Surely right, left, act is simpler, faster and straightforwardly better? This is a really important question, and it deserves a good response.

The rationale for the first two steps, 'right, left': the crux of the question is about what should happen in the third step: simply do what the LH advises, or pass back to the RH for further discernment before action. There are two good reasons to return to the RH.

First, the LH will not have analysed the full situation, but only those Clear-cut aspects it considers relevant. Its considerations are limited and simplified, and are skewed towards Clear-cut content and conclusions. Yes, they will often prove enlightening and relevant. However, the input on which they are based is partial: it would be very surprising if their output always proved accurate. This is true of the content of the input. It's also true of LH assumptions regarding 'how things work' – their accuracy and relevance will vary from context to context. Many decisions involve weighing one type of consideration against another utterly different kind of factor. This is a matter of discernment rather than calculation. The hemispheres may differ in their judgement. And it is the RH that is much better equipped to judge wisely: it is attentive to the reality rather than the simplification; and it is skilled at integrating and synthesizing diverse considerations.

It is for these reasons that the initial preserve phase is appropriate. The RH should expect that there may well be insight worth preserving, and it may be worth preserving in its entirety. Nevertheless, it would be naïve to accept it all routinely: there are good reasons why, sometimes, some of it should be held lightly, or set aside.

The second reason for the return to the RH relates to the second phase: transform. Having chosen what to preserve from LH analysis, it is the RH again that is best placed to discern how to enact it. The key word is how: transformation is needed because deciding what to do (serve the dinner) still leaves many options for how it is done (more or less sensitively). The Clear-cut LH focuses on the important question of what is done. The RH is highly attentive to the significant how considerations, and skilled in shaping a good response. This is why both the preserve and the transform phases are needed, and why both are best overseen by the RH.

Right, left, act is indeed simpler and faster, but will often not be better. Having started with 'right, left', the wisest next step is a return to 'right', enabling preserve and transform.

One further point is worth making at this stage. In contrast to the meal just described, in some scenarios the LH analysis will be highly detailed and complicated. The quantity of LH input will be substantial. (Perhaps we are considering detailed plans for a new building.) In such a context, we could easily assume that the RH is much less relevant, and so primary control should shift to the LH.

This, however, is not correct. The quantity of LH input is a different consideration from the roles that the two hemispheres take. The balance of input may be different in terms of quantity, but the need for Holistic RH discernment is unchanged. What this type of scenario usefully illustrates is that the RH is very happy to welcome and incorporate large amounts of good-quality LH input.

The fruit of healthy hemisphere relating

Let me offer another example of hemisphere partnership – which can also function as an analogy for healthy hemisphere relating in general. Imagine me setting out to learn to play a new piece of cello or piano music. I may start by listening to a recording, to get a rough feel for the whole piece. When it comes to learning to play it, some parts may be straightforward. But where the music is technically demanding, I will focus on one small section at a time. Each small section I will often repeat many times, gradually gaining the necessary technical skill. Practising in this way is both effective and necessary. However, when I've learnt the notes of the whole piece, I still haven't finished.

The next stage is to join back together what I had split into pieces. This leads to the short sections being put into their broader context. What's more, when I re-engage with the full flow of the music I begin to find ways to convey the shading, the expressiveness and the vitality within it. To polish this latter stage without having gained technical mastery would be farcical, but to end the process when the technical had been mastered would lead to mechanical playing: technically excellent, but lacking soul and vitality. In preserving and transforming the work of the Clear-cut LH, the Holistic RH has elevated the contents of the static musical map on the page up into the realm of living music.

This gives a further indication of how the hemispheres ideally relate: beginning with an RH sense of the whole, then the LH deploying detailed analysis on small parts. The final return to the RH preserves the technical mastery, and transforms it into expressive and living music. Both hemispheres have had distinctive but complementary roles. The end result is significantly enhanced and enriched, both by the detailed analysis, and also by the integrating reunification.

In the two previous chapters, I noted how each hemisphere on its own falls short of offering fullness of vision. The perspective of the LH, through its deliberate contraction of attention and simplified mapping, offers strategically reduced vision. The viewpoint of the RH offers vision that is broad and deep – and yet lacks the intensity of focus of the LH, or its strength of follow-through.

Now, however, we have explored the basic pattern by which the specialized strengths of both hemispheres can be combined. We have sketched the contours of collaborative hemisphere partnership. Such cooperation is not machine-like. It does not rely on a fixed formula, or static balance. Rather, this is a hemisphere relationship with an equilibrium centred in the RH, drawing dynamically and responsively on the specialized skills of both hemispheres. It is just such a collaborative partnership of the hemispheres that will enable a truthful and life-giving fullness of vision. Having focused on pattern, we now turn to posture.

In our engagement with the world, healthy hemisphere relating enables a posture of clarity anchored in compassion. Our centring in the Holistic RH offers stability from which we can attend with openness and care. Our discerning incorporation of Clear-cut LH perspectives strengthens and enriches the clarity with which we view the world around us. Synthesizing these forms of attention gives rise to a single integrated posture of poised attentiveness: strong, caring and discerning. Such poised attentiveness sets us up to respond appropriately to the very varied unfolding requirements of the different situations we encounter.

Thus far, we have seen the patterns, posture and rationale of healthy hemisphere relating. Our next step is to appreciate how such relating easily tends to become skewed. In doing so, we will see that the appeal of the simpler, shorter alternative pattern, *right, left, act*, is considerable.

How hemisphere relating tends to become skewed[2]

LH scepticism

I have set out what I see as a clear and strong rationale for the basic pattern of healthy hemisphere relating. The argument I have summarized makes a lot of sense – but there is a caveat. The 'problem' with its reasoning is that it relies on Holistic wisdom. Holistic wisdom, however, has little traction with the LH. View the rationale from a LH perspective, and much of its force seems to evaporate.

For the LH to be convinced by the rationale, it would need to recognize that the reality beyond its own simplifications not only exists, but is important. It would need to accept that its assumptions are often flawed to a greater or lesser extent. Underlying both of these, it would need to own the fact that it is itself limited.

As we have previously registered, however, the LH is blind to its own limitations. It does not see that its powers are restricted, never mind where the limits of its capability lie. As a consequence, *nothing* in the previous paragraph consistently rings true for the LH regarding itself.

Not only that, but the LH understanding of the RH is very different from what I have been describing. From an LH perspective, RH considerations (such as the manner in which something is done, the state of relationships, the local context) easily seem irrelevant. They may appear as fancy trimmings, an indulgence or distractions from the real work. Consequently, from an LH perspective, it seems downright irresponsible to let the RH make final decisions about action. It feels like an insult – and foolish – to ask the RH to sift its own (LH) recommendations and potentially reject some of them, or to transform them for use in this particular context. Overall, then, the rationale I have offered carries little if any weight for the Clear-cut LH.

LH rationale for its own superiority

The LH, therefore, tends to reject any notion that the RH is well suited to play the role of senior partner in the relationship. Instead, the LH seems (to itself) very well-equipped to be trusted as the leader (never mind senior partner). From an LH perspective, there are several reasons for its superiority.

First, its take on the world is clear and convincing. With the LH, you get a clear sense of knowing where you are and what is what.

Second, a strong sense of power adds energy to the clarity. This is the hemisphere that wants to get things done, and believes in its ability to achieve what is needed. Its *raison d'être*, as McGilchrist puts it, is 'narrowing things down to a certainty, so that we can grasp them'.[3]

Third, the LH holds several of the tools of powerful rhetoric. When it pulls together its analysis and its gift of clear logic, its arguments can sound very convincing. It is like a 'political heavyweight who has control of the media'. For the RH, in contrast, 'what it knows is too complex, [and] hasn't the advantage of having been carved up into pieces'[4] – so it can be hard for it to gain a hearing.

Taking these considerations together, and staying with a LH perspective, if either hemisphere is going to be the senior partner of the pair, it should clearly be the left. From a LH perspective, right, left, act seems not just perfectly adequate, but far superior: simpler, faster and straightforwardly better than any longer alternative.

This is how it seems to the LH. However, the clarity, power and certainty contained in these arguments all arise from the simplified mapping of the LH. In parallel, these arguments are much weaker than they seem, precisely because they rest on simplification, rather than on reality.

Let's consider again the meal cameo described in the previous section, and how the host responded. Here, the relationship between hemispheres was dynamic and cooperative, making the most of the specialized skills of each part of the brain. These strengths are contrasting and complementary, and we saw that what flowed from their cooperative partnership was a fullness of vision unmatched by either hemisphere on its own.

When, in contrast, the LH takes over as senior partner, this gift is lost. Rather than fullness of vision, we are left with a deficient form of perception. Yes, such sight has clarity and a sense of certainty. But the certainty is illusory, and the clarity is based on approximation. It is thus deceptive as well as shallow. In Chapter 2 I described LH vision as strategically reduced – which sounds positive. LH vision on its own is certainly reduced. But the strategy is only effective if LH vision is combined well with RH insight. If and when the LH tries to go it alone, its vision is both detrimentally simplified and unhelpfully skewed.

Falling out of equilibrium

The LH does not find the rationale for RH-centred cooperation attractive or convincing. The LH, moreover, is strong and determined. We should not, then, be surprised if there are occasions when hemisphere relating falls out of equilibrium, and the LH becomes the senior, and dominant, partner.

When this happens, and when we register that all is not ideal, there are two conceivable responses. The first is that we redress the balance. The pendulum, as it were, swings back again. We become centred in the RH once more, and healthy equilibrium is restored.

There is, however, also a second possibility. Here the lack of equilibrium is interpreted differently. With this option, any emerging negatives are taken to indicate that this shift *hasn't yet gone far enough*. Here the assumption is that we need to go further in the same direction: it is *more LH* that is needed, rather than a re-welcoming of the RH.

Let's take a brief example. Vicar Clare is feeling out of control. She regularly wakes in the night worrying about what she may have forgotten to do, and not infrequently double-books her diary. Something needs to change. Clare's response is to introduce a much stronger and clearer organizing system, including better planning, a default weekly schedule, and tight task management. This leads to significant improvements. At this point, the initial underuse of the LH has been redressed. We have a good equilibrium.

Over the weeks, however, things become more difficult. She finds herself treating her relationships as tasks to be ticked off – which is not appreciated. She also struggles to adjust her plans in response to important events at short notice – such as the funeral of a church member. At this point, it seems that the balance has shifted towards LH dominance. How will Clare respond? She has two broad options:

One option is focused on fine-tuning her planning and organization. Perhaps she needs to increase her default time allowance for relationships. Perhaps she should create a protocol that helps her adjust when a funeral request comes in. In this first option, a solution is sought in going further in the same LH direction.

The second broad option is not closed to refinements of the organizing system, but that's not its essence. Rather, this option is about going back to treating people as people. It's about relationships and responsiveness. The second option preserves all that is good in Clare's new system, but it shifts to treating her plans as a useful servant, rather than as a master. In the second option, Clare stops trying to be a machine. The second option is about re-centring in the RH. Falling out of equilibrium is recognized for what it was, and the pendulum swings back towards healthy cooperation.

Cultural shifts

At this point, we make a key move in the overall argument of this book. Our focus thus far has been centred on individual human beings. The step we now take is from the individual to the group.

The important claim here is that the hemisphere understanding I have summarized can offer striking insight at the cultural level, not just the individual. The principles we have been discussing can offer fresh perspective and helpful wisdom when we bring them to bear on broad patterns of human behaviour, not just on the attention and action of individuals. When we view a culture from a hemisphere-informed perspective, we notice significant features we would otherwise easily have missed. Moreover, we find ourselves spotting interconnections between characteristics that would otherwise have seemed distinct and unrelated.

When McGilchrist first considered the cultural implications of his hemisphere understanding, a major question quickly surfaced. If insight could be gained by viewing *contemporary* culture in this way, what further understanding might arise from looking at *previous periods* of human history? This question drew on his pre-medical academic expertise, where he had increasingly focused on the history of cultures and ideas.

McGilchrist's unusual career path made him remarkably well placed to respond. He did so by collating a whistle-stop overview of Western cultural history, from the time of ancient Greece to the present day, informed by a hemisphere perspective. He attends in particular to significant cultural shifts.[5] The patterns that he points out make surprising sense. This overview forms the second half of *The Master and His Emissary*.

In order to summarize Western cultural history in 220 pages, McGilchrist clearly has to generalize hugely, and paint a broad-brush picture. In the next section of this chapter, I offer a far more succinct summary of his potted history. I do so to remind us that our church life is situated in a cultural context which is not a blank canvas. Looking at how that context has been shaped will help us to see in sharper relief key features of contemporary church life (in subsequent chapters). Moreover, attending to the patterns in the broad historical canvas will help us notice patterns in the recent history of church leadership culture.

The divided brain and the shaping of Western history

Overview

In McGilchrist's historical survey, he points to evidence of the signature characteristics of each hemisphere in the cultural life of broad historical eras. He focuses especially on cultural shifts, times when new developments, emphases and patterns of thinking became influential. Particular attention is paid to times when the hemisphere relationship seems to have fallen out of equilibrium. As will be clear, sometimes the subsequent cultural response redresses the balance. But not always: at other times what follows is a push further in the same direction.

To address this section, I have summarized McGilchrist's broad conclusions in a diagram below.

The position of the arrows in the middle column gives some indication of McGilchrist's broad diagnosis of each period. If there is a 'Left Hemisphere' arrow, it indicates a strengthening of the left hemisphere influence in that era. When there is no 'Right Hemisphere' arrow for an era, the point being made is the lack of development of right hemisphere influence, or indeed its decline. It is not that all right hemispheres ceased to function.

HEMISPHERE INTERACTION AND HISTORY

Approx. Centuries	Left hemisphere	Right hemisphere	Key features
11th to 2nd BC		Ancient Greece	Initial advance in both Hs, e.g. in art. Then further shift to LH. E.g. Philosophy, currency.
8th BC to 5th AD	Ancient Rome		Initial advance in both Hs – literature. Uniform plans e.g. forts, towns, villas. Then shift to LH – increased codification & rigid systematization.
15th and 16th		Renaissance	Big strides in both science and art. Balance & breadth valued.
16th	Reformation		Shift away from symbol & metaphor, towards literal. 'Flesh became word'.
17th and 18th	Enlightenment		Rise of science to dominance. Clarity & certainty eclipse balance & reason.
19th		Romantic Movement	About how, disposition; lived experience; nature, arts, childhood, the particular. Depth, evocation.
18th and 19th	Industrial Revolution		Bid for power over natural world; manufacturing enables world increasingly aligned with LH view. Context, history, culture set aside.
20th and 21st	Modern & Post-Modern Words		Algorithms, bureaucratization, protocols outweigh wisdom. Virtual worlds, often cut off from nature.

The column on the left gives an indication of the broad time period of each era.

The position (left, central or right) of the name of each era, such as 'Ancient Greece', gives an approximate feel for the degree of balance between hemispheres in that period. The right-hand column mentions some relevant features of the period that inform McGilchrist's interpretation.

Overall, McGilchrist argues that each of these significant shifts in cultural history is associated with a strengthening of the influence of one or both hemispheres. Within this overview, two main overarching features are worth noting.

First, McGilchrist highlights three periods in Western history during which creative cultural development seems to have happened in a particularly fertile and balanced way. These three eras are: Ancient Greece (especially the earlier centuries); early in the Roman Empire; and the European Renaissance. McGilchrist sees these times as periods in which, broadly speaking, the mindset of that society appears to have had a healthy relationship of dynamic equilibrium between the two brain hemispheres.

Second, crucially, the narrative since the European Renaissance is broadly one of steadily increasing LH ascendancy. There are some exceptions to this pattern, but the centre of gravity has very much been moving towards the LH.

This second point is of considerable significance. It is not just that the 'centre of gravity' has shifted backwards and forwards, like a very protracted tug-of-war in which both teams are still more or less equal. Rather, it is as if the left hemisphere team is steadily and inexorably moving towards full domination of their opponents (in spite of some periods of greater equality). In one sense, this continued shift to the left should not surprise us. We have explored the attractiveness of LH dominance. What's more, the stronger the LH becomes, the less receptive it is to the perspective of the RH. What this overview suggests is that this pattern at an individual level is reflected on a grand scale in the shaping of societies and culture. Rather than the loss of equilibrium being followed by a return swing of the pendulum, here we see the second possible response: pushing further away from the equilibrium that has been lost.

If the general shape of this analysis is even approximately true, it is a matter of great importance. It suggests that Western culture may be increasingly dominated by a Clear-cut LH perspective. We would expect such a trend to lead to yet further dismissal of the RH's concerns, and away from healthy hemisphere relating. We turn now to some concise comment on each of the broad historical eras.

Ancient Greece[6]

Ancient Greece enjoyed a remarkable flowering of human culture, to an extent unprecedented in the West. This included new features that were very expressive of the RH, and also fresh innovations that are typical of the LH. There was a sustained period of creative balance between the two hemispheres. However, as the centuries of the Greek Empire proceeded, this creatively harmonious relationship began to shift towards a favouring of the LH. One important aspect of this shift was in the world of ideas. The richness and complexity of some earlier Greek philosophy was overtaken by more systematic approaches. While the latter still offer much insight, they are also Clear-cut in important and unhelpful senses. Here, for instance, theory begins to be given priority over what our senses and lived experience tell us.

One further intriguing change is memorably suggestive of the hemisphere shift. This concerns the direction in which text was written. In the earlier centuries of Ancient Greece, the language was written from right to left. This direction preferences the engagement of the RH. A new development emerged around the eighth century BC. At this time, Greek began to be written with its direction alternating line by line, backwards and forwards.[7] By the fourth century BC, however, the direction had fully switched, and Greek was universally being written left-to-right (favouring the LH).[8] Did the shift in writing lead to the shift in hemispheres, or was it the other way round? McGilchrist argues that the change in textual direction was a consequence of a more fundamental growth in LH emphasis.[9]

Ancient Rome[10]

The pattern for Ancient Rome is similar to that of Ancient Greece, but somewhat truncated: an initial fertile balance, followed by a shift in favour of the LH. For instance, the first century BC, early in the Roman Empire, saw, on the one hand, a well-codified legal system, and on the other, works of psychological sophistication and empathetic insight from the likes of Virgil and Ovid. Over the following centuries, however, many aspects of Roman culture became ever more rigidly systematized. One example is the practice of importing (or imposing) a standard Roman fort (or town, or villa) in whichever colony they had just conquered. Each single model was seen as universally applicable. Roman desire for power and control saw sameness being 'replicated' over an increasingly vast empire: strong LH characteristics.

The Renaissance[11]

The European Renaissance is the third of the three eras which most clearly demonstrate the hemispheres in full expression and healthy cooperation. A rise in the fullness of LH expression can be seen in the beginnings of modern science, history and philosophy. The expansion of RH characteristics can be seen in several areas. For instance, there was particular emphasis on harmony, in its broadest sense, and (relatedly) how parts in any context related to the whole (e.g. in musical polyphony, and in the development of perspective in art). RH longing also lies near the heart of much of the poetry and music of the Renaissance. This is not the task-focused, LH wanting of something we can grasp or complete. Rather, that for which we long, which may be relational or spiritual, can neither be made fully explicit, nor be fully achieved.

The Reformation[12]

One striking aspect of the Reformation, that turbulent and remarkable European period, is its desire for unambiguous certainty. So, for instance, visual images, with all their metaphor and symbolism, were largely set aside, along with their deep links to the RH. Focus shifted to the word, the literal and the explicit: very much the domain of the LH. An aim and a consequence was the exclusion of ambiguity. For instance, in understanding the Mass or Holy Communion, the two choices on offer were literal body and blood, or literal bread and wine. 'In essence the cardinal tenet of Christianity – the Word is made Flesh – becomes reversed, and the Flesh is made Word.'[13] We have moved from the rich equilibrium and communion of the Renaissance, into a more individualized and explicit realm.

The Enlightenment[14]

Although the best of the Enlightenment featured a balanced and humane outlook, and it saw many remarkable developments, some of its key principles led to increasing left hemisphere ascendancy.

One strong feature of the Enlightenment can be summarized in terms of the contrast between what can be described as 'rationality' on the one hand, and 'reason' on the other. McGilchrist uses the word 'reason' to refer to a broad faculty of understanding and judgement. This correlates with the broad integration of the Holistic RH, being informed by the specifics of context, and by the wisdom of lived experience. 'Rationality' can contribute to such reason, but forms only one part of it. Rationality, correlated with the LH, is much more explicitly rule-based and abstracted, setting aside considerations of context. LH rationality enabled great progress in parts of the natural sciences during the Enlightenment. This tended to lead, however, to the assumption that such rationality, and its underlying principles, are superior to reason in all domains of life.

Romanticism[15]

For McGilchrist, the nineteenth-century Romantic movement, featuring figures such as Goethe, Beethoven and Wordsworth, incorporated the best of Enlightenment values, but taken up into a richer integration. Within Romanticism, individual difference was, if anything, more important than generalizations. Rather than apparent opposites being dismissed as incompatible, holding them together in creative tension was often found to result in a fruitful union. For these and other reasons, McGilchrist discerns a significant increase in RH influence within the Romantic movement. Where the Enlightenment, broadly, saw the hemispheres fall out of equilibrium, the Romantic movement, in response, redressed the balance.

To mention one specific indicative feature, Romantics often had a particular interest in childhood, and especially in qualities of attentiveness frequently experienced in our early years, then often lost. For instance, William Wordsworth, recollecting his own childhood, described his experience as having 'the glory and freshness of a dream'.[16] McGilchrist points out that, in the early years of child development, we rely especially on the right hemisphere. It is later, as we encounter things no longer for the first time, that left hemisphere processing and re-presentation is increasingly deployed, and the experience of freshness and vitality tends to fade.

A longer summary would mention other RH-correlated priorities of Romanticism such as: depth; valuing the past; and the redemptive power of nature. The healthy hemisphere combination of the Romantic movement, however, was not to last.

The Industrial Revolution, leading into the modern world[17]

As the Enlightenment led into the Industrial Revolution, science was increasingly deemed the single source of understanding and knowledge about the world. Scientific developments were applied with increasing breadth and pace, with the manufacture of standardized products replacing the more individual, idiosyncratic and 'imperfect' craftsmanship of previous generations. The 'myth of the sovereignty of the scientific method' implied that a planned, methodical approach was not only legitimate but superior, coming to dominate many aspects of life.

This trajectory has broadly continued and increased into the modern world. One important consequence is that many people are increasingly surrounded by manufactured human products, and have much less contact with nature. The RH desires to reach out towards that which is 'other': both other humans, and the more-than-human world. Beginning with the Industrial Revolution, however, what surrounds many of us is typically significantly less 'other' than in earlier generations. With our tarmac roads, factory-made goods, screens, procedures and protocols, our lives are lived within a substantially LH world. Even if we do remember to reach for something beyond ourselves, for richer and deeper dimensions, what we often encounter is the straight lines and two-dimensional screens of yet more human products.

A broadly Clear-cut mindset has also often been applied to the shaping of organizations and society. Again, there have been some benefits. However, it is also now common to hold perspectives on society, and on organizational arrangements, that are simplified and reductionist, more than humane and relational.

Signature characteristics of the Clear-cut LH can be seen in the substantial reach of bureaucratic approaches. The world of social media, as well as enabling positive relational contact, has strong LH features. These include the virtual re-presentation of human beings, and simplified categories such as 'friend', 'follower', 'like' – all of which can be (and are) easily counted and compared. The influence of algorithms is noteworthy. They have remarkable LH-like power to manipulate 'data', but they are incapable of understanding the reality to which the data is related.

There are counter-currents as well, not least the increasing eco-concerns of recent decades, and growing awareness of interconnection. Nevertheless, it would seem over-optimistic to suggest that the long trend towards increased LH dominance has begun to be reversed.

Summing up

Overall, the evidence supporting McGilchrist's broad argument is strong. There have been important eras in Western cultural history in which the signature of left or right hemisphere influence can be particularly discerned. Moreover, in spite of some trends in the opposite direction, recent centuries have very much seen the increasing ascendancy of the left hemisphere. Rather than redressing the balance after losing equilibrium, society's response has often been to push further in the wrong direction. If there is even some truth in the patterns that he discerns, the impact of these shifts is of great significance.

The Master and His Emissary was going to press around the time of the 2008 global financial crash. That event offers just one example of what can happen when too much attention is paid to the simplified map (in this case, the computerized algorithms of the brokers) rather than to the reality of people's lived experience. If a further example is needed, of yet greater impact, we need look no further than the climate crisis in which we continue to live. The natural world has been treated as a 'resource' for us to grasp and manipulate for our purposes, rather than forming a living whole, of which we ourselves are part.

As we have seen, it is the RH that is more in touch with reality, that is more concerned with the whole picture, and that has a humane and holistic concern with relationships and flourishing. It is the LH that is prone to jump to quick conclusions based on simplifications, that resists alternative explanations once it has formed a view, that, in the absence of evidence, will make up a story to save face. It is the RH, therefore, that is able to harness the wonderful gifts of the LH, and integrate them into a broader partnership and vision. It is being centred in the Holistic RH that enables wise and humane presence and action in the world. If it is true that there are significant influences and trends towards LH dominance, these need understanding and redressing as a matter of importance and urgency.

Encapsulating McGilchrist

In summary, then, McGilchrist's broad hypothesis is that our lives as human beings need the strengths of both hemispheres, enriched by cooperation between them. This is true both for individuals, and for the shared life of groups and organizations. The ideal way of being is centred in the Holistic RH, drawing on LH strength with discerning generosity, and transforming LH contributions as appropriate in each situation. If we stray from this ideal, the downsides soon outweigh any initial apparent positives.

There are two ways in which we can stray from this ideal. The first happens if we draw too little on the Clear-cut LH. This might be because, when we encounter genuine problems, we fail to think them through. It might be that, when we communicate, we do so with insufficient clarity or detail. It might be that having greater clarity of structure, purpose or direction would be helpful. There is a range of possible ways in which under-using the LH can inhibit human flourishing.

However, it is possible to go too far. A certain amount of LH input is beneficial – but doubling the amount doesn't always lead to double the benefit. Sometimes such an increase will help, but often it will make things worse. The specifics will vary considerably, but the general point is clear: tipping into LH centring is unhelpful, and typically counter-productive. Such tipping may consist of going too far in an LH direction. Or it may be acting on a LH contribution without appropriate discernment or transformation.

This, then, outlines the patterns we should expect. Growing in our awareness of these considerations, and in how to respond to them, will prove helpful. These patterns and considerations are accurate, but these descriptions of them are couched in abstract terms. Let me, therefore, complement the abstract descriptions with metaphors (which are also examples), for ongoing illumination and reference.

The mountain summit of achievement

To encapsulate the ethos of having tipped into Clear-cut LH centring, let me offer the image of a certain type of mountain expedition.[18] The central purpose of this trip is to reach the summit of Mount Clear-cut. To be precise, one or more expedition members must stand on the highest point of the mountain, and do so before the winter weather sets in. That is the goal. Judgement of success or failure will be very clear indeed. The best energies of all team members are focused on achieving the target. Careful preparation focuses on developing all relevant skills, increasing fitness levels, researching hazards and keeping a close eye on weather forecasts. A detailed schedule is prepared, allowing for likely progress at different phases of the climb, and including 20% contingency factors. In the course of attacking the summit, the team find that there are unanticipated positives – a buzz from working together, hints of aesthetic pleasure when they occasionally raise their eyes and notice the surroundings. If such bonuses emerge, so be it, but the team are ruthless in not letting themselves be distracted from the raison d'être of their task: conquering the mountain, rather than being defeated by it.

With this metaphor, one of the primary Clear-cut features is that this is a task to complete, a problem to solve. Moreover, it is our task: it is our shoulders on which the responsibility sits – as will the achievement. It is also framed as having a binary outcome. There are only two possibilities: success or failure, yes or no. A range of Clear-cut strengths will be deployed in pursuit of the clear goal, not least linear analysis, and purposeful focus in pursuit of making things happen. Moreover, the central role of the mountain in all of this is as an object to be mastered. The Clear-cut LH is very strongly present. And the Holistic RH is peripheral at best. All in all, this analogy encapsulates the essence of strong and consistent centring in the Clear-cut LH. I will refer to this analogy as the mountain of achievement. Before moving on, two further comments are in order.

First, let me acknowledge a risk of using this metaphor – so that we can aim to sidestep it. The idea of standing on a mountain summit tends to have strong Holistic RH resonance. The embodied exhilaration of physical effort, the fresh air, the team experience and ideally the wonderful view all have rich RH connections. Particular mountains carry meaning, memory and significance for us. This includes theological significance: 'the mountain of God', a place of particular encounter with God, a 'thin place'. All this strong RH resonance naturally comes with the territory of mountains. So the risk of the mountain of achievement metaphor is that we focus too much on the Holistic attractiveness of the summit. Instead, a central point of the metaphor is to set aside all the evocation of awe and longing – and turn the peak into a problem and a project.

Second, the idea of standing atop the mountain captures some of the thrill of anticipation that the Clear-cut LH harnesses for energy. If achieving the summit seems feasible, such energy can feel positive. Experientially, however, the mountain summit of achievement easily morphs into the tightrope walk of doom.

The flowing dance of life together

The sheer breadth of Holistic RH concern makes it difficult to choose a single metaphor – and none will be perfect. Our meal with friends is not a bad example. Other alternatives include communal music-making, or dancing. So let's combine the three and imagine a social event featuring food, music and dance. It could be at a wedding feast. For now, I'll imagine a church and community ceilidh[19] (a Scottish or Irish form of country dance) in the church or village hall.

In contrast to climbing the mountain, putting into words the core purpose or aim of the ceilidh is rather more difficult. However, it includes a sense of many people participating, and finding it life-giving to do so. (One great thing about a ceilidh is that a one-year-old and a 103-year-old can both participate fully in the event. They may not dance in a literal sense, but their hearts and souls may be engrossed by the occasion.) Overall, there will be a sense of engaging – with the event and with (at least some) other people. There will be at least some deepening of relationship – with people familiar and unfamiliar. With the dancing itself, some will derive pleasure from demonstrating and stretching their skills. Others will be content to have a go, and not take mistakes (theirs or others) too seriously. The atmosphere will be important – that magical factor that can be influenced but never controlled. There will have been sufficient structure to feel confident and relaxed. And that structure will have been in service of a sense of flow. At the end of the evening, people will have felt a sense of connection – with their bodies, with the music, with other individuals, with the community – and perhaps even with life itself. There is something wholehearted and unreserved about it. We might describe it as a taste of fullness of life.

Such a ceilidh is shot through with many strong characteristics of the Holistic RH. A sense of connection is core: connection with other people, with the music, with our own body and that of others, and with the ongoing narrative of this community in this place. Participants will regularly draw on the broad, open, responsive attention of the Holistic RH: in looking out for others, within a given conversation, within the act of dancing. Participants will not generally know in advance exactly which dances will come up, in what sequence – there is a comfort with uncertainty. Indeed, it's better that way – the flux, the flow and the gradual unfolding of the evening are part of what makes it special. People will be in tune with, and appreciative of, the atmosphere of the occasion – even though that cannot be precisely articulated. The whole enterprise is very much about people as embodied beings. And the disposition of participants will play an important part – hopefully for the better. These are just some of the ways in which this occasion draws on the Holistic RH, and is shaped by it.

When we are centred in the Holistic RH, however, we also draw generously on the strengths of the LH. The RH knows its limitations so requests the assistance of the LH (but the converse does not happen). The extent of Clear-cut contribution to our occasion comes into focus if we imagine a ceilidh with insufficient Clear-cut thinking and action. What might be the consequences? It is easy to imagine, for instance: the publicizing of three different versions of the date, the time and the venue – and that at very short notice; food being provided in double quantity, by two different caterers, but no liquid refreshment; a band who seem very friendly, but entirely unfamiliar with ceilidh music; and the venue not being opened until very late, because the keyholder to the hall knew nothing of the event. In summary, we would expect insufficient narrow focus on solving the problems, making the decisions, completing the tasks necessary. Many aspects were under-clarified. The consequence was unhelpful disorder, and an event memorable for the wrong reasons.

What about the opposite: tipping too far into LH dominance? Rather than under-clarification, we would expect over-determination. For instance, we might find, on arrival, participants being given a personalized sheet detailing which dances they were expected/permitted to join, at which precise times, and with which other people. Moreover, the time between dances also being highly regimented. Rather than free-flowing social interaction, people being marshalled into pre-determined groups, asked to discuss pre-specified topics, and required to complete a standard summary sheet with their three key conclusions.

Standing back briefly, a good ceilidh needs good planning, planning which is content to retain a background profile, then recedes into the background. There is sufficient structure, and the structure then acts as a servant rather than master. The Clear-cut LH input acts like a trellis, whose purpose is to support the organic flourishing of wholehearted personhood, relationship, and indeed life. An overdeveloped structure, however, turns into a cage, constraining life, freedom and spaciousness. It is painful even to contemplate the second scenario, because it feels so wrong.

These examples of too little LH input, and of too much, help us appreciate two things: the vital role of the LH in an event such as our ceilidh; and the counter-productive consequences of going too far in that direction. Returning to our original ceilidh cameo, the hemisphere cooperation was just about right. The fruit was an engaging, spacious event, with depth, flow and connection. I will refer to this analogy of Holistic RH centring as the flowing dance of life together.

I offer these two metaphors, the mountain summit of achievement, and the flowing dance of life together, as encapsulations of the two broad forms of centring. As we approach any situation, we never simply 'see' that situation. Rather, to at least some degree, we are always 'seeing as'. We are always framing our perceptions in one way or another – seeing what is before us with reference to, in the light of its resemblance to, some analogy or metaphor or another.

Concluding comments

Within this chapter we have covered substantial ground: healthy and unhealthy relating between hemispheres, and a 3,000-year overview of Western cultural history. The patterns and principles I have articulated form the primary background for the later chapters of the book. Chapter 7 will bring McGilchrist's perspective into conversation with Christian theology, but first, in the next chapter, we will introduce several more (smaller) building blocks, including some from McGilchrist's later work.

Questions for reflection

1 If you were in a situation along the lines of the meal cameo 'with a twist', would you be more inclined to stick rigidly to the plan, or to forget about the food in the oven?
2 Can you think of times when a group you've been part of has had too much Clear-cut input? What were the consequences?
3 Can you think of times when a group you've been part of would have benefited from rather more Clear-cut input? What specifically would have made it better?
4 Which parts of the historical context particularly struck you?

Chapter 5 thumbnail summary – Hemisphere interaction and history

1 *Good hemisphere relating*

- It is not that one hemisphere is good and the other bad, but neither is the ideal a case of static, symmetrical balance.
- A frequent pattern of good relating is: right, left, right – preserve and transform. This is centred in the RH, and draws generously on LH strengths:
- First the RH notices something new, or deserving detailed attention.
- Second, the LH analyses the situation, and passes back to the RH its results.
- The third, RH, stage has two phases. First, LH analysis is sifted, and the RH preserves all that is relevant. (Some, based on a simplified map, may not be.) Second, the LH will have recommended what to do. The RH discerns how to do it, transforming the recommendation as necessary.

2 *Hemispheres skewed towards LH dominance*

- However, the LH is not convinced by this rationale. It is blind to its own limitations. Its preferred pattern, therefore, is right, left, act: why should the RH adjust its Clear-cut recommendations?
- When the hemispheres fall out of equilibrium, this will often be in the direction of increased LH. From here, there are two possible responses. One is for the pendulum to swing back, redressing the balance with more RH. An alternative is to push further in the same LH direction.

3 *Hemispheres and cultural history*

- Hemisphere perspective can shed light on cultural shifts, not just individual behaviour. McGilchrist has explored the whole of Western cultural history in this light. He suggests that the last period of fruitful equilibrium was with the European Renaissance. Since then, the broad trend has been of increasing LH dominance – away from equilibrium.

Notes

1 Iain McGilchrist, 2009, *The Master and His Emissary: The Divided Brain and the Making of the Western World*, New Haven, CT: Yale University Press, p. 14.

2 McGilchrist, *Master*, pp. 209–37.

3 Rowson, Jonathan and McGilchrist, Iain, 2018, p. 14. Divided brain, divided world, https://www.researchgate.net/publication/345512479_Divided_brain_divided_world, accessed 21.05.2025.

4 McGilchrist, *Master*, p. 229.

5 For a discussion of quite *how* such shifts might have taken place, see his Chapter 7: Imitation and the Evolution of Culture (McGilchrist, *Master*, pp. 240–56).

6 McGilchrist, *Master*, pp. 257–89.

7 '… in what is known as *boustrophedon*, literally "as the ox ploughs"' (McGilchrist, *Master*, p. 276).

8 McGilchrist, *Master*, p. 276.

9 McGilchrist, *Master*, pp. 277–9.

10 McGilchrist, *Master*, pp. 289–97.

11 McGilchrist, *Master*, pp. 298–313.

12 McGilchrist, *Master*, pp. 314–29.

13 McGilchrist, *Master*, p. 323.

14 McGilchrist, *Master*, pp. 330–51.

15 McGilchrist, *Master*, pp. 352–86.

16 From Wordsworth's 'Odes on Intimations of Immortality from Recollections of Early Childhood', quoted in McGilchrist, *Master*, p. 357.

17 McGilchrist, *Master*, p. 386–427.

18 An analogy focused on the functioning of a machine could arguably offer an even more precise metaphor, but let's stick with one in which human beings have a greater role.

19 Pronounced 'kay-lee', a ceilidh is a Scottish and Irish social gathering including dancing and folk music.

6

Further Foundations

The impact of McGilchrist's insights

McGilchrist's hypothesis has consistently resonated with my lived experience. As I have lived with it now for more than a dozen years, it has repeatedly rung true, and frequently proved helpful. Sometimes it helps me notice and attend to details and themes that, previously, I would never have registered. Often it has deepened my understanding of quite why something has gone well, or has ended up disappointingly. And I frequently bear it in mind as a sense-making framework, when seeking a good way forward. Let me flesh this out a little more, starting with two examples, the first of which needs some brief background.

Playing the cello was my primary hobby, from the age of eight until my early twenties. I loved solo pieces, orchestral playing and being part of a string quartet. When I then moved to London to work in computing, however, my playing more or less stopped. I would occasionally take my beautiful cello out of its case at a weekend, and play a little, then put it back for the next month or two. This pattern essentially continued until my late forties. Then in 2016 there was a turning point. I realized that the following November would mark the fortieth anniversary of my first cello lesson. And I made the decision to commit to playing a recital with a pianist friend to mark that occasion. I now had a goal in mind.

Some further LH input was needed, however. With a stretching job and teenage children, life was full. For the first time, I thought carefully about what had stopped me from playing more frequently. Having directed my attention to this question, in a focused and analytical mode, the nature of the problem quickly clarified. It took me most of five minutes to get my cello out of its case and set up to play, and another five to put it away afterwards. If I only had ten minutes spare at the end of the day, it wasn't even worth starting. These logistics formed a problem that could be solved. I invested in a cello stand, left a chair and music stand set up ready, and can now be playing the cello within

30 seconds. Ever since that analysis and adjustment, I have played about five times a week – sometimes for just five minutes, and often for longer. And I now know that a day with cello playing in it has a different quality, a richer essence, than one without. You will have already realized the point: clear LH analysis, coupled with a specific goal, formed a trellis that enabled ongoing RH-centred flourishing.

Second, as diocesan Director of Ministry and Discipleship, I found McGilchrist's framework a very helpful reference point in my regular organizing of conferences and residential training events. Was there sufficient focus and clarity? Was there sufficient breadth? Would the experience of participants be sufficiently spacious, and also sufficiently structured? I noticed that the 'gaps around the edges' of an in-person conference often enabled unplanned connections and conversations, which could be at least as valuable as the planned input. Had we allowed enough space around the edges? Moreover, rather than just paying attention to timings and session headings, how could we enable a conducive conference atmosphere? Overall, would the structure serve more as a trellis or as a cage?

These two cameos are genuine indicative examples, but they only begin to hint at the breadth and scale on which my life has been enriched. Articulating a fuller sense of that enrichment is not easy – not least because it arises largely from a greater valuing and rehabilitation of the RH domain, which itself resists straightforward summarization. Nevertheless, I can give some indication of it under four broad headings. First, awareness: McGilchrist's work has helped me direct more attention, for instance, to the quality of my own presence with other people. I have grown in my appreciation of 'betweenness', of tone and texture, and of how these are woven from subtle but fundamental qualities of attention. Such growth of awareness has led, second, to gradual shifts in my disposition. This learning has not been fast, and is certainly ongoing – but it has been transformative. The formation of my disposition is interwoven with the development of my skills – which have typically lagged some way behind the growth of my awareness. Chapter 10 offers further insight in this area.

Third, one of the great contributions of McGilchrist's work is the enabling of sense-making. He offers a framework which sheds radical new light across all sorts of contexts: from brief one-to-one interactions to large-scale cultural shifts and public discourse. I have benefited from the interpretive power of his perspective at three levels. It sheds light on its own (as in the previous two cameos). It offers a broad background context against which to understand other frameworks. (For instance, in the context of coaching, some approaches are very much goal-directed (more LH); others direct primary attention to the present moment (more RH); I seek to harness the interplay between the two.) Then, finally, I'm beginning to learn and explore how McGilchrist's understanding might be held alongside and integrated with other broad frameworks, for their mutual enhancement (the theological and improvisatory perspectives in the rest of this book are good examples[1]). As well as awareness, disposition and sense-making, my final heading is enrichment. My increasing understanding of McGilchrist, and of the many other thinkers on whom he draws, has enhanced my appreciation of so many dimensions of living, heightened my sensitivity to aspects previously undervalued, and expanded the vitality I notice in others, and experience myself. Of course, as I have been learning more from McGilchrist, so too have I been learning more from others, and from life. Nevertheless, this work has expanded my vision, and integrated my understanding, to quite a remarkable degree.

Our engagement with McGilchrist so far has been focused on the content of *The Master and His Emissary*. We turn next to give much more concise attention to McGilchrist's subsequent book. We will concentrate on a small number of selected themes which will inform the chapters ahead, but let's begin with an overview.

The Matter With Things

The Matter With Things, published in 2021, is a substantial work in size, and with a correspondingly ambitious scope. It begins by picking up the two main achievements of *The Master and His Emissary*: an understanding of the brain hemispheres and their typical relating, and a view of Western cultural history in the light of that understanding. From here, the argument proceeds broadly as follows: if our brain hemispheres are as they seem to be, and Western culture has tended towards Clear-cut LH domination, then we would expect the fruit of much Western culture – not least its philosophy and its science – to be shaped in a way that is biased towards an LH perspective. To gain a more truthful perspective on the world, then, what is needed is a sort of reverse translation, decoding the LH-biased presentation with which we have become familiar. McGilchrist's substantial project in *The Matter With Things* is this task of reverse translation. He begins the project by considering carefully those faculties by which we seek access to what is true, and re-examines them according to this principle.[2] He then offers a perspective on the nature of reality that is rebalanced to notice and appreciate more Holistic aspects that are easily undervalued by the Clear-cut LH – including, for instance, flow, consciousness and value. Throughout, McGilchrist pays particular attention to the most up-to-date findings of modern physics, which in fact are deeply congruent with his proposals. The final chapter of the book, 'The Sense of the Sacred', draws on all that has gone before it in putting forward an evocative and inviting case for the existence of God. It is a case richly informed by Christianity, and drawing deeply on its understanding, and on that of many theologians. McGilchrist sees this chapter as the 'culmination' of the book.[3] Overall, *The Matter With Things* seeks to offer a reconfigured way of looking at the world.

Subsequent chapters will draw especially on three of the human capacities that McGilchrist highlights as important. Each of these requires the cooperative contribution of both left and right hemispheres, but is frequently undervalued by the Clear-cut LH on its own. We turn first to the faculty of imagination.

Imagination[4]

Imagination is not only about coming up with good ideas for the future. It also plays a vital role in our engagement with the present. The more we can offer a poised imaginative attentiveness, the greater will be the depth of our perception. Without such engagement, we easily miss the subtleties, possibilities and nuances that form an important part of life, but are unlikely to feature on a Clear-cut simplified mapping. It is not surprising, therefore, that imagination is easily under-appreciated by the Clear-cut LH. In the absence of imagination, however, we would assume that what is obviously the case at a surface level is all that there is. We would assume that a simplified mapping of reality contained all relevant information. By contrast, it is in imagination that 'we experience intimations of matters that are glimpsed, but only partly seen'.[5] Moreover, 'It alone can put us in touch with aspects of reality to which our habits of thought have rendered us blind. It leads not to an escape from reality, but a sudden seeing into its depths.'[6] If we are to have any depth or substance of encounter, the ongoing cultivation of imagination is vital. Such imagination is distinct from nosiness, but overlaps with a degree of curiosity. It's not necessarily about needing to know, but recognizing that each individual and group has a backstory, a hinterland and also a 'front story' of future potential waiting to unfold.

In an encounter of any substance between people, we can normally sense the degree of imaginative depth which the other is bringing to the meeting. Are they assuming I am essentially two-dimensional? I'm reminded of a phrase of Cynthia Bourgeault: she describes how Jesus 'infused' situations he encountered 'with his own interior spaciousness',[7] inviting us to join him in deeper life together.

The depth of our imaginative engagement is interwoven with the posture of poised attentiveness, of clarity anchored in compassion, from which we seek to relate. Both compassion and clarity can increase the more we understand of how people (including ourselves) have come to be as they are, to view things as they do and to act as they do. And vice versa, bringing more compassion and clarity to bear in our attending will increase the depth of our imaginative appreciation of what may be going on in a situation, and for the people involved.

Our imaginative spaciousness needs to take seriously the fact that, as Aleksandr Solzhenitsyn put it, 'the line separating good and evil passes … right through every human heart'.[8] As well as looking for the good in everyone, we need imaginative clear-sightedness as we retain attentiveness – actively in the background, perhaps – for indications (anywhere on a spectrum between blatant and infinitesimal) of what is not good. That which is negative may be in others, and it may also be in ourselves (might I be missing something here? might I be wrong? might my motivation have become skewed?). Overall, a posture of clarity anchored in compassion retains the attentive poise that can respond appropriately to whatever it encounters.

Reason[9]

By reason, McGilchrist means an approach that is broader and richer than linear rationality alone. Reason includes Clear-cut logic, but goes beyond it. It is inclusive, integrating multiple perspectives. It engages not only with general categories, but with specific contexts and people, taking seriously our embodied nature. Reason knows that certainty is not always possible, and is therefore tentative where appropriate. Reason incorporates something of the scanning behaviour of our hungry chaffinch from Chapter 1 – looking out for and incorporating a broad range of factors, to help discern what seems the best way forward.

Reason and reasonableness, then, take us significantly further than

Clear-cut rationality alone. And yet reason alone is often insufficient for our purposes. For instance, it is frequently not obvious how one consideration should be weighed against another very different factor: they are incommensurate. It is often possible to give a reasonable argument in favour of each of several different approaches. In such a scenario, which is not uncommon, how should we proceed? I will offer my best understanding, informed by McGilchrist's analysis, in response.

The depth and breadth of our imagination holds open a space in which we can attend to all considerations that may be relevant. This may include our listening to people concerned, our own experience in other contexts with some similarity, our understanding of people in general, and of the Christian faith in particular. All this varied 'soup' of information is welcomed into the melting pot of our imaginations. We stir it and ponder it with our shared reason, probing, exploring and considering as we do so. There is then no formula that will tell us the right answer. Rather, prayerfully bringing to the situation the combined wisdom of all our experience, we seek to settle on what seems best, under God. In doing so, we draw substantially on our informed intuition.

Intuition[10]

One good description of intuition is 'the synthesis of experience with unconscious reasoning on the basis of that experience'.[11] Intuition incorporates knowledge and experience, but goes beyond our conscious processing and articulation of them. Intuition is often connected with an embodied sense of knowing, and with a sense of spiritual discernment. It relates to a sense of a whole interrelated situation, and not just to parts in isolation. The art historian Bernard Berenson described in this way his ability to validate masterpieces: 'It is very largely a question of accumulated experience upon which your spirit sets unconsciously.'[12]

Just as linear rationality in isolation can lead us astray, so also intuition is not infallible. What we need is informed intuition, in partnership with our other faculties. Jonas Salk, the discoverer of the polio vaccine, describes reason and intuition as both being necessary:

> The way I like to put it is that when I have an intuition about something, I send it over to the reason department. Then after I've checked it out in the reason department, I send it back to the intuition department to make sure that it's still all right.[13]

Readers will recognize the RH–LH–RH pattern of good hemisphere interaction.

Ideally, our processes of shared discussion and discernment will give appropriate space for the mutual testing of different intuitions, of different lines of reasoning. When it comes to making decisions, there is normally no formula or algorithm to tell us the right answer. We can rarely prove objectively what approach will be best. Instead, after appropriate preparation, it will be our best shared sense of informed intuitive judgement that leads us forward. We will seek an approach that rings true, that seems 'about right'.[14] Moreover, it's not just that this is how we should proceed. I believe this is a reasonable description of how we do actually come to decisions – allowing for the fact that the intuitions of different people may incline in different directions. Overall, then, our decision-making – and also our life in general – is much enhanced by these three rich human faculties: imaginative depth, broad reasonableness and informed intuition. With this backdrop in mind, we step sideways next, to focus on the processes by which we grow.

Processes and contexts

Punctuated processes

Gavin Wakefield offers the term 'punctuated process' to describe the typical pattern of how people come to Christian faith. The idea of a punctuated process holds together two considerations. On the one hand, coming to faith is nearly always a process, aspects of which take place over some extended duration of time. On the other, the process is 'nearly always punctuated by significant events or moments'.[15] The 'punctuation marks' or 'points' may vary considerably in their nature and magnitude. Many of them may seem very small at the time, but their cumulative effect can be considerable. The punctuation points themselves might include: a conversation (pre-planned or by chance); an encounter with beauty or suffering; the beginning or end of a relationship; engaging as a participant in a church course; a feeling or thought that won't go away; the sustained care and kindness of a friend; a word or phrase. Sometimes we will feel ourselves deeply stirred inside in the moment itself, without necessarily understanding quite why. At other times, it will be the next morning, or a few weeks later, that insight hits us. It's not just the punctuation points themselves that matter. The time between points is also important, allowing space for the import of what we've experienced to germinate and take root.

Wakefield's focus is on people's journeys to faith, but his concept is more broadly applicable. Our growth in faith, and in maturity, is also a punctuated process. Moreover, we can extend the idea further, and apply it to the life of a community – such as a family, a church or a group of churches. Again, this takes place over time, and some events or experiences will prove particularly significant for some or all of those involved. The punctuated process of each person's journey forms the story, interconnecting with other events, smaller and larger. The punctuated process of the life of the church forms a further, larger story, composed of the intertwining stories of individuals, friendships, the wider world and the life of God.

In all these cases, some punctuation points may have involved deliberate planning (by somebody), whereas others appear random, or perhaps serendipitous. Some punctuation marks feature events that 'just' happen, that impact us to whatever degree. Important punctuation marks can include obviously good experiences, but also a wide range of challenging *or* experiences. Crucially, it is not just what happens that matters, but how it is interpreted and received – individually and corporately. If the 'punctuation mark' is like a seed, does the seed land on good soil? If the 'punctuation mark' is like a spark, does that spark meet an atmosphere that kindles it into flame – or not?

The process that Wakefield describes relates not only to the steady passing of days, months and years (*chronos* time), but also to *kairos* time, which, in Chapter 3, we linked with the Holistic RH.[16] The developments and shifts that he describes depend not only on what happens, but also on when it happens. It is when events unfold at the 'right time', at opportune moments, even at the appointed time, that their impact is often greatest.

Clear, complicated, complex – and beyond

What we've been discussing is complicated, but is described even more accurately as *complex*. I draw here on a distinction that has been very impactful for organizational thinking, developed by Dave Snowden, a Welsh management consultant.[17] Snowden highlights the fact that different contexts (or domains) have different properties, different degrees of predictability. He uses the term *clear* to denote the most straightforward context: a stable and predictable domain in which we can select a pre-existing best-practice solution. Here there will be a clear process to follow: for instance, making a cup of tea in a well-equipped kitchen. A second domain is described as *complicated*. A good example here would be the inner workings of a Ferrari. Cause and effect still run in largely predictable ways, but expert knowledge is needed. In the case of a Ferrari, that would involve an engineer.

A *complex* situation (or system) is fundamentally different. Think not of a Ferrari, but of a rainforest. Multiple interconnecting factors affect what happens. A seemingly small shift in one place can have reverberations of surprising magnitude in a different part of the ecosystem – and those reverberations may be for better or for worse. Impacts ripple outwards, and back again, in surprising and unpredictable ways. In such a domain, don't expect a controlled journey towards pre-defined outcomes. Instead, Snowden recommends a much more *experimental and interactive* approach. Rather than expecting to plan it all in advance, he commends an appropriate degree of preparation, then taking a step at a time, seeing after each step what response is evoked, and choosing the following step accordingly.

As I expect will be apparent, both clear and complicated contexts fit well with the strengths of the Clear-cut LH. A complex domain, however, although likely to include Clear-cut aspects, stretches into the territory of the Holistic RH. Faced with a complex domain, an approach reliant solely on the Clear-cut LH would relate instead to a simplified mapping – which would be likely to be complicated, and thus misleading. To use a term offered by the sociologist Hartmut Rosa, a complex domain is 'nonengineerable'.[18] That is not to say that there is nothing we can do to shape its working, but it is to say that such domains are not controllable.

How does this relate to the life of the church? There may be some clear aspects (perhaps some of the rotas – or perhaps not), and some complicated aspects. Of Snowden's categories, however, communal life in a church (or elsewhere) will always be complex. Unpredictable ripples are part of the territory. McGilchrist uses the term reverberative in similar contexts. The complexity that Snowden describes helpfully highlights both the impossibility of direct control, and also the potential for the emergence of good.

I find myself, however, wanting to reach beyond Snowden's categories. The rainforest image conveys rich interrelationships, and emergent organic growth. In my own conception of church life, I also want to make explicit space for two further aspects. The first is the punctuated processes involved, for each individual and group: the often slow growth of each person, each soul, through different seasons of life. This includes our unique hopes and wounding, our gifts and longings, our opportunities and frustrations, our relationships with people and practices, our unique calling to make God manifest in the world, and the unfolding practicalities of our personal context. This punctuated process includes a maturing that unfolds in *kairos* time, not *chronos*. So too does the second aspect to acknowledge and welcome, namely the animating dance of God's Holy Spirit. Much harder to describe – never mind define – this is nonetheless essential to name, or at least gesture towards the sometimes subtle, sometimes insistent, nudging, inviting, challenging and sustaining work of God, without which there would be no life.

Church life, therefore, cannot accurately be described as clear or complicated in Snowden's terms. His description of a complex context, with its ripples and unpredictable reverberations, does ring true – but is not enough. Church life has dimensions beyond this description of complex. My suggested term is that this is an *animate* system. The Latin root *anima* points both to the depth, complexity and potential of human souls, and also to the animating work of God's Spirit. Moreover, healthy animation speaks of fullness of life, 'connected to the forcefield of God's aliveness'.[19] If churches were simply complicated, or even clear, life might seem easier – if rather dull. But we are not given that choice. The intertwined stories of our lives together, with others and with God, is complex, and animate.

In this chapter we have drawn attention to a number of concepts, from McGilchrist and other writers, which will inform what follows. One further concept deserves some unpacking: why it is that I have chosen to describe the recent leadership developments in the church as a *discourse*.

A word on 'discourse'

First, let me distinguish between two senses of the word 'discourse'. One sense is that a discourse can be a specific single conversation, or a speech.[20] The other sense, the one I am using, is more broad, and a little harder to grasp. In this second sense, a discourse is a way of speaking, writing and indeed thinking. Sometimes a discourse is focused on a particular topic (such as chess or politics), or it can be very broad indeed. A given discourse may be indicated in part by the vocabulary it uses.

And it also often carries an implicit stance or perspective. For instance, we could think of the contrasting discourses of left-wing and right-wing politics. So when a newspaper representing one perspective hails the 'cutting of red tape for business', we may not be surprised when another bemoans the 'removal of worker protection'. We recognize that well-established discourses are at play here, and we have learned something of navigating their disagreement. Different words are used to describe the same policy change. But it's not simply a question of switching synonyms: the difference in vocabulary in these short phrases acts as a surface-level indicator of a much deeper and more substantial contrast of perspective. The actual words are just the tip of the iceberg – of which more shortly.

In our life journey to date, we will have adopted some discourses, but not others – not least in our church engagement. Some discourses we may have gained familiarity with, and then rejected. With other discourses, our adoption of them may have happened with much less conscious deliberation, if any. By describing recent leadership-focused developments as the Church Strategic Leadership *Discourse* (Church SLD), I want to increase our awareness and understanding of the nature of this discourse – and of other discourses in comparison. This especially includes exploration of what is implicit in discourses, of what lies below the surface.

For a discourse often resembles a proverbial iceberg. The section above water represents the relatively small part of the discourse that is normally made explicit (such as 'cutting red tape'). As with an iceberg, there is substantially more hidden below the metaphorical waterline. This hidden content will include assumptions, perspectives and ways of interpreting reality. Any discourse will highlight some things, and hide others. It will treat some forms of reasoning as valid, and not others. Overall, a discourse significantly shapes how we pay attention. It influences what we consider valuable, and what we ignore. So when I adopt a particular discourse, it's not simply that I'm using it because I find it the most accurate way of expressing what I want to. In addition, I have also been – and I am also being – shaped by it. I am shaped not only in the words that I use, but also in the forms of perception and reasoning that I adopt. I am likely to operate according to its rules. Crucially, I can easily be unaware that I'm doing so. But it is only when the particular emphases and assumptions of a discourse are made explicit that proper critical evaluation becomes possible.

Some people, of course, will be substantially aware of the whole metaphorical iceberg, and will have considered all its assumptions in detail. For most of us, however, that is not the case. Indeed, we can easily be only vaguely conscious – if at all – that there is anything going on beneath the metaphorical water. Given this background, it's really not surprising when there is a clash of opinion between people using different discourses (the highly varied responses of participants on my diocesan leadership course offers just one example).[21] Moreover, we would expect any attempts to find a common way forward to be quite a struggle – and that is frequently what we find. In order for constructive progress to be possible, people need to start by *understanding* what's going on beneath the waterline – both with respect to their own iceberg, and also regarding the other one.[22] It is only by growing in our awareness and understanding of the foundations of our discourse, only by raising these to consciousness, that progress will be possible. This is my aim: to help increase both our perception of what lies beneath the surface, and our comprehension of it.

These comments on discourse in general will offer helpful illumination when we focus specifically on the Church SLD throughout Chapter 8. They will also shed light within our next chapter, within which we explore the congruence and compatibility between, on the one hand, McGilchrist's hemisphere hypothesis and, on the other, the Bible and Christian theology.

Questions for reflection

1 Can you remember a time when another person engaged with you, but without obvious imaginative depth? How was that experience for you?
2 What most helps you bring imaginative spaciousness to your perceiving?
3 How would you describe your relationship to intuition?
4 What did you make of the description of punctuated processes, and *kairos* moments?

Notes

1 I have also begun exploring the potential for synthesis with the adult development perspectives offered by writers including Robert Kegan and Jennifer Garvey Berger. See, for instance, Robert Kegan, 1997, *In Over Our Heads: The Mental Demands of Modern Life*, Cambridge, MA: Harvard University Press; Jennifer Garvey Berger, 2012, *Changing on the Job: Developing Leaders for a Complex World*, Stanford, CA: Stanford University Press.

2 Faculties considered include perception, judgement, emotional and social intelligence, imagination and intuition.

3 This paragraph draws on his comments in his 'Understanding the Matter with Things' dialogue on YouTube on the chapter: https://www.youtube.com/watch?v=fWGra8qBsPM, accessed 21.05.2025.

4 Iain McGilchrist, 2021, *The Matter With Things*, London: Perspectiva Press, chapter 19: 'Intuition, Imagination and the Unveiling of the World', pp. 753–76.

5 McGilchrist, *Things*, p. 768.

6 McGilchrist, *Things*, p. 768.

7 Cynthia Bourgeault, 2008, *The Wisdom Jesus: Transforming Heart and Mind – A New Perspective on Christ and His Message*, Boston, MA: Shambhala Publications, p. 134.

8 Aleksandr Solzhenitsyn, 2018, *The Gulag Archipelago*, London: Vintage Classics.

9 McGilchrist, *Things*, chapters 14 ('Reason's Claims on Truth', pp. 547–70) and 15 ('Reason's Progeny', pp. 571–640).

10 McGilchrist, *Things*, chapters 17 ('Intuition's Claims on Truth', pp. 673–706) and 18 ('The Untimely Demise of Intuition', pp. 707–52).

11 McGilchrist, *Things*, p. 256.

12 McGilchrist, *Things*, p. 693.

13 McGilchrist, *Things*, pp. 722–3.

14 In some scenarios, this may be the option that seems least bad.

15 Gavin Wakefield, 2006, *Conversion Today*, Cambridge: Grove Books, p. 26.

16 See p. 51 for *chronos* and *kairos*.

17 See, for instance, https://en.wikipedia.org/wiki/Cynefin_framework, accessed 21.05.2025.

18 Hartmut Rosa, trans. James C. Wagner, 2020, *The Uncontrollability of the World*, Cambridge, UK and Medford, MA: Polity Press, [ebook: 'Beyond Control: a Note from the Author on the Key Term of This Book']. In this introductory note, Rosa describes the challenge that faced him in offering an adequate translation of a particular German word, *Unverfügbarkeit*, which is the key German term in the original title of his book. For a long time his word of choice in English was 'non-engineerability', but in the end, 'uncontrollability' was deemed a slightly better translation. Rosa is a sociologist whose work has considerable and remarkable consonance with that of McGilchrist, despite their different angles of approach. See further his *Resonance: A Sociology of Our Relationship to the World*, 2019, Cambridge, UK and Medford, MA: Polity Press.

19 Bourgeault, *The Wisdom Jesus*, p. 44.

20 This is sometimes referred to as 'small "d"' discourse, and the other as 'large "D"' discourse. For a concise introduction to discourse, see Simon Western, 2008, *Leadership: A Critical Text*, Los Angeles, CA: Sage Publications, pp. 80–1; and Norman Fairclough, 2013, *Critical Discourse Analysis: The Critical Study of Language*, 2nd edn, London: Routledge.

21 Chapter 1, p. 7.

22 There may, of course, be more than two discourses in operation.

7

The Bible, Theology and the Hemispheres

Introduction

How might McGilchrist's hemisphere hypothesis relate to Christian theology? As I have lived with both over the last dozen years, I have repeatedly been struck by the congruence between them. Moreover, my understanding of the hemispheres has frequently enabled fresh insight – often searching – on the nature of God, and of Christian living. In this chapter, I don't seek to prove compatibility between the hemisphere hypothesis and Christianity. Instead, I offer a number of short perspectives in and around which I sense congruence and enrichment. In doing so, I aim to discern what is both above and below the waterline of Christian discourse – seeking accurately to depict something of the centre of gravity of faithful Christian living.

Holistic relational response to God

The prime focus of my Christian faith can never be my own agenda. At the centre is God. Everything, and everyone, is seen in the light of God, and in relation to God. Indeed, to use a significant biblical idiom, we live our lives before the face of God. The blessing with which Israelite priests were to bless the people includes the beautiful phrase 'The Lord make his face to shine upon you, and be gracious to you' (Num. 6.25). And it is in the face of Jesus Christ that we see most clearly the light of the glory of God (2 Cor. 4.6).

God is the source, the fount, the creator, the primary originator. When God creates, God pauses, recognizes, appreciates – that which is good and beautiful, and not only that which is useful (Gen. 1). God has given, and continues to give.

Christianity, then, is concerned with our response to God's initiative, to God's invitation and calling into a way of being. At the heart of this way of being is our relating to God – increasingly wholeheartedly, unreservedly, truthfully, from the depths of our being. Such relating is inevitably bound up with our relating to other people – to our neighbour. The way of being to which God calls us is not a problem to solve, or a task that we will ever complete (although there will be tasks and problems along the way). Rather, it is an ongoing process of gradual deepening, undertaken in partnership with God and others, of participating ever more fully in the divine life, love and mission. That said, the deepening is rarely smooth or linear. Within this participation we receive; we struggle; we cooperate in our own transformation; we pause our cooperation; we respond, fitfully, in love, trust and obedience; we slowly, often reluctantly, learn to love others as God loves us and them, as we let go of all that hinders such loving. The Christian God is concerned not only with what we do, but at least as much with the manner in which we do it.

We are called to know ever more deeply the God who makes Godself known most fully in the face of Jesus Christ. Such knowing can be enabled and inspired by the fact-focused knowing of theory and theology. But the knowing of God that is eternal life is fundamentally personal knowing (as I introduced that term in Chapter 2). We can know God genuinely, but never completely. As St Augustine of Hippo put it, 'If you understand, it is not God you understand.'[1]

Overall, any such wholehearted relational response to the face of God revealed in Jesus Christ, with personal knowing ever deepening but never complete, carries the hallmarks of strong centring in the Holistic RH.

On simplified maps

McGilchrist has made clear that we often need a simplified map of reality to help us get our bearings. This need holds true within Christian living. One well-known example of such a simplified map is the Ten Commandments (Ex. 20.1–17). These Commandments do not cover all we need to know for Christian life, but they can get us off to a very good start. An even richer and more distilled map is given by Jesus. When asked which is the greatest commandment, he spoke of wholehearted love, first for God, and then for our neighbour (Matt. 22.34–40). His next phrase – 'On these two commandments hang [or 'depend'] all the law and the prophets' (Matt. 22.40) – highlights quite how excellent is this simplified map. These two greatest commandments offer not simply a summary, but a distilled articulation of the source principles of Godly living. With most simplified maps, the contents are themselves fairly Clear-cut. Not so here. Not only is the central concern, love itself, deeply Holistic (though always with Clear-cut implications), but this love is to be with all of our heart and soul, and with all of our mind. Moreover, although the two greatest commandments are distinct, they are also deeply interrelated. In summary, in this short cameo, we can see the strength of a Clear-cut simplified map being adopted and elevated for profoundly Holistic purposes.

A similar pattern applies to the whole body of Old Testament law, and New Testament injunctions. This structure often features LH clarity and attention to detail, with seemingly neat category boundaries describing different types of action, situation and person. But the purpose is for blessing: for the protection and flourishing of people, of relationships (with God, and with other people), and of the whole community.

The same principle applies when it comes, for instance, to Christian spiritual practice. Many over the centuries have found helpful the idea of a 'rule of life' – a pattern of prayer, service, worship and learning as we seek to follow God. The pattern can be helpful, but it itself is not the point. The pattern is to act as a trellis, supporting our Christian living and relating in every season. The pattern is not to be a constricting cage – or indeed an accomplishment, a task to complete, or a spiritual feather in our cap.

Great insight on the content and disposition of any rule of life comes from the Anglican solitary contemplative, Maggie Ross, who has drawn substantially on McGilchrist's insights, integrating them into her understanding of life under God.[2] She uses the term 'self-conscious mind' to describe the left hemisphere, and 'deep mind' to describe the right hemisphere. From her long experience and wide reading, she uses McGilchrist's framework to offer a powerful articulation of what is true about human living. For her, story, myth, metaphor and especially silence (all with strong Holistic RH resonance) can be doorways towards God, and towards 'living the ordinary through trans-figured perception'.[3]

> It is only by attentive, responsive, receptivity to the silence, by allowing the deep mind to do its work out of sight, and by relocating the person's source of animating energy from the self-conscious to the deep mind, that outward behaviour undergoes permanent change. This process cannot be taught in the way chemistry can be taught.[4]

On truth and depth

It is easy to state the two greatest commandments, but not possible to fulfil them completely. That is, in part, because there will always be scope for our love to grow deeper and broader. It is also because of our nature as human beings. There are depths to our nature, and those depths include elements in mutual tension. Scripture is replete with examples. For instance, David Ford highlights how the apostle Peter is 'complex and ambivalent', demonstrating courage, misunderstanding, stability, faith, resistance, overcompensation and denial.[5] Not only are the depths of our nature complex, but they are also often hidden to us. We are often blind to our own reality. Self-deception is endemic within the human condition, and those committed to the life of faith are in no way immune or exempt. In fact, the very desire to be a good disciple of Christ, a faithful follower of God, can itself increase the likelihood of our own self-deception.

In the face of such complexity, we find God's desire for truth, probing more deeply than the surface clarity of the LH. And yet the Clear-cut LH still has a vital role to play. For instance, Jesus was masterfully imaginative at using Clear-cut figures within his teaching, in a way that probed deep into the motivation and self-knowledge of his hearers. Think, for instance, of logs and specks in eyes, or of the Pharisee and the tax collector (or of the Sunday school teacher who, having told the story of the Pharisee and tax collector, went on to say: 'So, girls and boys, let's shut our eyes and fold our hands and thank God that we are not like the Pharisee in the parable' – see Luke 18.8–14).

Again, the biblical narrative repeatedly portrays people being tested by God, such as Abraham, Jonah, Job, Shadrach, Meshach and Abednego and, not least, Jesus.[6] There is a Clear-cut choice before each of these – will they or won't they make the right decision? And this Clear-cut choice reveals – and perhaps further shapes – the true state of the depths of their heart. The truth matters to God: not a superficial summary, but the full depth of the reality. Moreover, biblical truth is frequently relational: it has strong connotations of faithfulness. We are called to be utterly true to God – and, in so doing, to discover more deeply that God is utterly true to us. Truth is thus closely related to trust. Such a sense of truth has strong RH resonance.

Before leaving the topic of truth, let me register consistent biblical truthfulness regarding the full breadth of human emotional range. There is jubilation, and there is lament. There is steely determination and candid quailing; conflict and reconciliation; sadness and joy. Access to such a range of emotion requires healthy engagement of the Holistic RH. The Clear-cut LH on its own, by contrast, prefers to focus on that which is explicitly 'positive' and optimistic (as well as having ready access to anger and anxiety).[7]

In this section we have seen once more a primary concern with Holistic depth of truth, enabled and increased by skilled and sensitive use of the Clear-cut LH. This is epitomized in Hebrews 4.12, where the sharp and piercing word of God is described as 'able to judge the thoughts and intentions of the heart'. We turn next for some observations in another domain in which the Clear-cut LH has much to contribute.

On structure and plans

There are frequent examples throughout Scripture of the introduction of helpful structure. In the Old Testament, for instance, Moses learning to delegate (Ex. 18); the construction of the Temple (1 Kings 6); Nehemiah leading a reconstruction project (Neh. 2—6). The introduction of kingship to Israel as an example of a societal structure that came with clear warnings of its likely downsides (1 Sam. 8.6–22). In the New Testament we see, for instance, Jesus sending out his disciples in pairs (e.g. Mark 6.7–13), and the appointment of deacons in Acts 6.

Several brief points are in order. First, such structures and plans are portrayed as being in service of people and communities, rather than being an end in themselves. This includes serving individuals as they are now, and also their ongoing formation. It also includes shaping appropriate structures to address (current or potential) issues, reducing conflict and contributing to healthy relating – towards the rich concept of *shalom*: not only the absence of conflict, but flourishing, safety and well-being for individuals and communities.

Second, structures can lead to negative consequences. The existence of structure does not guarantee that it will be used well. They can, instead, lead to the domination of other people (for instance, some of the many abuses of kingship). And they can lead to distortion of, or distraction from, what is best. For instance, in the parable of the good Samaritan, a generous interpretation sees the priest and Levite, passing by, as being distracted from the requirement of love, by the lesser requirement of the law. A less generous interpretation sees this as them distorting the law for their own benefit.

Third, the closely related concept of order is one that has received considerable theological attention. Dan Hardy and David Ford note that, theologically, order has often been equated with good, and disorder with evil. Certainly, too little order, insufficient LH clarity, can be unhelpful. Hardy and Ford's primary emphasis is that there is 'another dimension of goodness' which sits beyond order. Within the realm of this goodness they mention experiences such as laughter, freedom and joy, play and delight, and they term it non-order. Along with their examples, we might add qualities such as welcome, friendship, grace and love, noting the strong RH associations of all of these. Such experiences often overflow and spread, 'creating a new atmosphere and producing all sorts of unpredictable results'. They see this realm as being good: 'to be valued in itself, whatever its practical consequences', rather than to be harnessed instrumentally. Moreover, they note that 'many forces, psychological, social and spiritual, try their best to order the non-order out of existence, often labelling it disorder. The result is dullness and boredom.'[8]

The realm of plans and planning deserves our attention, not least because it is a substantial focus within the Church SLD. Once again, evidence of plans can be seen in many contexts across Scripture. In comparison to the Church SLD, however, one striking scriptural feature is the general lack of explicit deadlines. Yes, there may often be a clear sense of purpose and direction. But that very rarely translates into more detailed pre-planned timelines or milestones (as far as we know). One central biblical journey, for instance, is that of the people of Israel after their delivery from slavery in Egypt. Perhaps the central feature of that journey is that its timing was neither specified in advance, nor under the control of the Israelites themselves. Rather, it was to be a repeated daily responsive exercise of trust and obedience. The people were to follow the pillar of cloud by day, and the pillar of fire by night. They were to stay put or move on as directed – whether for one night or one year, never knowing in advance.

Overall, under this heading we see, once again, a wide range of biblical insight and Christian practice resonating with McGilchrist's principles. We also see further instances of negative consequences from treating Clear-cut LH structures as master rather than servant. We turn next to a brief overview of the life and ministry of Jesus, connecting in different ways to the strengths of the two hemispheres, and to their interaction.

The life, ministry and teaching of Jesus

Let's begin by continuing one of the considerations of the previous section – the degree to which Jesus' movements and activities appear to have been pre-planned. Here we can see strong evidence of both hemispheres. On the one hand, in the later stages of his ministry there is a clear shift, as Jesus sets his face towards Jerusalem. We can see this as an increase in Clear-cut LH focus, and yet, alongside that fact, we have no immediate sense of undue haste – there is still ample time for both storytelling and interruption. Nevertheless, the timescale becomes clear as the narrative progresses: Jesus wished to arrive in Jerusalem in good time for the Passover. On the other hand, throughout Jesus' ministry he was remarkably responsive. He held together both a strong sense of purpose, and a remarkable willingness to be interrupted.[9] Overall, he was both proactive and responsive, both focused and flexible, with his discernment in each day and moment deeply connected with his sense of what the Father wanted.

A second striking theme is the way in which Jesus repeatedly engaged, face-to-face, with each unique person he encountered. He embodied imaginative depth. Their station or status in life appeared irrelevant to him. He saw through or past the category labels of society, and engaged, offering full imaginative depth, with the unique human in front of him.[10] On the one hand, we have his genuine engagements with 'higher status' people, such as Nicodemus, and indeed Herod. On the other hand, we encounter his clear determination that those easily undervalued by society should know God's love. In particular, he was attentive to how the structures of the powerful impact on those with less power. And he was unafraid to be radical and subversive in his response.[11] This leads on, third, to the fact that his ministry seamlessly combined both an integrity and a great variety. If he had a single theme, it was a very broad one. His core and congruent emphases led to uniquely tailored interactions in each different context. This was no replicated algorithm. If he had a method, it was to be fully engaged, bringing both grace and truth, in interaction with the unique person with whom he was face-to-face. Jesus epitomizes a posture of poised attentiveness, of clarity anchored in compassion, strong, caring, discerning and flexible to respond as fitting in each unique context.

Fourth, Jesus frequently appears to have been remarkably unconcerned with the effectiveness of much of his approach. With his public teaching, he was apparently content to offer memorable stories, and leave it to his hearers to make of them what they would. There is no indication that Jesus needed to be energized by the setting of pre-determined targets. He found ample motivation elsewhere, from a different source, and of a different quality.[12] This links, fifth, with the pace of his ministry – namely, walking pace. Stephen Pickard, noting that 'nothing can be loved at speed',[13] sees Jesus' walking as providing 'the space and rhythm for his ministry of saving presence'.[14] This pace enabled the depth of his attention and presence. It signalled his willingness to be interrupted, and no doubt facilitated his responsiveness.

Sixth, Jesus seems to have seen each thing and person afresh. There is the simplicity, almost a naïveté, in how he draws attention to the lilies of the field, to the everyday experiences of his contemporary world – weeds in a field; labourers waiting for work; marriage feasts. He sees with the eyes of a child, and with the wisdom of a sage – both of which manifest the Holistic RH, rather than being stuck in any simplified Clear-cut map.

Finally, Jesus lived by different values, and sought to upend those of his hearers. The implicit assumptions of the 'iceberg' of his discourse contrast starkly with those of most others. He was disinterested in power or apparent success. Notably, although he was frequently ready to take initiative, to do and to act, he was also willing to be done to, to be acted on. Jesus did not need to be in control, or to feel in control. Instead, the depth and intimacy of Jesus' relationship with his Father led to radical trust, and a consequent sense of security. This trust was deeply tested, especially in Gethsemane – tested, and found to be strong and true. Not only was this total trust and self-centring in God the source of his own security, but it also forms the heart of his invitation to those who would follow him. 'Abide in me as I abide in you … As the Father has loved me, so I have loved you; abide in my love' (John 15.4, 9). From such a disposition of trust and obedience, we are free to follow God's leading in taking initiative, in responding to others, and in being done to, knowing the limits of our responsibility, and thus increasingly liberated from anxiety. At the end of Matthew 11, Jesus describes the depth of the mutual knowledge of the Father and the Son. It is as we learn from Jesus to share his knowledge of his Father that we can receive his remarkable invitation: 'Come to me, all you that are weary and are carrying heavy burdens, and I will give you rest. Take my yoke upon you, and learn from me; for I am gentle and humble in heart, and you will find rest for your souls. For my yoke is easy, and my burden is light' (Matt. 11.28–30). This is not a temporary exception to a general disposition of focused and determined spiritual accomplishment, but a combination and distillation of the heart of the gospel.

Trusting participation with God

Such trust in God, demonstrated supremely in the life of Jesus, lies right at the heart of the Christian calling. This trust is utterly interwoven with obedience – trust and obey, as the hymn has it. A crucial point is that the obedience is interwoven with ongoing trusting relationship. It is not that God gives us a list of tasks, then leaves us to complete them on our own. Rather, we are called to learn ever-increasing participation and collaboration, with God and with others, in and as we seek to play our part. It is not our role to carry the weight of that which is God's responsibility.

A central recurring question through the Scriptures is this: in what or whom do we put our trust? Where is our primary centre of gravity? Is it in our own strength? Is it in the strength of other nations, or their ways of going about things? This is a persistent question throughout the Psalms and Isaiah. It is repeatedly highlighted in the narratives of Abraham, Moses and David. The nature of trust is portrayed with sharp clarity in the story of the burning fiery furnace (Dan. 3). Here, Shadrach, Meshach and Abednego declare their expectation that God will deliver them. Crucially, even if he does not, their trust and obedience will be unchanged. The centrality of trust continues into the New Testament. Both Testaments repeatedly make clear that it can be very difficult to retain our trust in God, especially when God does not act according to prevailing cultural expectations.

David Ford draws particular attention to the ending of John's Gospel, and to Jesus' interaction with Peter (John 21.17–23). Here, the culmination of history will be centred on Christ. 'Everything else is left vague, and curiosity about precise details is discouraged … The positive emphasis is on "Follow me!"'[15] To be clear, trust in God is rightly combined with appropriate action. It does not mean abdicating all responsibility. Neither, however, does it mean assuming all responsibility, taking on our shoulders that which is God's, thereby stepping out of a relationship of trusting participation.

It is worth underlining the degree to which this contrasts with some other narratives of leadership, starkly summarized as 'command and control'. And we should not be surprised by such a stark contrast. As

Richard Bauckham puts it, commenting on the biblical narrative as a whole, the way of God is not 'merely a more powerful or more successful version of the imperial powers, but ... an altogether different kind of rule'.

Such deepening trust and participation with God is inevitably centred in the Holistic RH, with its ongoing relational attentiveness and responsiveness. And the vision towards which we are summoned continues Holistic RH themes: the transcending of division; the reconciliation of creation with God; and the spread of joy and shalom.

Ecclesiology: the nature of the church

We draw this chapter to a close with a reflection on the nature of the church. In recent writing, the church has very helpfully been described as a 'sign, instrument and foretaste' of God's kingdom (with this phrase widely adopted in a number of ecumenical agreements).[16] The church is a sign, pointing to the utter goodness of God, the paradoxical wisdom of the gospel, and the hope of God working even in and through frail and fallen human beings. It is an instrument, in and through which God continues to work. And it is a partial foretaste of the fullness of blessing of the kingdom of God. Drawing on all three of these, the missiologist David Bosch describes the church as 'challenged to be God's experimental garden on earth, a fragment of the reign of God, having "the first fruits of the spirit" (Rom. 8.23) as a pledge of what is to come (2 Cor. 1.22)'.[17]

These descriptors of the function of the church can be helpfully complemented by one further term, namely church as communion.[18] The concept of communion, with its connotations of reconciliation, friendship, unity, shared participation and love, summarizes much of what we have discussed in this chapter. 'This communion is participation in the life of God through Christ in the Holy Spirit, making Christians one with each other'[19] although such unity is always partial and fragile. Such participation in the life of God holds together divine and human action in the world, rather than setting the one against the other, or indeed seeing them as separable. The concept of communion enriches and intersects with our understanding of the church as a sign, instrument and foretaste. Viewing the church without communion at its centre would be to significantly reduce its nature, to render it two-dimensional at best. As *Church as Communion* puts it:

> [The Church] is therefore itself rightly described as a visible sign which both points to and embodies our communion with God and with one another; as an instrument through which God effects this communion; and as a foretaste of the fullness of communion to be consummated when Christ is all in all.[20]

We have, then, four terms which, taken together, offer a rich description of the nature of the church: sign, instrument, foretaste and communion. Of these, instrument is the one with the strongest LH connotations. An instrument can often legitimately serve as a means to an end, to be deployed in pursuit of problem-solving or task completion. The notion of a sign also carries some LH characteristics, perhaps with more obvious space for RH resonance. Both foretaste and communion, however, are substantially centred in the relational and Holistic RH. Taking them together, the framing offered by the report *Church as Communion* is, overall, deeply congruent with McGilchrist's proposals. Here, sign, instrument and foretaste are all infused with the notion of communion with others, and centred with and in the dynamic life and purposes of God:

> Communion implies that the Church is a dynamic reality moving towards its fulfilment. Communion embraces both the visible gathering of God's people and its divine life-giving source. We are thus directed to the life of God, Father, Son and Holy Spirit, the life God wills to share with all people.[21]

The notion of the church as 'instrument' normally carries connotations of direct causation, which can be accurate. But let me broaden the resonance of the term by mentioning musical instruments – which is to say, instruments of music, instruments through which music comes into being. Might the church also be an instrument through which God's music is heard in the world, shaping the atmosphere around it, conveying at least a little more of the grace and truth of God. The effects of music are much less linear or predictable than the term 'instrument' normally suggests. Nevertheless, living in a world imbued with the music of life is very different from inhabiting a world without music. The church as 'instrument' may itself resonate as a sign and foretaste of communion in and with the divine life.

Conclusion

This chapter has considered, in brief, some of the main themes of the Bible and Christian life, alongside McGilchrist's hypothesis. On the one hand, his understanding of the distinctive strengths of the two hemispheres, and of their interaction, has repeatedly enabled new insight and depth of appreciation. On the other, there have been no obvious instances in which the priorities of Christian theology have been at odds with his proposals. There is plentiful space in the life of faith for wise harnessing of Clear-cut LH strength, but its centre of gravity is much more holistically and relationally RH. The metaphor of a journey can accurately illustrate some aspects of the life of faith. Such a journey, however, rarely if ever has the degree of pre-knowledge and control beloved of the LH. Moreover, what is important about it incorporates a much richer and broader perspective than the narrow focus of that hemisphere. In particular, we are called to a rich communion before the faces of God and others, characterized by trust, obedience and love.

Questions for reflection

1 Thinking of your primary experience of Christianity, how does it relate to both the Clear-cut LH and the Holistic RH?
2 What structures or patterns have proved most helpful in your own spiritual life? Have you ever found such structures beginning to become master rather than servant?
3 From what you read in this chapter, what insight was most obviously helpful? What seemed unconvincing or provocative? What questions are you taking away?
4 What do you find yourself seeing in a new light?

Notes

1 'Si comprehendus, non est Deus', Augustine, Sermon 117, quoted in Iain McGilchrist, 2021, *The Matter With Things*, London: Perspectiva Press, p. 1201.
2 Maggie Ross, 2014, *Silence: A User's Guide: Volume 1: Process*, London: Darton, Longman & Todd. This work combines remarkable depth of insight with an occasional tendency to lose sight of the genuine gifts of the Clear-cut LH. See also her *Writing the Icon of the Heart: In Silence Beholding*, 2011, Abingdon, BRF. Another who draws explicitly on McGilchrist's work is Rowan Williams,

2018, *Being Human: Bodies, Minds, Persons*, London, SPCK (see especially chapter 3: Bodies, Minds and Thoughts, pp. 49–68).

3 Ross, *Silence: A User's Guide*, p. 33.

4 Ross, *Silence: A User's Guide*, pp. 46–7. A passage such as this encapsulates for me both why disciplines of regular spiritual retreat are so important and potent, and also why those steeped in our Western Clear-cut culture can find that claim baffling, unconvincing or incomprehensible.

5 David Ford, 2021, *The Gospel of John: A Theological Commentary*, Grand Rapids, MI: Baker Academic, pp. 416–17.

6 See, respectively: Genesis 22; Jonah; Job 1—2; Daniel 3; Matthew 4.1–11; 26.36–46.

7 For an insightful biblical analysis in this territory, see Philip Plyming, 2023, *Being Real*, London: SCM Press. Plyming focuses especially on St Paul's hardship narratives in 2 Corinthians. He suggests considerable cultural parallels between first-century Corinth and contemporary Western culture, centred on a pressure primarily to show a positive and optimistic front. (We might describe this as a smiling mask, rather than our real face.) I can't help noting that, if McGilchrist's epic sweep of Western cultural history were broadly true, we would expect first-century Corinth to be influenced by Clear-cut LH dominance.

8 Daniel W. Hardy and David Ford, 1985, *Praising and Knowing God*, 1st US edn, Philadelphia, PA: Westminster Press, p. 97.

9 For a rich and thorough exposition of the importance of the latter, see Al Barrett and Ruth Harley, 2020, *Being Interrupted: Reimagining the Church's Mission From the Outside, In*, London: SCM Press.

10 Or indeed above him, hiding in a tree. I can't help thinking that in the remarkable account of Zacchaeus, his turning was sparked primarily by Jesus treating him as Zacchaeus, as himself, rather than as 'a tax collector' (Luke 19.1–10). See also Christopher Cocksworth, 2014, *Seeing Jesus and Being Seen by Him*, London: SPCK.

11 See for instance Walter Wink's reading of Matt. 5.41, on 'going the second mile'. Wink puts a convincing case that this offers the oppressed a chance to recover the initiative and assert their human dignity, at the same time putting the occupying soldier at the risk of military punishment. Walter Wink, 1992, *Engaging the Powers: Discernment and Resistance in a World of Domination*, Minneapolis, MN: Fortress Press, pp. 179–84.

12 For more on motivation, see Chapter 10.

13 Stephen K. Pickard, 2012, *Seeking the Church: An Introduction to Ecclesiology*, London: SCM Press, p. 213. See also Kosuke Koyama, 2021, *Three Mile an Hour God*, London: SCM Press.

14 Pickard, *Seeking the Church*, p. 221.

15 Ford, *The Gospel of John*, p. 34.

16 This description is expounded, among other places, in the ARCIC agreed statement *Church as Communion*, and the Meissen, Porvoo and Reuilly statements with the Continental Protestant churches.

17 David Bosch, 1991, *Transforming Mission: Paradigm Shifts in Theology of Mission*, Maryknoll, NY: Orbis Books, p. 11, quoted in Mark Ireland and Mike Chew, 2009, *How to Do Mission Action Planning: A Vision-centred Approach*, 1st edn, London: SPCK, 1st edn, p. 44.

18 This term, translated from the Greek word *koinonia*, has been a recurring focus of recent ecumenical discussion and agreement, especially *Church as Communion*.

19 *Church as Communion*, paragraph 13, www.anglicancommunion.org/media/105242/ARCIC_II_The_Church_as_Communion.pdf, accessed 27.09.2024.

20 *Church as Communion*, paragraph 17, www.anglicancommunion.org/media/105242/ARCIC_II_The_Church_as_Communion.pdf, accessed 27.09.2024.

21 *Church as Communion*, paragraph 3, www.anglicancommunion.org/media/105242/ARCIC_II_The_Church_as_Communion.pdf, accessed 27.09.2024.

8

Making Sense of the Strategic Leadership Discourse (Church SLD)

Introduction

On the desk in front of me sit two small paperbacks. Published just four years apart, in the 1970s, both are concerned with Christian ministry and the life of the church. Their style, however, could hardly be more different. The earlier book is entitled *The Christian Priest Today*.[1] Written by Michael Ramsey, then Archbishop of Canterbury, the book is primarily composed of addresses given by Ramsey to those about to be ordained. Although its language may now feel somewhat dated, much of its core content is timeless. (This is why, more than half a century later, this text still features on reading lists for those considering ordination.) In his description of the role of the ordained priest, Ramsey groups his thoughts under four subheadings: the priest is to be a person of theology, of reconciliation, of prayer and of the Eucharist. Leadership, we note, is not one of the subheadings. In fact, the terminology of leadership does not feature in the book.

The second paperback is *Your Church Can Grow: Seven Vital Signs of a Healthy Church*. Its author, Peter Wagner, was a disciple of Donald McGavran, founder of the 'Church Growth movement' not many years previously in California. Wagner's style of communicating is very different from that of Ramsey. More importantly, he also has very different emphases. First, Wagner's 'Vital Sign Number One' is the *'dynamic leadership'* of a pastor motivating the entire church into action for growth.[2] Second, Wagner emphasized the importance of good *methods*. For Wagner, a good method is an effective one. In this, he follows McGavran: 'Constantly measuring the effectiveness for church growth of all activities is both feasible and necessary.'[3] Third, and relatedly, Wagner calls for 'clearly defined *objectives*'.[4] Underlying his perspective, Wagner is happy to describe a 'church growth' approach as a *science*. This science he sees as seeking to understand 'God's work in the world with more precision' than has previously been possible, enabling highly effective church methods.⁵ Overall, if pressed to choose a single book that marked the beginning of (what I term) the Church SLD, it would be this one: *Your Church Can Grow*. Our aim for the rest of this chapter is to gain a broad understanding of this discourse, and to explore those aspects that come into clearer relief in the light of McGilchrist's work. This will include increasing our awareness and understanding of all that lies below the surface of the iceberg of discourse.⁶

The Church SLD

Within the pages of *Your Church Can Grow*, most of the main themes and assumptions of the Church SLD are already apparent:

- stress on the importance of method, frequently linked to objectives;
- an underlying 'scientific' assumption that 'how things work' for the church is substantially predictable;
- a striking optimism, explicit in the title of the book;
- and an emphasis on leadership itself, understood to imply dynamic action, ongoing change, and the assumptions and emphases already mentioned.

Following Wagner's book, the Church SLD continued with a steady stream of titles such as *Understanding Leadership*,⁷ *A Call to Excellence*,⁸ *Leadership for New Life*,⁹ *Growing Leaders*,¹⁰ *The Road to Growth*¹¹ and *Developing Visionary Leadership*.¹² These and other titles consistently emphasize some or all of the themes already mentioned, and approach church life with a broadly comparable mindset.

Authors have described very similar forms of method using some variations in terminology. Of these, the approach known as Mission Action Planning has become probably the best-known within the Church. *How to Do Mission Action Planning* is the go-to handbook on the subject, written by an experienced priest (now an archdeacon), Mark Ireland, and a business consultant, Mike Chew.¹³ (More of this later, including the interesting developments in its second edition.)

Alongside written publications, the Church SLD has been very influential on practice, at several levels. In 2011, the use of Mission Action Planning was approved and encouraged by General Synod. Many or most dioceses support parishes in such planning, and some have strongly encouraged churches to produce such plans. Additionally, most dioceses have adopted some form of strategic planning. A significant development nationally was the Strategic Development Funding programme, which ran from 2014 to 2022. Over that period, a total of £198 million was awarded to dioceses, in support of 92 different projects.[14] Applications to this fund needed to convince decision-makers that the project would result in a significant difference to missional and/or financial health. In doing so, applicants were asked to specify the intended outcomes of their project. A particular focus was on the number of 'new disciples' envisaged.

The Church SLD takes its most focused and intense form in connection with funded projects. The number of such projects, along with the substantial sums involved, has called for new forms of oversight and accountability, with new committees at diocesan and national levels. The approach taken around such grants has also led to many dioceses employing project managers, and/or programme managers (where the latter typically oversee several different funded projects). In a recent *Church Times* advertisement for such a post – termed the diocesan 'Strategic Programme and Change Lead' – the role was described as follows:

> ... to drive the development of our strategic programme and to structure and monitor its implementation to deliver the diocesan vision. The successful candidate will lead on planned development, advise on delivery mechanisms, monitor progress against objectives, and communicate this well to our stakeholders.[15]

This is familiar and reassuring language for some, and rather less so for others. Its vocabulary and assumptions are certainly in some contrast to the discourse of Michael Ramsey.

As soon as we begin to consider the hemisphere characteristics of the Church SLD, the signature presence of the Clear-cut LH becomes obvious. Its characteristics are strong, pervasive and clear throughout the discourse. It is worth giving brief attention to several indicative aspects of the discourse, crystallizing such LH presence.

The Church SLD primary metaphor: a pre-planned journey to a pre-identified destination

Within the Church SLD literature, the concept of a journey forms the primary metaphor for church life. The consistent focus within the literature is on a certain type of journey.[16] First, we work out where we are supposed to get to. Then we invest energy in planning how to get there – and quite possibly imbue a sense of urgency by warning of the perils of doing nothing. Finally, according to this approach, we take the journey, persevering until we arrive at our intended destination.

How does this analogy relate to the hemispheres? We should first note that the use of metaphor is particularly linked to the Holistic RH. Moreover, the concept of a journey can easily carry a range of RH connotations, suggesting a wide range of Holistic qualities and attributes. These can include: openness to the new; engaging responsively with who and what we encounter; savouring new experiences; enjoying friendships old and new along the way. And journeys come in a range of forms, such as leisurely roundtrips, open-ended explorations, adventurous forays into new territory, and perilous quests.

Such gifts and possibilities, however, do not come into focus in a Church SLD journey. Instead, it is purposeful and pre-planned, and clearly directed towards a pre-identified destination. It resonates strongly with the mountain summit of achievement described in Chapter 6. This is indeed the territory of the Clear-cut LH, in several respects.

Narrow focus

First, the tunnel vision of Clear-cut focus plays a foundational role. Just as the chaffinch ignores everything else in order to pick up its seed, so the SLD encourages the focus of the whole church to be narrowly directed towards the desired endpoint. Naming it as a priority, or *the* priority, would be one way of enabling such focus. For the Church SLD, however, this is not enough. It wants us to narrow down further, to be even more specific. Our priority needs to be sharpened into an objective, with an explicit endpoint. And the universal recommendation is that every objective needs to be SMART (Specific; Measurable; Achievable; Realistic/Resourced; Timed).[17] We need to know in advance much more precisely where we want to get to, and by when. For instance, here is one such example SMART objective, as offered in *How to Do MAP*: 'To engage more with young adults aged 18 to 30 so that we see an increase in Sunday and midweek regular attendance of 10% within 12 months.'[18] The clarification that turns a priority into an objective, and then the further honing to make it a SMART objective, both involve a narrowing of focus. Moving from a priority to a SMART objective is a journey of increasing LH input and impact. This strong Clear-cut LH characteristic is ubiquitous in the Church SLD.

Method

For the Church SLD, there is a method by which any church can proceed. As noted, Mission Action Planning (MAP) is the best-known of these. Any church can follow the recommended steps, and doing so will lead to the necessary clarity. Ireland and Chew offer a '10-point health check' for the steps needed. These 10 steps are supported by a total of 52 questions for reflection.

Several aspects of the MAP method carry the signature characteristics of the Clear-cut LH. The MAP process is seen as generally applicable. It is a clear and fixed simplified mapping of what should be involved. Later in the chapter we will engage with an account that highlights many of the (Holistic) aspects not emphasized by the method. The method is shaped by a Clear-cut sense of purpose, and designed to increase the sense of purpose of those using it. This method can help a local church to clarify tasks they want to complete, or problems they want or need to solve. We might suggest that it also encourages people to view the life of the church primarily in terms of tasks or problems.

Optimism and positivity

Church SLD writing carries *a high degree of optimism*. This is in line with the positive, but constrained, emotional range of the Clear-cut LH. Such optimism is often implicit, for instance in the titles of books and chapters. Along with *Your Church Can Grow, I Believe in Church Growth*[19] and *The Road to Growth* we have, for example, *Leaders Discern, Articulate and Implement God's Vision*[20] and *Fantastic Leaders – God's Changemakers.*[21] There is optimism regarding the potency of leadership. There is optimism regarding the reliability and effectiveness of the proposed method. The optimism is marked by consistent positivity – sometimes expressed with heightened rhetoric: 'Fantastic organisations ... have fantastic leaders. With great leadership churches can be transformed into places where people are excited to belong ... What we are saying is that if you are a church leader then the future is in your hands...'[22]

Along with the presence of such positivity, most 'negative' aspects of human experience are unmentioned within the literature, giving it a somewhat distorted feel. There is one exception, as previously mentioned. Fear or anxiety regarding the likely consequence of doing nothing is harnessed to imbue a sense of urgency: Something must be done, and fast; this method sounds compelling and optimistic; given that something must be done, let's get on and do *this* thing, using this method. Both the consistently optimistic tone (including unrealistic optimism), and the link with anxiety, carry the hallmark of the Clear-cut LH.

Seeing the life of the church primarily in terms of a task to complete, or a problem to solve

We saw in Chapter 2 how the left hemisphere's purposeful way of being is bound up with how it tends to view the world: primarily in terms of problems to solve, and tasks to complete. Such a perspective, I suggest, is strong within the Church SLD, but also largely implicit – we might not immediately notice it. Moreover, Western culture typically shares this perspective. We are therefore even more likely simply to see it as 'normal', if we register it at all. Clearly, the ability to complete tasks and solve problems is indeed important, and church life will include examples of both which merit appropriate attention. Nevertheless, this should be neither the only frame, or even the dominant frame, through which we should conceive of church life. The Diocese of Oxford, recognizing and underlining this point, have recently made good use of the phrase 'A parish is not a problem to be solved'.

The key factor that leads me to understand the Church SLD in this way is its consistent desire for a clear binary outcome. A clear and certain answer to the question 'Have we finished?' is seen as a necessity. If this is a task, we want to be able to complete it, and to know that we have done so. If it is a problem we are addressing, we want to solve it, and know that we have done so. Those operating from this approach would find it simply unthinkable to set out to address an issue without knowing in advance the criteria for 'success'. Turning a priority into an objective makes such a response possible. Making the objective SMART further cements the sense of clarity and certainty.

What is the problem to be solved? What is the task to be completed?

The numerical growth of the church is clearly at the centre of answers to these questions.

Ecclesiology and the Church SLD: what is the nature of the church?

The Church SLD offers very little explicit reflection on the nature of the church. Assumptions on the subject largely lie hidden below the metaphorical waterline. I offer several reflections. The first is to note that the purposeful LH has a strong drive towards action, so the lack of reflection is not surprising.

Overall, the Church SLD seems to see the church primarily as an organization, and to understand the nature of organizations in a particularly Clear-cut LH way. For the SLD in general, a good organization is one that prioritizes clarity of purpose, and a lean task-focused disposition. This appears to be seen as obvious and uncontroversial, and so the discourse views its own recommendations as theologically neutral, as 'consecrated pragmatism'.[23] What, then, is the purpose of the church? The strong bias here is towards a focus on the salvation of more individuals. Such a focus is interwoven with a much greater SLD emphasis on the Great Commission (understood substantially in LH terms of increasing numbers) than on the greatest commandments.

Ireland does offer an explicit reflection on the nature of the church, rare within the Church SLD. Although he does cite the phrase 'sign, instrument and foretaste', the word instrument is very clearly the centre of his attention.[24] Tellingly, Ireland does offer a rich RH quotation from the missiologist David Bosch, describing the church as God's experimental garden.[25] This image, with its biblical resonance, easily suggests, for instance, overflowing bounty, generously given as blessing, in which time can be taken for enjoyment and wholesome pleasure. It holds potential as an image for our working with God in restored communion and trust, and for fruitful living unfolding in both planned and unexpected ways. However, following this quotation, there is not even one phrase recognizing such richness. Rather, he moves immediately to an anecdote about moving to a new house: it seems that the point of the garden image is that even a garden requires an 'action plan'.

In the previous chapter, we described the nature of the church in four terms: sign, instrument, foretaste and communion. Of these, instrument was seen to have the strongest LH connotations. In this section we have seen a strong Church SLD bias towards seeing the church as instrumental. Moreover, more anecdotally, Church SLD discourse sees responsibility for such instrumental 'making things happen' lying squarely on the shoulders of church leaders and members. It is we who are to be instrumental. An aphorism I have heard in a Church SLD context is this: 'Pray as if everything depended on God; work as if everything depended on you' (variously attributed to St Ignatius, St Augustine and to John Wesley). The second phrase in particular – work as if everything depended on you – rings true to my experience of the mode of the Church SLD. At first glance, this may sound an attractive and compelling call to responsible engagement. Importantly, however, it seems to me both untrue to experience, and out of line with biblical Christianity. Yes, we should respond wholeheartedly in obedience to God, and in response to the world. But no: everything does not depend on us – so we should not act as if it does. Once again, in this aphorism we see the hallmark separation instinct of the Clear-cut LH. Here it cuts across all notions of working with God, trusting God and fellowship with God and others in service of the kingdom.

As with the Clear-cut LH, the Church SLD seems to assume that the only way to achieve what one desires is by direct and targeted pursuit. And yet, might it be that, in engaging with church, alongside a proper degree of purpose and direction, people might also be looking for more 'hopeful, profound and transcendent forms of living'?[26] Might it be that the church is called to offer much more of an alternative to the outcome-focused narrow preoccupations with success that are so widespread in contemporary culture? Might doing so, with modesty, truthfulness and a Holistic desire to keep growing in our ability to love, trusting in God's presence and action in and beyond our midst, be something of the foretaste of God's kingdom that we are called to offer.

Overall, then, the broad, flowing expansiveness of the joyful dance of grace does not ring true as a primary image of the Church SLD. This leadership discourse does not resonate with the ceilidh's evocation of a rich, multi-faceted occasion, for participation and enjoyment, for connection and relation, for memories, joy and unfolding narrative. Rather, the Church SLD operates by identifying (or more frequently constructing) fresh mountain summits to conquer, then setting out in their pursuit, with the clarity, determination and focus of the Clear-cut LH.

Significantly, here we encounter a very important distinction. Thus far we have focused on Church SLD literature: how this approach is described and prescribed in published work. This literature forms a very important consideration – but it is not the only one. Arguably even more important is what actually happens in practice. What is the experience when real people – including experienced church members and clergy – are guided by Church SLD advice? What is the manner in which they incorporate its clear prescriptions (and perhaps adjust, nuance or transform them on occasion)?

The use of the Clear-cut Church SLD in practice

Let's frame our discussion with two questions. First, is it possible to adopt a Church SLD approach, and still retain healthy hemisphere cooperation, centred in the Holistic RH?

Question 1 – Can the Church SLD approach be used well?

I'll address this question using the best account I know of some Church SLD practice being adopted in a healthy and constructive manner. Before turning to the content of the description, first some brief context. In 2016, Ireland and Chew brought out a second edition of their *How to Do MAP*.[27] Some chapters had been cut, and some new terminology introduced (interestingly, all more Holistic RH than what was there before). This account comes from one of several new chapters, in which different practitioners each focused on their experience of one aspect of Mission Action Planning. I will describe a chapter by Damian Feeney, a parish priest and the Catholic Missioner of Lichfield Diocese. This chapter is entitled 'Prayer and Desire' – introduced to the second edition of the book, as a new first (and preparatory) stage of Mission Action Planning. Feeney describes the experience of one church as they engaged with MAP.

Damian Feeney's account of using MAP

As Feeney describes this engagement, Holistic centring and strengths come across in most of the areas he spotlights as significant. Let me give a flavour of his account. First, as Feeney describes initial planning and consultation meetings, he repeatedly emphasizes the contribution made by their (RH) tone and texture. He mentions 'relaxed, informal storytelling … copious quantities of coffee and bacon sandwiches …'

An away day was held in a parish in a neighbouring town with excellent facilities – there was a Eucharist to start, and a magnificent cooked lunch. Overall, participants 'were astonished by the difference this made both to relationship and deliberation ... there was further storytelling, and much laughter. Such an atmosphere was essential in creating the climate for positive engagement.'[28]

Feeney highlights not just (LH) optimistic looking to the future, but also honesty: 'We looked at historical factors that were helpful and some that were destructive ... We felt very strongly that the formulation of a vision for the church's future had to be built on a truthful, joyful and realistic understanding of the past.' He draws attention not just to general issues, but to specifics: 'We looked at some of the distinctive personalities who had shaped the local church for the present generation.'

Whereas the Clear-cut SLD separates one thing from another, to sharpen clarity, Feeney's description is repeatedly characterized by the Holistic bringing together of things and of people. The parish developed a 'principle of paired responsibility' (he himself was paired with 'the inspirational Sunday School teacher, known to all as Aunty Chris'). He points to the importance of (RH) connection between the PCC and the whole congregation, and the listening role of the council. 'The fusion of local personality and a good strategic planning' was vital. And 'it was the coming together of the intuitive, relationship-based thinking and the application of strategic principles that bore fruit'. Overall, those involved came to recognize 'that process is as significant as outcomes': this process led to 'the [Holistic] growth of individual souls, the development of collaborative ministry and the maturing of a worshipping community in self-awareness'.

Importantly, Feeney has noted and successfully navigated the risk that the plan could 'become a harsh task master' (especially with regard to estimated timescales).[29] But they found a way of using the process flexibly 'according to circumstance and context'. Mission Action Planning thus offered a 'framework' that 'made mission manageable without foreclosing potential'. Rather than letting it become their master, or finding it to be 'the straitjacket that some had feared', they found ways of working with MAP as an 'effective ally'.

Feeney emphasizes the need for learning to desire (RH) what God desires (a consistent emphasis on desire being a welcome addition in the second edition of the book). Such desire will lead us to change often if we are to be faithful to the loving purposes of God. And this 'implies an ever greater [RH] trust and delight in the loving purposes of ... God'.

MAKING SENSE OF THE STRATEGIC LEADERSHIP DISCOURSE

In hemisphere terms, we can see the church here remaining centred in the Holistic RH, and also being receptive to constructive input from the LH. We may note that much of the effectiveness in this account arose from factors to which the Church SLD is blind. As we've seen, there are clear signs of the Holistic RH transforming the manner in which LH input was integrated. We are not able to judge from this description the degree to which there was also a careful sifting of which aspects of the SLD were adopted. Nevertheless, overall, this was an approach that clearly bore Godly fruit, seen in an integrated RH combination of effective action, personal maturing and strengthened relationships.

Our initial question was this: is it possible to adopt a Church SLD approach, and still retain healthy hemisphere cooperation, centred in the Holistic RH? In Feeney's skilful practice, we can see the complementary ways of being of the two hemispheres in constructive collaboration. His account demonstrates the authentic life of the church being strengthened as a consequence. Feeney's narrative, in sum, enables us to give our question a positive response, tempered by one significant qualification: in Feeney's account we heard nothing of the adoption or impact of the later stages of the MAP process. These later stages come into focus as we turn now to explore our second question, watching out for potential downsides of adopting the Church SLD.

Question 2 – How might the Church SLD approach prove less than positive?

To address this second question, we will again look at a specific published account. This time, it's a brief cameo. The cameo itself is of one moment in time, but it offers a way into exploring the impact and the assumptions of the Church SLD. It comes in a book by Emma Ineson, *Ambition: What Jesus Said about Power, Success and Counting Stuff*.[30] She describes it as one of the two key moments that informed the book.[31]

At the centre of this brief cameo is Ineson's husband, whom she describes as a 'very good' vicar of a 'very good' church, which is to be a 'Resourcing Church'.[32] It therefore receives 'Quite A Lot Of Money'. In return for this, 'everything must be measured and accounted for' and so now 'his every move is being watched'. Then she describes a day when the stats for that particular month are just in, and they aren't quite as good as they should be. The key moment is not that itself, but rather, 'When I see written on his face what these numbers are doing to his soul

... I see in that moment glimpses of self-doubt and disappointment that should never have been part of this journey.'[33]

There is a lot going on in this short cameo. Its central character will not be the only vicar or minister who has experienced something similar. As we explore this incident, rather than repeatedly referring to Emma's husband, I'll use the name 'Jo' to represent 'someone with church leadership responsibility in a situation like this one'. Let's assume that Jo has been working sensibly hard, with colleagues, all offering their best skills and judgements towards the flourishing of the church (as seems to have been the case in the Ineson account). However, how people have responded, at this point in time, falls short of what was hoped for. 'The churches aren't growing in numbers quite as much or as fast as they were expected to.'[34] I want to use this cameo to explore indications of the hidden assumptions below the waterline of the iceberg of the Church SLD. I will do so by suggesting three possible ways in which a Church SLD proponent might feasibly interpret the cameo described by Ineson.

Interpretation 1 – Failure to control

The first interpretation is straightforward, and indeed clear-cut: if the statistics don't match what's in the plan, Jo is to blame. The whole point of determining a SMART objective is to energize those involved to achieve it. Quite simply, she should have made it happen. In response to such an interpretation, we might point out that is not actually possible to make people come to faith, or even to attend church. To this, our interpreters might just stand their ground: she accepted the grant, and so she should have found a way to make it happen.

This first interpretation is problematic because it assumes that control is possible. Moreover, it assumes that control is desirable. Its argument may start by seeing Jo as responsible for how things develop. And then it jumps from a broad sense of responsibility to a false assumption that 'being responsible' implies 'being able to make it happen'. But this is simply not true to experience, and even less true to the Christian faith. If I believe because you've made me believe, my faith is not genuine.

Interpretation 2 – How the game works

A second interpretation is very different. From this perspective, there isn't actually a problem. The only trouble is that Jo is taking the scenario personally. If she can learn to lighten up and just play the game, then all will be fine. According to this perspective, everybody knows that she can't make the statistics come to pass – of course not! So on the one hand, she should keep doing what she's doing. And on the other hand, she needs to learn to play the game, without taking it too seriously. Part of the game, of course, is that those overseeing the project will need to seem somewhat disappointed with the recently received figures. When they make this move, her response is to be appropriately contrite, summarize what she has learned already, and reassure them that she will try harder next time.

As it happens, I once heard of such a governance and oversight meeting in which the vicar responsible for a funded project offered as his opening gambit something like, 'Can I just check – we all know these numbers are unrealistic, don't we?' It is perhaps not surprising that those responsible for oversight evidently said nothing at all in response. For to reply, 'No, we think they are very realistic' would probably be untrue. But to say, 'Of course we know they are unrealistic' would be to undercut 'the game' being played.

What should we make of this second interpretation? It is at least more realistic than the first interpretation. Control is neither possible nor indeed desirable. This second interpretation may be roughly how the system tends to work. However, it relies on a foundation that is not truthful. It is thus inappropriate for the life of the church.

Interpretation 3 – The challenge of prediction

Prediction is very difficult – especially about the future, as the physicist Niels Bohr is said to have said.[35] Sometimes it's just that our timing is a little optimistic (as Feeney experienced). When the thing we are predicting depends on other people's responses, as in this cameo, it is often not at all surprising if the eventual outcome is nowhere near what we predicted.

This third interpretation of our cameo takes a very different tack from the previous two. Its comment is straightforward: 'It turns out that our initial estimate was over-optimistic. Jo and the team have acted appropriately, but now we know that the prediction was inaccurate.' Rather than blaming Jo, and treating her as having failed, this interpretation locates the cause in the challenge of accurate prediction. Moreover, it could do so in a humane way.

Interestingly, the Church SLD gives very little attention to how one might make good predictions in the first place. Similarly, what we should do if they prove inaccurate also appears to be of relatively low interest. Ireland and Chew give more attention than many to the latter question, and prescribe a low-key approach. Ireland describes how 'we will find ourselves naturally adjusting our plans as needed'.[36] The second edition of *MAP* puts extra emphasis on Mission Action Planning as a learning cycle, and describes such adjusting as part of 'the learning cycle of life'.[37] It is clear from 'Jo's' response, as described by Emma, that a simple 'natural adjustment' of the plan is not what she was expecting – however sensible and humane that may seem. What she was expecting, it seems, was Interpretation 1, and a clear sense of blame and failure.

It appears, then, that within the Church SLD there is more than one type of response to this sort of scenario. We might, therefore, simply conclude that Ireland and Chew have got it right: Interpretation 3 is the way forward, and Interpretations 1 and 2 have got it wrong. But we should not move so quickly, jumping to accept a straightforward resolution. This cameo highlights a tension which deserves deeper consideration. It has important truth to offer regarding the whole Church SLD approach.

The tension is formed by the gap between what actually happened, and what 'should have happened' (the pre-specified outcome in the plan). Such pre-specified outcomes form an integral part of the Church SLD. It has been asserted confidently that we need to know the destination of our journey before we set off. This is partly so we know whether or not we've 'got there'. Additionally, we are told, having a clear goal will be energizing for us. The desire to reach the summit will lead us forward, and we need to know precisely where the summit is. If this is a good rationale, it makes no sense simply to move the summit when it suits us. Our trust in the whole system would be undercut. The foundation would be removed. Our energy would be cut off at its source. All this is true – if the rationale is a good one.

These first three interpretations each offer a different way of making sense of the cameo. The three interpretations make contrasting moves, all broadly within the assumptions of the Church SLD. Each interpretation on its own is problematic, and there is tension between them. Clearly, then, we need a fourth interpretation, and we need this interpretation to take a different approach. Our fourth interpretation, therefore, draws on the strengths of the Holistic RH, and steps away from the assumptions of the Church SLD.

Interpretation 4 – A helpfully clear anomaly

Our fourth interpretation takes a very different tack. It welcomes this cameo as a great gift of truth. Drawing on an earlier metaphor, the truth unveiled by this cameo is that the foundations of the iceberg on which the Church SLD is resting are unstable and unreliable – when they are asked to carry all the weight. As this cameo makes clear, the assumptions that underpin its proposals turn out to be flawed and insufficient on their own. The gift of this cameo is that it exposes the anomaly of an approach, such as the Church SLD, that is centred in the Clear-cut LH. It is worth unpacking further quite why the recognition of an anomaly should be received as a great gift. To do so, we begin with a short detour via sixteenth-century astronomy.

In the year 1500, astronomical consensus was that the universe had the earth at its centre, as described by Ptolemy around AD 150. Ptolemy's understanding is known as the geocentric model: 'geo' relating to the Greek word for 'earth'. Since that time, as astronomical instruments had become more accurate over the centuries, so astronomers had been able to map the movements of the planets more precisely. These observations had revealed that planetary movements did not, in fact, match the model very well. To put it another way, there was a gap, a tension, between where the planets were and where they 'should have been'. For quite some decades, such anomalies were treated as minor discrepancies. With each new discrepancy, astronomers would make a further minor adjustment to the basic geocentric model, making it ever more complex. However, as the evidence of anomalies increased, awareness gradually dawned that the underlying model itself was flawed. Such awareness offered the necessary conditions for a decisive shift, and the emergence of a new model.[38] This new model was 'heliocentric', with the sun understood to be at the centre.[39]

With the earlier, geocentric model, aspects of planetary movements seemed irritating discrepancies, which just needed to be accommodated. Shifting the discourse to the heliocentric model made a radical difference: now the planets were moving just as expected. The apparent anomalies simply disappeared. Adjusting expectations to be based on a truthful model removed all sense of irritating discrepancy.

Anomalies can be irritating, and it is often tempting to ignore them. They may, however, be highly significant. They deserve our attention. Moreover, the two hemispheres relate to anomalies in different ways. One of the particular strengths of the Holistic RH is as an 'anomaly detector'.[40] This strength is enabled by the breadth of its perspective, its openness to new information, and its ability to hold open multiple possibilities at once. These capacities combine to help it find a perspective, an understanding, that is as truthful as possible. The RH is good at recognizing the flaws in one model, then letting go, and embracing a different interpretation. In contrast, once the Clear-cut LH has committed to an understanding, its default is to resist any apparent anomalies, and to try and explain them away. (You may remember the protestations of the stroke patient in Chapter 3, who denied that it was his arm that was paralysed.) LH 'stickiness' makes it reluctant even to consider an alternative understanding.[41]

This cameo of Jo, and of what the numbers were doing to her soul, offers a similarly clear anomaly, and can play a broadly similar role. None of the three Clear-cut LH interpretations are satisfactory: all have irritating discrepancies, in different ways. In each case, there is a clash between the theory and the reality. In the first, the clash is about whether Jo could make the desired responses happen. In the second, the anomaly is about truthfulness between her and those with oversight. In the third, the anomaly is the suggestion that a pivotal part of the rationale can be dispensed with when it suits. It seems that there is no satisfactory way of reconciling reality with what the Church SLD recommends. There is an anomaly between the theory and the reality. It may be tempting to ignore the anomaly, but the wiser way is to let go of the theory that is revealed as problematic.

The nature of the anomaly

Thanks to the substantial ground we have covered, we can diagnose this anomaly concisely. For fullness of life and flourishing, human beings in general, and Christians in particular, need to be centred in the Holistic RH. The Church SLD literature, however, is substantially centred in the Clear-cut LH. The assumptions on which that discourse rests have their centre of gravity on a Clear-cut LH iceberg. The tensions and contradictions at the heart of this cameo all arise from this mis-centring.

The core of the tension is caused by the difference between the actual attendance statistics, and what was predicted: what is described as a 'falling short'. For the Clear-cut LH, this falling short proves that there is a problem. However, any problem is entirely of our own making. Any sense of a problem comes into existence because of the repeated simplifications that have led to the scenario, and because of false assumptions as to the nature of the church, and how it 'works'. In keeping with the LH way of being, the Church SLD repeatedly works with strategically reduced vision, which is always much narrower and shallower than actual life or God's calling. The rich vocation of the church is primarily reduced to growth in numbers. Quite who should be included within those numbers is determined by simplified criteria. It is assumed that we can know (with precision, and well in advance) what will be the rate of increase of those numbers. The combined weight of all of these over-simplified assumptions ends up bearing down on the shoulders of Jo.

Such narrowness of focus sucks attention away from much that is good, and much that is important. Relationships, creativity and the slow healing of wounds are unlikely to be recognized or appreciated under the Clear-cut Church SLD gaze. The Clear-cut Church SLD perspective tends to see everything in terms of its potential usefulness. People are inevitably viewed substantially as means to an end. Relating, rather than I–thou, becomes much more I–it. Not only will this easily be counter-productive, but it will also be damaging. If the sustained focus is towards a determined assault on the summit, come what may, there will be human casualties along the way. The Clear-cut structures of the Church SLD, constructed with the best of intentions to serve the purposes of the church, have ended up as a constraining cage, rather than a supportive trellis. The servant has become the master. Our own work (in the form of numerical predictions) has become that to which we make ourselves accountable.[42]

It is thus sad, but not surprising, that the consequent experience is not that of grateful, trusting participation with God and others, in the flowing dance of life together. Neither, it turns out, is it the promised exhilaration of the mountain summit of achievement. What Jo experienced, rather, sounds much more like the tightrope walk of doom.

Such a description may seem bleak. Describing it concisely may have heightened its negative features. However, we should receive as good news this diagnosis – that the Church CLD is problematically centred in the Clear-cut LH. This is good news because it is straightforwardly truthful, making good sense of the phenomena we have encountered. The truth shall set us free (John 8.32). It is a relief not to have to contort ourselves into one of the three previous interpretations.

Having recognized the presence and significance of the anomaly, it becomes clear what should happen next. Interpretation 4, drawing straightforwardly on the breadth of a Holistic RH perspective, recognizes the strong signs that we need to centre our weight on a different iceberg. We need a different perspective, and a contrasting form of sense-making. We need to be centred in a different way of being in God's world.

Two concluding comments

Before drawing the chapter to a close, two further points are worth registering. The first is to underline the impact on 'Jo' of the type of attention she felt she was receiving, given the structures and assumptions of the Church SLD. The implicit gaze under which she was living was not poised attentiveness, with clear-sightedness anchored in compassion, but much more that of scrutinizing judgement. The understanding we will develop in the remaining chapters will offer alternative ways of seeing – and thus different forms of implicit gaze – along with some sketches of different ways of framing developments in the church.

Second, one helpful angle of illumination on the cameo we have just explored comes from the work of Dave Snowden, introduced in Chapter 6. We can reasonably describe the Church SLD as assuming that the life and work of the church is essentially a 'complicated system'. In particular, the assumption is that accurate predictions can sensibly be made regarding how others will respond to our ministry and mission initiatives (roughly parallel to predicting the fuel consumption of a particular car on a specific journey). As we discussed, in a complicated system, which is typically machine-like, cause and effect are largely conformed with LH assumptions about linear causality. The Church SLD effectively treats the church as if it were a complicated system. This, however, is a classic example of one of the main weaknesses of the Clear-cut LH: misunderstanding the nature of what it is dealing with. The reality of people's lives and faith journeys is very different from a complicated system. This realm of life is 'nonengineerable', to use Rosa's term.[43] It is complex, and it is 'animate': soul is involved. People's responses are shaped by a multidimensional tapestry of factors, influences and constraints, by intertwined stories and by individual dispositions. Moreover, the punctuated process of our individual and shared journeys is significantly shaped by unanticipated *kairos* moments, within and around which the Holy Spirit of God is always present. This is not at all to say that there is nothing the church can do. But it is very much to reconstrue our understanding of our role, our context and our purpose.

Making sense of the Church SLD

Several factors have combined to make the Church SLD appear an attractive proposition. First, many churches and clergy, I suspect, have historically tended to underuse Clear-cut LH strengths, to the detriment of church life. Second, traditional ministerial discourse has perhaps struggled to address practical questions of structure, focus and planning – encouraging a ready hearing for the Church SLD. Third, the significant overall decline in church engagement over recent decades plays into the LH tendency to view the church itself as a problem to be solved. Fourth, optimistic LH rhetoric can indeed sound very convincing, and is consistently adopted by the Church SLD. Fifth, as McGilchrist has persuasively argued, our Western host culture has increasingly come to see a predominantly LH approach simply as 'normal'. Finally, much of what is problematic in the Church SLD frequently remains implicit – hidden below the waterline of the iceberg of discourse. It is easy not to recognize its existence, never mind its shortcomings. Taking into account the combined weight of all these factors, it is hardly surprising that this approach has come to have such substantial influence in recent years across the life of the church.

Nevertheless, as we have argued, there are serious anomalies running through the core of the Church SLD. Its basic disposition and manner of attention lead to the overlooking and undervaluing of much that is most important. They lead to a distortion of priorities and of relationships. And they rely upon unfounded and counter-productive assumptions regarding our capacity to predict and control – our ability to 'make things happen'.

We need, therefore, to be centred in a different way of being and acting in God's world. We need a way of conceiving life and ministry that welcomes and values both our initiative and our responsiveness, both our action and our disposition, and that manages to give proper space for our own priorities, for those of others, and for those of God. To help address these requirements, and more, we turn in the next chapter to familiarize ourselves with the practice and potential of *improvisation*.

Questions for reflection

1 What experience, if any, have you had of the Church SLD? What did you find most helpful about it?
2 How did you respond to Damian Feeney's account? Would you like to have been part of that process?
3 If you had been in Emma Ineson's kitchen at the moment she described, what might you have said to her husband (or to our imagined vicar, Jo, in an equivalent situation)?
4 How convincing – or not – do you find the diagnosis that the Church SLD is overly centred in the Clear-cut LH? What are the main factors that lead you to that conclusion?

Notes

1 Michael Ramsey, 1985, *The Christian Priest Today*, London: SPCK.

2 C. Peter Wagner, 1976, *Your Church Can Grow: Seven Vital Signs of a Healthy Church*, Ventura, CA: Regal Books, pp. 55–68.

3 Donald McGavran, 1955, *The Bridges of God; A Study in the Strategy of Missions*, London: World Dominion Press, p. 51.

4 Wagner, *Your Church Can Grow*, p. 30.

5 Wagner, *Your Church Can Grow*, p. 41. Few, if any, writers after Wagner choose to use the term 'scientific' for their approach. That said, it's not obvious that their working assumptions are substantially different.

6 See pp. 90–2.

7 John Finney, 1989, *Understanding Leadership*, London: Darton, Longman & Todd.

8 Paul Beasley-Murray, 1995, *A Call to Excellence: An Essential Guide to Christian Leadership*, London: Hodder & Stoughton.

9 David Pytches, 1998, *Leadership for New Life*, London: Hodder & Stoughton.

10 James Lawrence, 2004, *Growing Leaders: Reflections on Leadership, Life and Jesus*, Oxford: BRF.

11 Bob Jackson, 2005, *The Road to Growth: Towards a Thriving Church*, London: Church House Publishing.

12 Richard Williams and Mark Tanner, 2004, *Developing Visionary Leadership*, Cambridge: Grove Books.

13 Mark Ireland and Mike Chew, 2009, *How to Do Mission Action Planning: A Vision-centred Approach* (hereafter referred to as *MAP* in the notes), 1st edn, London: SPCK.

14 A successor scheme to Strategic Development Funding is now underway. My understanding is that the way it is structured includes some Holistic RH shifts,

including greater timescales, and the desire for an integrated approach, rather than simply separate projects.

15 *Church Times* advertisement, January 2024.

16 See, for instance, Bill Hybels, 2002, *Courageous Leadership*, Grand Rapids, MI: Zondervan.

17 See, for instance, Williams and Tanner, 2004, *Developing Visionary Leadership*, p. 10.

18 Ireland and Chew, *MAP*, 1st edn, p. 72.

19 Eddie Gibbs, 1990, *I Believe in Church Growth*, London: Hodder & Stoughton.

20 Lawrence, 2004, chapter 10 in *Growing Leaders*, pp. 192–214.

21 Williams and Tanner, 2004, *Developing Visionary Leadership*, p. 3.

22 Williams and Tanner, p. 3.

23 Wagner, *Your Church Can Grow*, p. 31.

24 For instance, the relevant section heading is 'Church as an instrument of God's mission', Ireland and Chew, *MAP*, 1st edn, pp. 43–5. The relevant chapter is attributed to Mark Ireland.

25 As quoted in the previous chapter: see p. 104.

26 Percy, 1998, *Power and the Church: Ecclesiology in an Age of Transition*, London: Cassell, p. 134.

27 Mark Ireland and Mike Chew, 2016, *How to do Mission Action Planning: Prayer, Process and Practice*, rev. and expanded 2nd edn, London: SPCK.

28 All quotes in this section are taken from *MAP*, 2nd edn, chapter 4, ebook.

29 Hofstadter's Law is normally pertinent: 'It always takes longer than you expect, even when you take into account Hofstadter's Law.'

30 Emma Ineson, 2019, *Ambition: What Jesus Said about Power, Success and Counting Stuff*, London: SPCK.

31 The other was her own appointment as a bishop: when she began writing the book, Ineson was the principal of Trinity College, Bristol. By the time she completed it, she had been appointed Bishop of Penrith. She is now Bishop of Kensington.

32 Ineson, *Ambition*, p. 1.

33 Ineson, *Ambition*, p. 2.

34 Ineson, *Ambition*, p. 2.

35 Iain McGilchrist, 2021, *The Matter With Things*, London: Perspectiva Press, p. 727.

36 *MAP*, 2nd edn, chapter 2, 'Towards a Theology of MAP', ebook. I expect that Ireland is assuming that the 'oversight' of our SMART outcomes lies entirely with us – rather than involving any grant funders, or broader church body.

37 *MAP*, 2nd edn, Chapter 3.

38 Albeit one that seems to have been anticipated long before Ptolemy, for instance by Aristarchus, in the third century BC.

39 This shift in understanding is often referred to as the Copernican revolution due to the key contribution of the astronomer Copernicus.

40 As mentioned earlier: see p. 47.

41 For more on the role of anomalies in paradigms more generally, see the seminal work of Thomas Kuhn, 1962, *The Structure of Scientific Revolutions*, Chicago, IL: University of Chicago Press. Reading this with McGilchrist's hemisphere perspective in mind adds yet more interest to an already fascinating book.

42 In such a move (a staple of the Church SLD) it is hard to avoid being reminded of what the Bible repeatedly condemns as idolatry. See, for instance, Isaiah 44.9–20.

43 See p. 89 in Chapter 6.

9

Improvisation

Introduction

McGilchrist's perspective, then, helps us make sense of some of the potential shortcomings of the Church SLD. We turn now to look towards a constructive alternative. What form of discourse and description can help us approach ministerial leadership in an even better way? If life and leadership in the church were richly informed by McGilchrist's hemisphere understanding, what might it look like?

My best answer to these questions centres on *improvisation*. As we will go on to explore, the practice of improvisation is remarkably relevant for our purposes. Good improvisation requires constructive cooperation between the hemispheres. The shape of God's relating to the world can be described as improvised, as can the nature of Christian living. Improvisation together (with God and others) depends on, and develops, attentive and courageous relating. In particular, Christian leadership, in ministry and mission, involves us and others improvising together as we seek to enable ever deeper participation in the divine life and love.

In our exploration of improvisation, we will draw especially on the work of the theologian Jeremy Begbie, who trained first as a musician. In his *Theology, Music and Time*, Begbie explores how the nature of music can enrich our understanding of human lived experience under God.[1] His chapters on improvisation, from which I will be drawing, come at the end of his book, summarizing much of the previous insight. Begbie himself draws very helpfully on the insights of Keith Johnstone, a British-Canadian pioneer of improvisational theatre, some of which we will incorporate. I also draw (more sparingly) on the work of another theologian, Samuel Wells (who also draws on Keith Johnstone's insights). It was in Wells's *Improvisation: The Drama of Christian Ethics* that I first encountered theological engagement with improvisation.[2] Whereas Begbie's focus is primarily musical, Wells's is mainly theatrical. Both are concerned with the interplay between improvisation, theology and Christian life.

In this chapter, then, I invite you to explore with me the subject of improvisation. We will see how attending to the ways in which improvisation is present can highlight important aspects that we might otherwise miss, in a very wide range of contexts. We turn first to register some key aspects of the nature of improvisation, gaining a feel along the way for how it shows up in a wide range of contexts.

Features of improvisation

Improvisation has already been present within many examples in this book. Consider, for instance, the meal with friends. Here the conversation, at most points of the evening, was substantially unplanned, leaving plenty of space for exploration, response and innovation. Moreover, when George's concern for his mother called for a reconsideration of the timetable, the host adjusted accordingly. For another example, consider the ceilidh from Chapter 5. The dance caller and the band will probably have brought with them a clear idea of the 'agenda' for the evening, but may well have adjusted this as time went by. Those who came along to dance will have exercised considerable choice through the evening. They will have made decisions about when to dance, and when to take time out. They may have chosen which other groups of dancers to join on different occasions, and with whom to join in conversation. Moreover, they will have had considerable flexibility – within their own physical limits – regarding quite *how* they have danced: with what degree of energy, skill, exuberance.

These two events, the ceilidh and the meal with friends, are both substantially improvised. They begin to bring to life the nature of improvisation. With these in mind, let's continue by registering a number of factors that characterize improvisation. Additionally, we'll aim to dispense with some common misconceptions along the way.

Normally partially planned, but never fully known

Improvisation often incorporates a substantial degree of preset structure. For instance, as we explored in Chapter 5, the ceilidh depended on substantial planning in advance.[3] Many details needed unambiguous decision, and clear allocation of responsibility. Providing this degree of planning did not remove the space for improvisation. Rather, it provided a clear structure and a safe space within which to improvise.

The amount of prior planning can vary substantially. When we are chatting with a good friend, for instance, we may or may not have any idea in advance what way the conversation will go. And even if there are two or three things we know we want to talk about with them, the conversation will still be substantially improvised. Indeed, the same is true at the level of speaking a sentence. When we start to speak, we typically have some sense of what we want to convey – a degree of pre-planning – but we are happy to start speaking without full prior knowledge of the entirety of the sentence.

The normal presence of some planning rules out the common misconception that improvisation is about being utterly original, with no preparation. Such an assumption easily implies that improvisation is only for people of outstanding talent and wit, and not for the majority of humanity.[4] But these assumptions are not true. As our examples have already begun to suggest, all of us are routinely involved in everyday improvisation.

In Chapter 5, one of the things we imagined was what it would be like to participate in a ceilidh that had been over-determined.[5] Here, too much detail had been specified in advance, essentially shutting down any space for improvisation. The etymological root of 'improvisation' is the Latin *improvisus*, literally meaning 'not foreseen'. For there to be some degree of improvisation, there needs to be a corresponding degree of 'not knowing in advance'. With improvisation, this fact of not knowing is welcomed and embraced. This by no means removes the need for preparation. The basic approach of improvisation is to make appropriate space for the unexpected, and then, rather than being braced against it, to greet it when it arrives.

Concerned with the manner in which, not just what

Our engagement with improvisation normally focuses not only on what is done, but also on how it is done. We are attentive to the manner in which our friend is conversing, or in which the music is played. Tone, pacing and mood are all experienced as significant.

This point can help us recognize the degree to which improvisation is frequently present even in highly pre-planned situations. For instance, when I lead a church service, quite a few of the words I speak may come from a set liturgy, and from the text of the Bible.[6] As I lead, I will seek to speak these pre-chosen words in a way likely to ring true for these people, on this day – perhaps looking out for resonance with the readings, or with recent events. In my speaking (and that of others involved), there will be questions of pace, emphasis and nuance. More broadly, there is the host of embodied ways in which all present contribute to the atmosphere of the occasion. All of these can properly be included within our understanding of improvisation. Each detail may seem small and subtle, yet the aggregated impact is substantial.

Importantly, it would be easy to assume that if the words (or notes) are already written down, there is no improvisation. But no: that is another misconception to dispel. Granted, the more the content is pre-planned, the less space there is for improvisation. Sometimes, however, this makes the manner of the improvisation all the more important – does it come across, for instance, as engaged or soulless, exaggerated or authentic?

A consequence, then, is that, with improvisation, the emphasis is on the process and the experience, and especially on the nature of that experience. We are no longer in a world of blunt binary questions – 'Have you done it?' or 'Is it completed?' We have moved instead into a realm replete with questions of nuance, shading and degree. 'How was it?' is one simple (and often profound) form of such a question.

In improvisation, tone and texture really matter. These considerations were repeatedly highlighted in Feeney's account of his church's Mission Action Planning process. The venue, the atmosphere, the mood, the space for honesty and laughter and stories – all of these formed rich parts of the partially planned improvisation of that experience.

This links to a further important detail, regarding the boundaries of involvement in improvisation. When I talk with a friend one-to-one, it is the two of us who are improvising together. When a music group at church play an instrumental piece before the service, it would be easy to think that only the instrumentalists are involved in the improvisation. There is some difference of degree, to be sure, between those playing and those not. Nevertheless, the 'audience' to an improvisation are never 'just the audience'. Rather, the quality of attentiveness of those listening can have a surprisingly large impact on how the improvisation develops and unfolds. It can be shaped to a surprising extent by the mood of the occasion – which itself can be considerably influenced by all of those present.

An ecology of gifts and giving

Good improvisation is not about force or imposition. Rather, it is characterized by both an openness of giving, and also a generosity in receiving. Underlining this sense of giving at the heart of improvisation, the theatrical improviser Keith Johnstone uses the word 'offer' to describe any 'move' made by an improvising actor. Any such offer can be either 'accepted' or 'blocked', where blocking means preventing it from developing. To accept the offer, on the other hand, means welcoming it as a gift, and 'being willing to treat the gift as fundamentally something from which fruit can come ... consistent with the "story" of the drama'.[7] According to Johnstone, good improvisers 'accept all offers made – which is something no "normal" person would do'.[8]

Why should the acceptance of all offers be a wise thing to do? Johnstone's experience is that, if actors focus on making interesting what they themselves are offering, the mood of the improvisation becomes unhelpfully competitive. Instead, therefore, he encourages actors to 'concentrate on making the gift they *receive* interesting'.[9] The term Johnstone uses for this focus on receiving is 'overaccepting'. The fundamental shift of attention is towards the previous contributor, and towards receiving well what they have offered. As Begbie puts it, 'What is given is received as inherently valuable.'[10] The way in which that offer is *received* can substantially change how it is then *perceived*: for instance, whether or not it comes across as interesting.

The generosity of this reception, however, should not lapse into naïveté. Not every gift that is offered is purely good. What Johnstone means by overaccepting is a 'first phase' in the reception of an offer – a 'front end', if you like. Accepting an offer as a gift is, on the one hand, a central improvisatory move but, on the other, not the final one. The reception of an offer then needs to be followed by discernment how this particular offer can best be incorporated in a life-giving continuation of the drama. This may happen in the moment, and at great pace, or following considered reflection (as we will explore in due course). Creativity and ingenuity may be required: a good incorporation may require a reframing or reinterpretation of the offer as it was intended. (Later in the chapter, we will see an example of Jesus receiving an 'offer' from the teachers of the law, and skilfully redirecting its direction and energy.)

Generous receptivity may be called for not only regarding the actions of others. It may also be needed in response to what we see as the unalterable facts of a situation. Begbie highlights that the word 'given' is sometimes used to describe what feel like constraints. The 'givens' of a situation easily evoke resentment or frustration in us. Examples might include government (or church) policies, the attitudes of some with whom we find ourselves engaging, or our own finite resources. With improvisation, however, the invitation is to learn to treat givens as gifts.[11] We may not always find this straightforward. We may, indeed, find ourselves feeling that we deserve givens that are (in some sense, and from our perspective) 'better'. Nevertheless, as the concept of overaccepting makes clear, the invitation is to invest effort and creativity into receiving as a gift that which is currently the case. There will be occasions on which this stretches our capacity – hence the adjective *generous*.

A sense of spaciousness

Near the core of the delight of improvisation is a sense of spaciousness. One of the joys of arriving for a meal with friends is the anticipation of an evening together offering room for conversation to flow where it will. Or again, imagine arriving at the ceilidh, setting aside the concerns of the day, and stepping forward into an expansive space of possibility. Feeney's description of the process in which his church engaged contains repeated indications of such spaciousness. There was relaxed, informal storytelling, over coffee and bacon sandwiches. There was an atmosphere including much laughter. The spaciousness included the need to be truthful and realistic, including naming some historical factors that were destructive. There was room as well for a sense of trust and delight in the loving purposes of God. Such a sense of spaciousness is one of the core gifts of improvisation.

One source of such spaciousness is the priority of overaccepting. Whether the context is informal conversation or a planning meeting, an ethos of overaccepting opens up space for possibilities, and for exploration. This comes partly from a confidence that suggestions will not immediately be shut down and negated. It also arises from trust that overacceptance will be coupled with discernment. I will voice my idea, even though I'm not sure it's spot on – because I trust that it will be properly sifted, and it may contribute to a better idea from somebody else. I trust that my fellow improvisers will take the time to unwrap the gift I offer, appreciate what is good within it, and then move forwards from it in whatever way seems most fitting. Without this sense of spaciousness, my gift would remain un-given.

Importantly, improvisation offers at least some space for what may seem like failure. What initially seems like an error comes to take on a new significance. Not only is it less bad than I might fear, but the aim will be to incorporate it such that it makes a positive contribution. Whatever 'note' we have just played, there will always be something that can be played which re-contextualizes what seemed like a mistake. The invitation of improvisation is so to accept each 'note', so as to find that which is valuable within it, that it can be incorporated into the ongoing story.[12] The jazz trumpeter, Miles Davis, put it like this: 'It's not the note you play that's the wrong note – it's the note you play afterwards that makes it right or wrong.' Some approaches to Christianity feel much more like the tightrope walk of doom, with the essence of the faith being avoiding error, and playing safe. The spaciousness of improvisation is different. It puts trust in grace and redemption, and opens out room for 'understanding and speaking about the expansive joy of Christian corporate living'.[13]

Improvisation, then, offers space for exploring and developing possibilities. The manner in which we respond to possibilities is deeply intertwined with how we are treating the persons who suggest them. Good improvisation gives space to each person involved.

This giving of space to the people involved plays a very significant part in the overall experience and effect of improvisation. To enrich our understanding of this, let me draw briefly on the concept of 'personhood', as developed by Alistair McFadyen.[14] Rather than seeing personhood as an attribute with which we are born, he describes how we learn to grow into our own personhood – how we come to appropriate it. Crucially, much of that learning comes from how other people treat us – for better or for worse. It is as others expect, intend and invite our own personhood that we find it deepening and maturing. The messages we receive from others, subtly or otherwise, significantly affect our confidence to take up space in the world. It is not uncommon for us to assume that the gift we have to offer is without value, and undeserving of consideration. Healthy improvising offers great scope for strengthening, welcoming and encouraging the personhood of all involved. If my tentative offer is 'received as inherently valuable'[15] and treated as 'fundamentally something from which fruit can come',[16] I may experience myself, also, as being 'received as inherently valuable', and find my personhood affirmed accordingly.

Relatedly, if improvisation is to be truly spacious, it must be free of domination. There will often be some appropriate constraints, but there must also be substantial liberty for each to improvise as seems fitting. Such liberty includes the possibility of another person's offer resisting or redirecting what I have just given – which resistance I am called to value. The giving of others may, indeed, require my own transformation. What others choose to give may at times be consonant with what I have offered – but it will also be unpredictably different.[17]

Western culture is often not good at offering the quality of spaciousness we have been considering. Coming to offer such spaciousness may, for many of us, require both learning and unlearning. Giving space may require disciplined self-restraint: a deliberate act of deciding not to act, in order to leave room to welcome forward the action and being of others. Begbie describes some of what may be involved in these terms: 'Giving "space" to the other through alert attentiveness, listening in patient silence, contributing to the growth of others by "making the best" of what is received from them such that they are encouraged to continue participating, sensitive decision-making, flexibility of response.'[18]

Begbie's description begins, rightly, with listening and alert attentiveness. As we explored in Chapter 2, the nature and depth of our attention makes a qualitative difference, both to our own experience, and to the experience of those to whom we attend. It is vital also to 'flip' the perspective of these phrases: sometimes 'we' will be the 'other' to whom space is given. Sometimes others will need to 'make the best' of what they receive from us.

If the giving of space will need at times to be a deliberate act, so also will the taking of space. For some of us, the invitation to step forward (at least metaphorically) and make an offer can be unfamiliar, and can feel vulnerable and uncomfortable. The offer I make may not always be expressed easily, smoothly or comfortably. Grace and graciousness may be called for in its receiving. But in and from such overaccepting reception can be forged the strength of relationship, founded on both grace and truth, on which improvisation depends, and towards the maturity of which improvisation contributes.

We have explored several facets of the spaciousness characteristic of improvisation. A major factor in such spaciousness is the nature of the relationship between improvisation and time.

Improvisation and time

The practice of improvisation sheds fresh light on our relating to time, and it forms a particular focus for Begbie: as noted on p. 131, his book is entitled *Theology, Music and Time*. He has wisdom to share regarding the creative poise required of a seasoned improviser.

Most fundamentally, we are invited to 'live peaceably with time'.[19] The belief is that sufficient time has been given for what God asks of us. One manifestation of this belief is that the improviser can be 'relaxed and unhurried because he knows that, wherever he lands up, there are a dozen different ways of getting from there to the next place'.[20] To be clear, being relaxed and unhurried need not imply being slow. Perhaps you can imagine a jazz pianist sitting comfortably at the keyboard, her fingers flowing over the keys, with speed but without angst. The key point is about trusting the sufficiency of what has been given – and thus learning to live peaceably with time.

Second, however, Begbie takes that concept and stretches it. While living peaceably with time, improvisation simultaneously invites us into a creative restlessness. And that restlessness is restful and joyful, rather than anxious. Yes, we can rest in the sufficiency of time. And we are also invited forward, to participate in the exploring and creating of what could be possible. The delight of this invitation evokes a restlessness, to be held in and alongside our trusting restfulness. How might we learn to hold together these apparent contradictions? Begbie highlights three things we need to learn (and relearn as necessary): 'the firm stability of divine grace'; that it is not our responsibility to 'make it happen'; and freedom from 'that "convulsive clutching" at "getting it right" which prevents us from throwing anything into the air'.[21]

Writing these paragraphs, I am very aware that this theory may seem in stark contrast to the lived experience of some readers. For a host of reasons, cultural and personal, to live peaceably with time can seem unattainable – and perhaps even indulgent. And yet, do we believe that God has not given sufficient time for what God wants of us? For a concise and insightful guide to practice and formation in this area I regularly commend *Beyond Busyness: Time Wisdom for Ministry* by Stephen Cherry.[22]

Improvisation, unfolding and flow

When then Prime Minister Harold Macmillan was asked what was the greatest challenge for a political leader, he is reputed to have replied, 'Events, dear boy, events'. Sometimes the events that happen are the events that we have planned. Macmillan was referring to the other ones.

Viewing life and ministry from an improvisatory perspective reminds us that the unexpected is to be expected. People will become ill, and die. The state of nations and economies will impact people's well-being and lifestyle, and how they express their calling. Policies of other organizations will affect funding possibilities. People will move away, and other people may move in. And the rain will fall, and the sun will shine, and birds will sing, and 'news just in' or a chance encounter can impact our mood and our action for the rest of the day, or longer. Unfolding events can be deeply frustrating, and worse. Nevertheless, the way of improvisation expects them to happen, for good and ill, and isn't surprised when we are regularly surprised by them. Our improvisation of life and ministry is played out against the unfolding of the lives of individuals, nations and of the whole earth.

If the ripples of 'external' unfolding events regularly impact on church life, there will also be ripples heading outwards from the life of the church and its people. These can be smaller or larger in their reach, and can also be positive or negative in their impact – or quite possibly positive with some people, and negative with others. We will explore further in the next chapter something of how such ripples can go on to impact on the lives of those involved.

The term unfolding suggests distinct steps or moves in how things develop. Alongside that, there is also flow. Flow suggests greater continuity, but the flow of a turbulent river incorporates no end of tensions, swells and strong counter-currents. Around and between the distinct events of our lives and our times there are the multiple currents of our relationships – to each other, to our contexts, to God and to ourselves.

A perspective informed by improvisation treats the unfolding and flow of life as part of the improvisation. It is attuned to seeking all that is gift within what unfolds. It combines discernment and creativity in judging what can best be incorporated and how. It sees our own roles not as detached observers, but as fellow-participants within the unfolding flow, the dynamic dance. The unfolding flow of events, only partially influenced by our own plans and actions, means that *control* is rarely what we can do, or what we should seek to do.

The way of relating to time I have been describing stands in some contrast to that of the Church SLD (and indeed other related leadership literature). Rather than going with the grain of time, strategic leadership approaches can seem to be battling against time. Some such approaches, for instance, recommend deliberately creating a sense of urgency. They do so by likening the current situation (whatever that is) to a 'burning platform'. If we were literally standing on a platform that was burning, swift and decisive action would be appropriate – namely, commencing a (swiftly) pre-planned journey to a pre-identified destination.

It's not that an improvised approach means always being slow – far from it. But what Begbie conveys is a belief that sufficient time has been given. Moreover, time is a precious unfolding gift. Our engagement with improvisation ideally draws on the Holistic RH ability to dwell within the flow of time and the flux of events, savouring and engaging with each present moment as it unfolds. In contrast, as mentioned in Chapter 3, the LH mode of being can be experienced as skating over the surface of time and of life, in its desire to complete the task and reach the end-point.

Two timescales of improvisation

It may be helpful to distinguish between two 'timescales' of improvisation. The first is perhaps most obvious, and I'll call it 'real-time' improvisation. The meal with friends, the evening of the ceilidh and the pecking and scanning of the chaffinch all fall into this category. Here, the improvisation is unfolding in each moment. There are no obvious gaps (although there may be pauses, or silences). In the context of any one particular conversation, meeting or event, real-time improvisation is most likely.

The second timescale I would describe as 'phased' improvisation, and Feeney's church engagement offers a good example. The main point is simple: it doesn't all happen on one occasion. Whether it is split over two events, or happens daily for years on end, phased improvisation repeatedly comes back to what has gone before. New ideas may have been generated; fresh events may impact previous thinking; personnel or energy may have changed; or it may largely be a case of picking up where we were before. Instances of phased improvisation in church life could include a process of planning, a study/discipleship/explorer course or series of services. It can also describe the development of any relationship, or the formation of any group or team. There will often be real-time improvisation within specific meetings or conversations, and there is also a phased aspect – picking up where we were, but affected by all that has happened in between.

These examples both focus on 'us', on things over which we have a reasonable degree of influence. So it's worth underlining the degree to which 'external events' can impact especially on phased improvisation over the medium- and long-term. The nature of that impact may initially seem positive or negative – and the invitation and challenge is to discern how best to interweave what has happened with our ongoing participation in the life of God.

Both real-time and phased improvisation will regularly feature individuals and groups making decisions. These include decisions in the moment – shall I speak out what's in my mind, or listen further first? These will often also include some degree of more formal process, and more careful and considered communal decision-making.

Four forms of improvisation

Improvisation occurs in several different forms, which can feel notably different. Here are four main forms.

First, then, we have *improvisation of* what has already been pre-shaped or pre-planned. Musically, we might offer an improvisation of 'Amazing Grace' – with two people, or 10,000. 'Improvisation of' can involve a greater or lesser degree of improvisation. Another example would be that of a substantially scripted service. Here, improvisation of tone, pace and emphasis will make a big difference to the experience of all involved.

Improvisation from is significantly different. Here we have a starting point, and (typically) an abundance of possibilities. For instance, imagine sitting beside a stranger on a train journey. What unfolds will be improvised, whether or not any degree of conversation develops. The life of any person, or of any church, can also be described as 'improvisation from' their current state.

Improvisation within refers to some form of constraint or boundaries. One example is that of improvising within a tradition – to which a later section of this chapter will give attention. Another example is a conversation or meeting with a clear timeframe, within which we have freedom to improvise. As we will go on to explore, the presence of the constraints and boundaries can be a helpfully energizing factor.

Finally, we have *improvisation towards* a goal of some sort. This could be a journey, literal or metaphorical – we want to find a way to get to a certain point. The intended goal may be held very tightly, but with considerable openness as to the means of achieving it. Alternatively, I may begin a conversation with a clear idea what I think it will lead to, and also an openness to adjusting that idea as the conversation continues.

We have thus far sketched a range of interrelated characteristics of improvisation, and their connections with life and ministry. It will now be helpful to make more explicit the connections between improvisation and McGilchrist's work, to which we turn now.

Improvisation and McGilchrist

Improvisation and the divided brain

We can imagine something of the contribution that each hemisphere makes to fluent improvisation, for instance using music as an example. We can summarize this as the Clear-cut LH primarily offering the framework and structure of the music. It provides sufficient order for the occasion, and contributes clarity as needed. It can also be drawn in to come up with solutions to technical problems, musically or organizationally. (What musical key shall we play this in? How many verses shall we sing? Is there a trumpeter here today?) The Holistic RH complements this with responsiveness, nuance and flexibility. It enriches the music itself, and the unfolding experience as a whole, through its attentiveness to subtleties of tone and texture, to a sense of flow and flux, and to the relationships between instruments, between notes, between chords, between sound and silence.

If there is too much LH influence, this may lead to a performance that is technically perfect – except (importantly) for its lack of vitality. Over-planning and over-effort can lead to constriction and lifelessness. Receiving too little LH input also leads into undesirable territory. This would again be characterized by lifelessness, but this time it's the lack of structure, the formlessness that leads to lethargy. There is insufficient order and forward rhythm against which to spark, and the result is a lack of vitality.

For another example, let's think again of the 'meal with a twist' described in Chapter 5. Here, just as the host was about to usher guests through to eat their meal, Geoff began to unburden himself regarding his concerns for his mother. The host could have intervened, saying, 'I'm sorry, Geoff – you clearly have a lot going on – but I need to interrupt. If we don't serve the dinner now, it will be burnt – so can you all please come through to the dining room.' (One might describe this move as deploying a 'burning lasagne' strategy to generate a sense of urgency.)

What the host actually did was to use gesture to usher guests through, thus avoiding cutting across Geoff's sharing. In the context of Chapter 5, this example illustrated excellent hemisphere relating – incorporating the relevant fruit of LH analysis (regarding timing), but transforming the manner in which this was then offered forward (silent gesture). In the context of this chapter, however, let me flip the point being emphasized. Hearing of the host's response in this scenario, we might well describe it as improvisation – and skilful and sensitive improvisation at that. And so the point is this: the nature of improvisation at its best is to embody and enable a constructive relationship between brain hemispheres. The nature of that constructive relationship, required, embodied and developed by improvisation, is in line with the principles we have learned from McGilchrist.

What's more, we can go a step further. The nature of a cooperative relationship between the brain hemispheres is itself improvised. Each hemisphere offers its distinctive gifts; there is discerning, valuing and incorporation of what is helpful; there is often an underlying alternating rhythm between the hemispheres; what emerges from the interplay of hemispheres is much richer and more potent than either could offer on its own.

The importance and potential of tension

I recently had the privilege of sailing with yacht-owning friends. Despite being a relative beginner, I was generously encouraged to take the helm (under supervision), and received helpfully clear instructions regarding the direction to seek. This required me to sail almost as close as possible towards the direction of the wind. After a while I voiced my experience: 'I'm feeling some tension between staying on our desired course, and heading too close into the wind.' Nigel's wise response was, 'That sounds about right.' In this context, the tension was to be inhabited and embraced, rather than resisted, resolved or avoided. Had I turned further away from the direction of the wind, the sails would have caught much less of the weather's energy, and our speed and dynamism would have slumped significantly.

IMPROVISATION

For McGilchrist, tension is often not only positive, but necessary. Across multiple contexts it plays a crucial role – and thus he devotes to it an entire chapter, early in the third and final part of *The Matter With Things*.[23] As we will see, tension makes an important contribution to improvisation, and to life.

Sometimes, tension is helpfully held between two opposing forces. Imagine, for instance, picking up an egg between your thumb and forefinger. Those two digits would be pressing in opposite directions. And you would intuitively moderate the force of one against the other, so that your grip was strong enough to lift the egg, but not so intense that the egg cracked or collapsed. Or again, the functioning of each string on my cello relies on the two ends being pulled in opposite directions. When an archer raises her bow, she flexes it to increase the tension, then judges at what point to release the arrow. It is the energy of the opposing forces that sends the arrow on its way.[24] There are several different systems within the physiology of the human body whose functioning depends on careful regulation between similar 'opponent processors'.[25]

Discernment in the good navigation of tensions forms an important part of wisdom for life in general, and ministerial leadership in particular. Tensions come in a range of forms, and can be conceptual as well as physical. They can be seen in physics: light is both wave and particle. They are also manifest in theology and religious life. God is one, and God is three. McGilchrist quotes with approval William James:

> The ethical and religious life is full of such contradictions held in solution. You hate your enemy? – Well, forgive him, and thereby heap coals of fire on his head; to realise yourself, renounce yourself; to save your soul, first lose it; in short, die to live.[26]

Overall, McGilchrist argues that such oppositions are frequently 'the ground of energy',[27] and necessary for both creativity and meaningful life.

How does the Clear-cut LH relate to tensions? McGilchrist suggests that it tends to 'resolve the necessary tension by pretending that one of the pairs of opposites either can safely be dispensed with, or is not real'.[28] This desire to clarify, and thus eliminate tension, rings true for much of the Church SLD. I suggest, however, that another aspect of its approach is to focus on one single, linear tension – typically the desire to complete the task, or solve a problem, perhaps within a pre-determined timescale – and thus to harness the energy from this tension alone. Either way, its default is to reduce the richness and complexity of tension, in line with its purposes.

Improvisation and tension

Begbie's understanding of improvisation similarly highlights the vital role played by tension. For instance, we have already encountered, on the one hand, living peaceably with time and, on the other, the need for restlessness – which is itself restful.

Sometimes, as with the lifting of an egg, opposing forces need to be held in a very steady manner. Importantly, they are not simply blended, or balanced out, resulting in a single force somewhere 'in the middle'. As McGilchrist puts it, what is needed is 'not a flabby compromise', but rather a situation of dynamic 'taut synergy'.[29] Nevertheless, at times there is a proper stability in our relating to tension. At other times, however, something much more dynamic is called for.

Improvisation draws substantially on tension, and often exemplifies such dynamism. For instance, it may be that the drummer in a jazz group maintains energy and momentum by playing the rhythm straight, keeping the musical beat absolutely steady. At the same time, however, the saxophonist and then the trumpeter bend the default timings of their melodic lines, both bouncing off the boundaries of the bar lines,[30] and stretching beyond them as well. The tension between the two – the regularity and the flexibility – significantly adds to the energy of the performance.

Another tension to be navigated is that between seeking high quality, on the one hand, and taking risks on the other. Performers know that seeking perfection is almost guaranteed to be counter-productive, constricting the liberation needed for the best music.

In his description of such creative tensions, Begbie chooses, and regularly refers back to, three terms: contrast, interplay and mutual enhancement.[31] The contrast is typically between what is more ordered, and what has the abundance that goes beyond order. Then there is interplay between the contrasting emphases – structure and flexibility, sound and silence, strict and fluid rhythms, and so on. And out of this dynamism, the structure and flexibility 'highlight and magnify each other' in a rich mutual enhancement. The combination of these three characteristics is remarkably powerful. These features give rise to much of our enjoyment of the music. Moreover, this combination of contrast, interplay and mutual enhancement can naturally give rise to a dynamic of some playfulness. And, in a further polarity, such playfulness is held alongside a proper seriousness: to take improvised music seriously is precisely to welcome and appreciate its playful dynamic.

The creative tension generated by this contrast and interplay is an ongoing source of energy. The unfolding mutual interplay carries a sense of spark and freshness. There is an overall vitality to the process at its best. The contributors wholeheartedly offer into the performance something of their very being, their very lives. And what arises in and from the performance carries the freshness – to at least some degree – of the emergence of new life.

Begbie wrote *Theology, Music and Time* about a decade before McGilchrist published *The Master and His Emissary*, but I am repeatedly struck by the congruence between the two perspectives. In particular, it seems to me that the trio of 'contrast, interplay and mutual enhancement' sheds helpful light not only on improvisation in general, but also on the nature of ideal hemisphere relating in particular.[32] Within this cooperative working, the hemispheres will each be doing what they do best. This will include the LH contributing structure, clarity and direction, and the RH preserving and transforming all that is relevant in the strengths of the LH. Overall, the interplay of the contrasting emphases of the hemispheres leads to mutual enhancement and the generating of a creative overflow of innovation, of energy and of life.

Improvisation and tradition

Early in this chapter we clarified that improvisation does not (normally) mean making things up from scratch at short notice. Rather, any improvisation has meaning primarily in the context of a particular tradition – whether musical, theatrical or more broadly. Rather than being an enemy of tradition, improvisation requires it. Indeed, there is no such thing as an environment free of tradition.

The concept of tradition is itself, of course, viewed and used in various ways. Some use the word 'tradition' primarily to describe an ongoing process, whereas others to refer to the fruit or deposit of that process. The concept of improvisation is a powerful one that can combine both of these meanings. Wells, for instance, describes the common desire to find a way forward that is both apposite in a new specific situation, and also faithful to the Christian tradition. His examples include 'seeking a harmonious breakthrough in church order or considering appropriate models for development work in the face of famine'. Both of these challenges he describes as 'a stimulus to faithful improvisation, fresh embodiment of the grace and truth of the scriptural witness'. Indeed, he asserts that 'improvisation is the only term that adequately describes the desire to cherish a tradition without being locked in the past'. For the record, both Wells and Begbie devote substantial space to exploring some of the ways and levels in which 'improvisation is scriptural'.[33] Indeed, Wells cites Begbie as describing the whole of the Acts of the Apostles as 'a stream of new, unpredictable, improvisations'.[34] Ecclesial improvisation will rightly include, as in the Acts of the Apostles, the testing and clarifying of which aspects of tradition are non-negotiable.

Three more points from Begbie are worth noting in this context. The first is to notice and value the informal in the passing on of tradition.[35] The bacon rolls and the laughter in Feeney's account played an important role in that church's ongoing tradition, both in and of themselves, and in their enabling of relationship, conversation and participation. Second, healthy appropriation of tradition does not stop with the past informing the present. Rather, it continues 'with generating a novel and fruitful future'.[36] Here we encounter 'an engagement of our past with our present for the sake of a future that is not strictly determined by either'.[37] Finally, one becomes a skilled improviser precisely by 'indwelling the corporate tradition', being shaped by it, learning it deeply as our 'native language'.[38] This notion of being formed in a tradition in order to improvise faithfully forms a central strand of Wells's argument.

Five vital dispositions of improvisation

As we have seen, the quality of any improvisation will depend on the qualities and attitudes of those involved. Let me single out five particular characteristics, which I will describe as dispositions. By 'disposition' I mean not a passing mood, but a consistent outlook, mindset and heartset. I see my disposition as my metaphorical posture towards a situation. It includes my attitudes, and is seamlessly interconnected with my actions. The following dispositions I see as vital in two senses: they are necessary, and also life-giving.

I default to thinking of these as the dispositions of an individual – and that is certainly necessary. There is also a sense in which each improvising group needs to cultivate its own shared dispositions, its own common ethos. The character of the members and their web of relationships will contribute to this. Similarly, the dispositions themselves are deeply connected: mutually dependent and mutually reinforcing.

Four of the five dispositions can also be seen as relating to phases of improvisation (namely, the first four). If we were to observe a film of five improvising actors, and we kept pressing 'pause' to slow the action right down, different dispositions would be prominent at various periods within each move or exchange. I'll introduce the five dispositions briefly at this point, and then each will receive some further expansion in a relevant subsequent chapter.

Responsive attunement

We start with responsive attunement, which begins with an open, attentive alertness to all that is going on right now. We seek attunement with God, with the other people involved, with the broader context (perhaps organizational, geographical, historical or political), and with ourselves. Attunement includes awareness, but goes beyond it, to some degree of sufficient alignment. There can often be both an initial attunement, which is especially important, and also an ongoing responsiveness to the flux and flow of events. As with good hemisphere engagement, starting with responsive attunement helps us to begin our improvisation by engaging the Holistic RH domain.

Generous receptivity

The overaccepting previously discussed will only ring true if it arises from a disposition of generous receptivity. This disposition affects not only how I relate to what has just been said, played or done. It describes (at least in aspiration) my posture towards each person, towards the whole situation, and towards the whole of life: seeking to treat the given as a gift, and to treasure what is valuable within it. We can, again, cultivate generous receptivity towards God, towards others, towards the broader context and towards all aspects of ourselves.

Discerning incorporation

This third disposition is a necessary counterpart to generous receptivity. Having focused on receiving an offer, skill, creativity and wisdom may be needed in discerning how 'fruit can come'[39] from it, consistent with the story of the drama. Such discerning incorporation follows the shape of healthy hemisphere relating: preserving all that is good within the offer, then transforming it, to whatever degree may be necessary, so that it is fitting for this place and this time.

Trusting courage

Fourth, we come to the posture of trusting courage that leads to the action – or sometimes the waiting – we have discerned as appropriate. The degree of courage required will vary substantially, but a wise way forward may often involve risk (sometimes more risk than we would prefer), and thus courage. Several forms of trust may be relevant: trust that our action will be 'good enough'; trust in the people who will take things forward; trust in our ability to keep improvising, in the light of initial response. There may be a trust in the ongoing process. Most fundamentally, our engagement in the improvisations of life is held by the degree of our trust that 'God has got it'.

Deepening desire

This final vital disposition of improvisation is a quality for the medium- and long-term. I am unlikely to grow and develop in my improvising unless I desire to do so. That desire may begin by focusing on my own capacity, and then steadily extend outwards: desire for fullness of life to flow from this improvisation; desire for this group to increase our capacity; desire to help other people and groups participate more fully. If such desire is genuine, it will lead to sustained and dedicated action – parallel to the thousands of unseen formational hours in which musical and theatrical improvisers invest. The term 'deepening desire' deliberately holds two meanings: both a desire for ever greater depth, and also a desire that itself continues to deepen and intensify.

Caught in the act: Jesus in the flow of improvisation

We now conclude the chapter with a 'case study' from the Gospel of John, looking at one episode in the life of Jesus as an example of improvisation. I have chosen to focus on the powerful account of the woman caught in adultery, found in John 8.1–11.[40]

As Jesus sat down to teach in the temple, the scribes and the Pharisees made a bold interruption, which Jesus did not resist. They brought in a woman, led her to stand at the front, and said to Jesus, 'Teacher, this woman was caught in the very act of committing adultery. Now in the law Moses commanded us to stone such women. Now what do you say?' (John 8.4–5). Their evident aim was to trap Jesus via a dilemma, and thus undermine and terminate at least Jesus' ministry, and ideally Jesus himself. Jesus, it seemed, must either condemn the woman to be stoned, or declare that she should not be so punished. The latter meant opposing the law of Moses, and the former meant opposing the law of Rome (which limited the right of execution to the Romans). Within the purposes of the scribes and Pharisees, the woman was treated purely as an object, as a pawn – and we note the absence of the man. Both the woman and Jesus were treated as 'it', rather than 'thou'. How would Jesus respond to this clear-cut and highly dramatic move, this improvisatory 'offer'?

Jesus is highly attuned to the multiple dynamics of the situation. He attends with remarkable imaginative depth. He does not aim to 'block' the unfolding drama, nor does he retaliate in kind. Moreover, he is generous in receiving, in making space for, the important underlying questions raised by the dilemma. His first move in response has striking resonance with the right hemisphere. 'Jesus bent down and wrote with his finger on the ground' (John 8.6). Jesus remained silent, stepping sideways from linear logic. He paused, slowed the pace. He averted his gaze, at the same time as deepening his presence. And the tension built as the seconds ticked by.

When Jesus eventually spoke, it was to take seriously the original question, and offer it back, but at a deeper level. 'Questioning Jesus leads to the questioners being questioned in a way that transforms the very terms of enquiry.'[41] Rather than critique and condemn the scribes and Pharisees (which would have been entirely justified), he practises what he himself is teaching, and abstains from condemnation. Jesus' poised attentiveness is strong, responsive and flexible, shot through with grace and truth, with clear-sightedness anchored in compassion, offered towards the woman, and also towards the scribes and Pharisees. The lack of condemnation was not because sin hadn't happened, or didn't merit attention. Rather, by presenting his offer as he did, Jesus invited his hearers to take the more challenging path of deeper transformation, and engage in self-examination. In this instance, the greatest need for such self-examination concerned 'habits of blame, judgement, condemnation, and punishment'.[42] In making the offer as he did, Jesus harnessed the momentum of their own hostile question and, with the skilled conversational *aikido* of a remarkable wisdom teacher, offered it back to them as a gracious invitation to deeper spiritual awareness.

Jesus' articulated offer is profound: 'Let anyone among you who is without sin be the first to throw a stone at her' (John 8.7). We see within it both LH clarity and RH depth, seamlessly integrated and precisely tailored for this moment. The words that Jesus spoke formed only part of his offer. He also then bent down again, and wrote once more with his finger on the ground. As previously, he offered space and silence, with slowing of the pace, with the averting of direct attention from the woman, from the scribes and the Pharisees, and from the other temple worshippers.

In all of this, rather than prescribing and constricting what the other actors should do, and rather than treating them as a means to an end (as they had done with the woman), Jesus intends and gives remarkable freedom of response to all of the others involved. He creates a spaciousness and invites deeper reflection. A passage from Begbie, quoted earlier, is worth repeating: a good improviser can be found 'giving space to the other through alert attentiveness, listening in patient silence, contributing to the growth of others by "making the best" of what is received from them such that they are encouraged to continue participating'.[43]

Jesus carefully listened to what the scribes and Pharisees offered, and found a way to make the best of it. Following Jesus' intervention, it would not have been surprising had the scribes and Pharisees responded in a legalistic Clear-cut manner. They could, for instance, have argued against Jesus' terms, highlighting that the law of Moses stipulated no such requirement for general sinlessness on the part of those carrying out execution. Why was this not their actual response? Perhaps the tone and quality of Jesus' engagement with them made some difference? Through his words and his manner of being, he may have helped them to move (to some degree, at least for a while) towards a different mode, a mode that was more compassionate, and more self-aware, more open, and essentially deeper. It seems that Jesus' response encouraged them 'to continue participating' in deepening their understanding about sin and condemnation through self-examination, rather than (for now) seeking Jesus' elimination. Perhaps at least some of them walked away with a greater degree of insight, rather than purely with embarrassment, or with heightened rage at having been outflanked.

And Jesus was left alone with the woman. He who could have

responded to his own invitation by stoning her, chose not to. Instead: 'Neither do I condemn you. Go your way, and from now on do not sin again' (John 8.11). This statement contains both liberation and challenge. Reading the final clause ('do not sin again') on its own, there is a spectrum of possible emphasis and intention. Do we hear it more as an implied threat, a command, an encouragement, or an aspiration – or as several of these? Did Jesus expect the woman to live a sin-free life from now on? (That he was only interested in sin relating to sex seems unlikely.) If not, what was his intention with such a Clear-cut utterance, and how does it relate to that other Clear-cut utterance 'neither do I condemn you'? Will condemnation remain absent only if there is no further sin? Do these phrases apply only to this woman at this point in time? Jesus makes no attempt to remove the tension. Rather, in the whole encounter, he has offered her a taste of the grace of God and the nature of holiness. He has left her with an invitation to reorientate her life accordingly. And so also with us: we are left with an invitation to view more clearly our own sinfulness, and to live more fully into the depth of God's grace. The episode is left without everything being fully clarified. Rather than nailing down all the specifics of an abstract understanding, the emphasis is towards improvising forwards in the light of this encounter.

Conclusion, and the way ahead

All human life is substantially improvised. With Christian living is added the call to improvise with God, and to let the manner of God's improvising shape the quality of our own. We are invited to share in the divine life, joining in the relationship of the Son with the Father by the Spirit.

This is an invitation to wholehearted self-offering, integrating initiative and responsiveness, action and relationship, attention and imagination. Whatever the context, improvisation starts where we currently are, and searches out that which is gift in what has already been given. Improvisation calls forth the best of our discernment, and of our creativity. Improvisation encourages us to dwell with full presence in each unfolding moment, with God and with our other fellow improvisers. With improvisation, we let go of any pretence at full control or substantial foreknowledge, but retain plentiful scope for wise influence and prudent anticipation. Improvisation requires and deepens our trusting cooperation with God and others.

The divine life into which we are drawn is shot through with expansive and invitational love. As Christians, and particularly in ministerial and missional leadership, our calling includes helping others join in participation in the divine life. It also includes being helped by others to do the same ourselves – cooperating and participating together into the improvisation, and into ever deeper participation in the life and love of God.

The practice of improvisation, then, offers a rich and truthful depiction of the nature of life together under God. Good improvisation embodies and requires a dynamic, healthy relationship between the two brain hemispheres. The qualities and disposition required for improvising well with others are deeply in tune with Christian virtues. We have explored one example in the life of Jesus – and there are many others – in which his courageous, wise, compassionate, poised improvisation proved powerful and life-changing. We turn next, in our final chapter, to connect and integrate further the themes of this book with its title: *Fullness of Vision, Fullness of Life*.

Questions for reflection

1 How do you find yourself responding to this description of life as improvised? To which aspects do you warm? Are there any that you find unconvincing or off-putting?
2 'The belief is that sufficient time has been given for what God asks of us.' How does this statement seem in theory? How does it feel in practice? If there is tension, where exactly does that tension lie?
3 Of the five dispositions of improvisation, which would colleagues say that you already embody well?
4 Which do you find more challenging: finding the courage to act, or relinquishing the desire for control? Whichever way you answer, what's your best understanding of why that is the case?

Notes

1 Jeremy Begbie, 2000, *Theology, Music and Time* (hereafter *TMT* in the notes), Cambridge: Cambridge University Press.

2 Samuel Wells, 2004, *Improvisation: The Drama of Christian Ethics*, London: SPCK. For a different approach, try Pippa Evans, 2021, *Improv Your Life: An Improviser's Guide to Embracing Whatever Life Throws at You*, London: Hodder & Stoughton.

3 See p. 77.

4 See Wells, *Improvisation*, pp. 67–8.

5 See p. 77.

6 For the record, I generally avoid preaching from a full script, but prefer to speak from a page of notes – which will often include some carefully crafted phrases. That said, even when I do speak from a full script, there is still improvisation in quite *how* I speak.

7 Begbie, *TMT*, p. 251.

8 Keith Johnstone, 1979, *Impro: Improvisation and the Theatre*, London: Faber, p. 99, quoted in Begbie, *TMT*, p. 250.

9 Johnstone, 1979, p. 101 quoted in Begbie, *TMT*, p. 250. Emphasis in the original.

10 Begbie, *TMT*, p. 240.

11 See Begbie, *TMT*, chapter 9: Giving and Giving Back; especially pp. 246–7.

12 John Sloboda, 1993, *The Musical Mind*, Oxford, Oxford University Press, pp. 148f., quoted in Begbie, *TMT*, p. 229.

13 Begbie, *TMT*, p. 269.

14 Alistair McFadyen, 1990, *The Call to Personhood: A Christian Theory of the Individual in Social Relationships*, Cambridge: Cambridge University Press.

15 Begbie, *TMT*, p. 240.

16 Begbie, *TMT*, p. 251.

17 See Begbie, *TMT*, p. 240.

18 Begbie, *TMT*, p. 206.

19 Begbie, *TMT*, p. 203.

20 Sloboda, *The Musical Mind*, pp. 148f. quoted in Begbie, *TMT*, p. 229.

21 Begbie, *TMT*, pp. 244–5.

22 Stephen Cherry, 2012, *Beyond Busyness: Time Wisdom for Ministry*, Durham: Sacristy Press.

23 Iain McGilchrist, 2021, *The Matter With Things*, London: Perspectiva Press, chapter 20, *The coincidentia oppositorum*, pp. 813–42.

24 The example of the archer and of the cello both arise from the work of the ancient Greek philosopher Heraclitus – albeit that Heraclitus referred to a lyre (an early string instrument) rather than a cello. See McGilchrist, *Things*, p. 817, and 2009, *The Master and His Emissary: The Divided Brain and the Making of the Western World*, New Haven, CT: Yale University Press, p. 270.

25 McGilchrist, *Things*, p. 54.

26 William James, 1909, *A Pluralistic Universe*, Longmans, Green & Co, pp. 98–9, quoted in McGilchrist, *Things*, p. 831.

27 McGilchrist, *Things*, p. 825.

28 McGilchrist, *Things*, p. 841.

29 McGilchrist, *Things*, p. 821, where McGilchrist goes on to say that 'For a good apple pie you need both tart apples and honey, both sourness and sweetness, not just apples that are bland.'

30 Most music is divided into short units known as 'bars'. In any given passage, each bar typically occupies exactly the same length of time. In written music, the end of each bar is signified by a vertical 'bar line'.

31 Begbie, *TMT*, p. 185.

32 In order to speak truthfully of good hemisphere relating, some care would be needed around the word 'mutual'. The contribution of each hemisphere does enhance that of the other, but in a way that is not symmetrical.

33 Wells, *Improvisation*, p. 66.

34 Begbie, *TMT*, pp. 222–3, quoted in Wells, *Improvisation*, p. 66.

35 Begbie, *TMT*, pp. 216–17.

36 Begbie, *TMT*, p. 220.

37 Begbie, *TMT*, p. 221.

38 Begbie, *TMT*, pp. 218–20.

39 Begbie, *TMT*, p. 251.

40 I am indebted in what follows to the insightful commentary of David Ford, 2021, *The Gospel of John: A Theological Commentary*, Grand Rapids, MI: Baker Academic, pp. 206–9.

41 Ford, *The Gospel of John*, p. 207.

42 Ford, *The Gospel of John*, p. 207.

43 Begbie, *TMT*, p. 206.

10

Fullness of Vision, Fullness of Life

Introduction

In earlier chapters we have surveyed neuroscience, the shaping of Western culture, Christian theology, and recent approaches to church leadership. Improvisation, the theme of the previous chapter, went some way towards indicating how all of these might fruitfully be integrated together. The tasks of this final chapter include continuing that integration, and offering some practical pointers. They also include making explicit the connections between what we have covered already and the two phrases of the title of this book.

Fullness of vision: attending with depth and clarity

The faculty of attending

From our first encounter with the chaffinch at the beginning of this book, we have been consistently concerned with the manner in which we pay attention. As we explored in Chapter 2, the nature of our attention is foundational. How we pay attention shapes the kind of world that we experience. Moreover, the manner of my attention to others impacts their own experience of the world.

Fullness of vision is primarily about the openness and sensitivity of our receiving. To use a radio analogy, it is concerned with reception, rather than transmission.[1] I am not speaking of 'sharing my vision with the world', but rather of coming to see the world more fully and richly. I am exploring a posture that is fully present to the world, reaching out towards it, in order to connect and understand, rather than primarily to change or manipulate.

Fullness of vision, then, describes a disposition, a way of being in the world. It encompasses the habit, skill and art of perceiving with greater sensitivity, range, depth and generosity. This foundational virtue encompasses not only an initial perception, but also the capacity to stay present. Such attending will at times lead to action, but the quality of the attending itself is primary.[2] It enables betweenness; it facilitates the possibility of relationship; and it shapes an atmosphere conducive to shared improvisation.

The nature of the disposition

The fullness of vision to which I aspire is rooted in grace and truth. On the one hand, this involves an openness to whatever is actually the case – the truth of the matter. On the other, I want my attending to be permeated by grace. If I jump to judgement, this will shut down openness to increasing perception and understanding. Our culture can assume that, at any given moment, we need to choose between clarity and compassion. For instance, in situations of oversight, auditing or review, a Clear-cut understanding of 'objective scrutiny' might seem to take priority over disposition of care. However, as so often with the Clear-cut LH, this is to create a false dichotomy. Fullness of vision integrates clarity and compassion, grace and truth – to the benefit of all involved. As Feeney's account illustrated, the more we trust that we are in an atmosphere of grace, the more we are able to articulate what is really going on. And the more we find that our truth is met with grace, then the deeper our trust in that grace, and the more we are liberated into greater depth of truthfulness and insight.

In Chapter 9 I touched on five dispositions of improvisation. The first three are especially relevant to fullness of vision. The notion of responsive attunement highlights the need to become personally present in our attending: centred in the Holistic RH, reaching out in order to connect in I–thou relationship. The second disposition, generous receptivity, resonates both with the idea of overaccepting, and also with grace. Here, we look for the gift in what the other has given, and we do so with the expectation of finding it, and receiving it well. We give space to the other, welcoming forward not only their offer, but also them as a person. Truth is relevant in our generous receiving – wanting to perceive truthfully both the nature of the offer, and the spirit and context from which it is offered. Truth also resonates with the need for discerning incorporation. Here we search out how this particular gift might contribute in a way that is consistent with the story. The discernment will often involve both the preservation of all that is good, and its transformation to some degree as it is integrated into what follows.

Depth, clarity and dynamism

Fullness of vision inhabits the imaginative depth offered by the Holistic RH. There will be times when we use the shorthand of simple categories, but our full vision regularly directs its gaze beyond the superficiality of a simplified map of reality. Fullness of vision does not let tidy-mindedness get in the way of the truth. It gives space for tension and ambiguity, and acknowledges what is uncertain, and what is transitory. Being centred in the relational RH, fullness of vision is about facing: facing the world, and attending to the faces of others. David Ford gives sustained attention to the importance of faces, in our selfhood and in our salvation. He highlights the link between a sense of depth and the human face, seen, for instance, in the language of 'gazing deeply into the face of another'.[3]

Healthy fullness of vision also draws on the clarity offered by the LH. It will regularly deploy simplified maps of reality, for instance using their shorthand approximations as a helpful introduction, or as a way of probing options and possibilities. Such use of simplified maps will be carried out in the consciousness that they are simplified maps, and not reality itself. The clarity offered by fullness of vision goes beyond the Clear-cut. It's clear-sightedness includes transparency about the boundaries of what can be clearly known, and a clear recognition of the limits of clarity. When we gaze deeply into the face of another, we may know clearly that there is a substantial backstory behind this face – and that it may never be our privilege to know very much of that backstory. When we engage with a simplified statistical mapping following a multiple-choice survey, we remember that each aggregated number represents real people. Indeed, the word 'data' is the Latin plural of 'datum', meaning 'something given'. Each unit of data represents a gift – and that gift frequently represents a unique human face. Whether faced with a statistical summary or a group of people, healthy fullness of vision offers poised attentiveness, with both strength and flexibility. Its imaginative depth integrates a caring clarity anchored in compassion.

Healthy fullness of vision is not static. With the chaffinch at the beginning of this book, we encountered a simple rhythmic alternation in modes of attention. This simple pattern offers a very good template and prototype. We regularly need periods of narrow focus, typically directed towards completion of a task, or solution of a problem. And these need to be interspersed with periods of open, broad vigilance. Crucially, the purpose of this broader scanning of our environment is not only light relief from focused intensity. It is also genuinely looking out for that which may merit fuller attention. When the narrow focus of our Clear-cut LH is locked on to a compelling task, it can be very challenging to turn away, to open ourselves to the possibility of other issues needing our attention. And yet, cultivating the ability to do so – and the capacity to adjust our plans if and when necessary – should be among our most important disciplines. Conversely, periods of broad relational connection typically need to be interspersed with periods of focused action, decision and task-completion. Simple alternation offers a basic template. The reality is ideally flexible, dynamic and responsive, built on the valuing of both the Clear-cut and the Holistic.

Dimensions and directions of attention

Fullness of vision incorporates the past. It knows the importance of truthfulness about what has been the case – and that onward movement will be hampered unless the past is properly faced. Fullness of vision is fully present in the present. It relies on a pace that enables such presence. It is broad and generously receptive, open to pain, frustration and lament, as well as joy, hope and celebration. Fullness of vision includes the imagining of future possibilities, and is wise to how these may be invoked and explored in the present. It is also realistic about the degree of knowledge or certainty we can have about the future, and is comfortable holding open multiple possible futures.

Most fundamentally, fullness of vision is anchored in God, and nurtured by ever-growing awareness of the unbounded richness of God's being: transcendence and immanence, power and tenderness, creativity and patience, holiness, grace and passionate love. However imperfectly and incompletely we do so, nurturing the desire and practice to turn towards God, in contemplation and beholding, must be the still centre around which all else turns. Here we learn depth of trust and obedience, patterned according to the life of Jesus, and receive afresh the life and love of God.

Fullness of vision is turned towards others: individually and collectively; within the church and beyond it. Fullness of vision attends carefully to context, in all its richness, for individuals, churches and groups. For instance, this could include: socio-economic background; history over months, years and centuries; significant life events; gifts and aspirations. Depth and clarity, grace and truth are to characterize such vision. Our vision will engage with simplified mappings of reality, in order to enrich our understanding, appreciating and relating. Such use of simplified mappings will always be to strengthen and deepen vision, rather than to reduce persons to objects.

Fullness of vision, then, attends in many dimensions: past, present and future; God, others and context. What's more, fullness of vision attends not only to the dimensions separately, but also to their interplay, their mutual enhancement or constraint. What is the relationship between this person and the group they co-lead? What are the aspects of enhancement? Are there any ways in which it constrains their life, or they constrain its flourishing?

Last, but by no means least, fullness of vision is reflexive. I seek to attend to myself, my own being, with the same imaginative depth, clarity, grace and desire for truth that I have been describing. I seek to understand more fully what has been, what is and what might be. I want to be clear-sighted regarding the impact of others on my own development, and also the impact of my own way of being on the groups and people with whom I interact. As we noted in Chapter 7, Scripture highlights how challenging it frequently is for any human being to see themselves clearly. For this reason, fullness of vision regarding ourselves is of particular importance – not least as we seek to grow in our fullness of vision.

Growing in fullness of vision

I recently heard of a survey in which participants had been asked whether their perspective on life had changed significantly in the last decade. The substantial majority replied that yes, their perspective was considerably different from what it had been ten years ago. The follow-up question was whether they expected much change in their perspective on life over the following decade. The substantial majority replied that no, they did not think that would happen, or be needed.

Despite the responses in this survey, whatever the current fullness of our vision, there is always more to see, for the sake of ourselves and of others. This includes, not least, seeing more clearly our patterns of attentiveness – including growing in awareness of our blind spots. Growing in fullness of vision includes coming to a greater depth and richness of truth, and also a fuller appreciation of grace. It is part of our participation with God in the ongoing work of transformation, of becoming more like Christ, of gradually growing in holiness.

I find insightful the comments of the American psychotherapist John Welwood. He notes that many of his clients who are committed to a spiritual tradition trip over the same stumbling block, which he terms 'spiritual bypassing'.[4] These clients assume that, by focusing on spiritual aspects of life (in whatever tradition), they are thereby exempted from the inner psychological work which is necessary for the growth of other human beings. It is as if their spiritual commitment, with its prayer and aspirations, offers them a shortcut to maturity, bypassing some or much of the sheer graft required of others. But this is not possible. The spiritual cannot be pursued separately from the psychological.[5] Although Jesus did not use the abstracted terminology of psychology, both the content of this teaching and the nature of his interactions point to the remarkable depth of his psychological insight. If we are to grow in fullness of vision, this will involve serious psychological work. It will not always be comfortable. This is substantial territory, in breadth and depth. For an excellent introduction to the domain, I commend *The Psychology of Christian Character Formation* by Joanna Collicutt, psychologist, priest and theological educator.[6] For now, given the importance of the subject matter, I offer some headline thoughts in this territory.

Simplified maps of reality feature in such psychological work, in two different ways. On the one hand, we may be repeatedly faced with the fact that we relate to others – individuals and groups – in a way that is overly simplified. Perhaps we have made the binary assumption that Freda would not be suited to a particular role. But then we come to realize that when Freda works with Jill, it brings out the best in her, and the two of them together would love to share the role together. Or again, we may have made clear-cut assumptions about our own strengths or weaknesses, which prove overly simplified when examined more deeply.

Simplified maps of reality can also be seen in many frameworks and models that can be enlightening in this territory. To give one example, Karpman's 'Drama Triangle' is a simplified model that describes some common patterns of behaviour. It does so by describing three roles (summarized as persecutor, victim and rescuer), and some of the common dynamics that can go with these roles. Self-examination and self-understanding can often be aided by exploring such a framework, helped by appropriate questions ('Might I ever like to see myself as the rescuer? When do I most feel like a victim?'). We noted in Chapter 7 Jesus' skilful use of Clear-cut questions and parables, offered to help his hearers probe more deeply into the Holistic depth of the attitudes and behaviours. In a similar way, frameworks such as Karpman's, used with skill and sensitivity, can help enable depth of insight, and shifts in understanding and disposition.[7]

We will also grow in fullness of vision from habits of open, attentive listening. There will be plentiful opportunity to broaden and deepen our understanding of humanity in general, and specific people in particular – both in our direct conversations, and in engagement with biographies, literature and films. Having the curiosity that genuinely seeks to understand what life is like from the perspective of another is invaluable.

Also invaluable is the insight that can arise from direct feedback – if we can receive it well. One potential source of truthful feedback is a recording, audio or video, of a service, meeting or event. We may not initially like what we see or hear, but it can be very helpful. The giving and receiving of feedback can feel very vulnerable, but there are approaches that can help both the giver and the receiver. For instance, one simple pattern that I have experienced very positively is to ask for feedback on one thing that the person really liked, and one thing that would have made what I did even better.[8]

One of the most difficult challenges in this area is often at the earliest stage: beginning to loosen our grip on how we currently understand things: ourselves, others and the world. We may be very familiar with our current simplified map of reality, and hold it with all the stickiness of the Clear-cut LH. A necessary initial step is becoming open to the possibility that other interpretations may be possible – or at least that our assumptions may not apply in every situation. The more we are centred in the Holistic RH, the more able we will be to loosen our grip. It is only by unlearning as needed that we can move into a greater fullness of vision.

The fifth disposition of improvisation I describe as deepening desire. And so the question arises: how deep is my desire to grow in fullness of vision? And if that desire is deep and genuine, what combination of habits and practices will I deploy, in order to see ever more fully and truthfully God, others, myself, and the strengths, assumptions and blind spots that I currently carry?

There will always be more such growing to be done. It is important work, liberating work, and sometimes hard work. It takes time – and giving it time, intention and appropriate forms of practice is likely to yield life-giving fruit. Many of us will benefit from skilled and committed accompaniment, more and less formal, in our quest for fullness of vision. This will often include friends, family members and colleagues with whom we can be candid, and from whom we can receive candour. The role of spiritual direction is frequently important. There may also be seasons in which we do well to engage with pastoral supervision, counselling, therapy or coaching.[9]

Fullness of vision, then, relies on the growing and skilful deployment of both hemispheres in healthy relationship. Fullness of vision is also foundational for good improvisation. From considering how we grow in fullness of vision, we now turn to consider how we might grow in improvisation more generally.

Growing in improvisation

A wide range of contexts calls on our improvisatory ability, both real-time and phased. These include informal conversation; small and large meetings; our personal organization of days, weeks and years; relationships with friends and colleagues; and reshaping patterns and structures of church life. We have seen how improvisation holds together the vital components of action and attention, initiative and responsiveness. Good improvisation enables the sharing of many people's gifts, and shared participation in the divine life and love. Desire for ever deeper participation can appropriately fuel our motivation to grow in our improvisatory ability. In this section, as in the previous one, I offer some indicative headings as to how we might direct energy and intention as we seek to improvise with ever greater sensitivity, skill and fullness of life.

Awareness

Good improvisation is immensely helped by the sensitivity and skill with which we are able to read our context. All that we have covered under fullness of vision, therefore, offers an excellent foundation for growing in improvisation. Once again, this is not a static vision, nor static awareness. And all dimensions are relevant: past, present and possible futures; God and others (in the room and beyond it); the broader context; our own selves, including our thoughts, emotions and behaviour as the improvisation unfolds.

Genuine self-presence

The more we can bring our full selves to be present within the improvisation, the more it will come alive. Moreover, the more we can help to shape an atmosphere which helps others show up fully, the greater the depth of our shared participation. Bringing my full self, therefore, must not be done in a way that leaves little space for others, but rather in a way that is fully engaged and attentive, and responsively poised to take up space or offer space as appropriate.

Trust

I identified the fourth vital disposition of improvisation as trusting courage. Courage is needed if we are to be fully present: offering my full self can be vulnerable and risky. Doing so may stretch my trust in God and in my own capabilities. It will also be linked to the degree to which I trust the other people involved. Do I trust them to receive sufficiently well that which I have to offer? Do I trust the strength and depth of our relationships? Do I trust that together we can discern a good way forward? Do I trust the process – either an existing predetermined one, or our ability to improvise an appropriate process together? Is there sufficient grace in this context for me to show up fully, and to put forward that which seems most important to offer?

These three areas – awareness, genuine self-presence and trust – offer a strong and flexible foundation from which to improvise. These alone, however, are not enough. Whether our context is musical, theatrical or ministerial leadership, our capacity to improvise will benefit significantly from a broadened repertoire of improvisatory material.

Broadening our improvisatory repertoire

Professional jazz musicians sometimes spend hours each week rehearsing musical patterns and motifs that may in due course enrich their playing. They do so at various speeds, in contrasting rhythms, and in every possible key. Their skill at improvisation rests in part on having at their fingertips an extensive repertoire of patterns and options from which to select.

Such commitment to development and disciplined practice can serve as an inspiration and a challenging provocation for us: how committed are we to developing our practice? It also serves as a useful analogy for us broadening our repertoire of improvisatory options for a range of scenarios. Such options include skills, techniques or approaches. It can include learning of a wider range of ministry and mission approaches. It can include expanding our repertoire of short phrases that we have to hand when leading a meeting. It can also include learning how to use gesture and body language to good effect. All this is in service of giving welcoming space to the contributions of others, and also enabling proper time for discernment before incorporation.

In an ideal world, we would be able to anticipate in advance each situation that will call for new options, and arrive at it well-prepared. In the real world, much of our learning will arise from muddling our way through unanticipated situations, perhaps feeling somewhat inept and awkward in the process, and then reflecting on them with hindsight. 'What else might we have done? What options did we have?'

As I look back on my own gradual learning over years of ministry, there are several areas in which I wish I had developed a broader range of strong skills much earlier. These areas include facilitating good discussion in a planning meeting; options for coming to a decision when there is no clear consensus; options for one-to-one conversation; the specific situations of receiving feedback, and of giving it. In each of these scenarios, having a broader repertoire of options – phrases and processes with which we are familiar – can be very helpful, and can also increase our confidence and relaxation. Moreover, in each of these scenarios, part of the challenge can be dealing with our own emotions that may arise in the middle of the discussion or feedback. Learning in these areas, therefore, is inextricably linked to the fullness of self-awareness described in the previous section. Learning in these areas, moreover, will never be wasted.[10]

In our repertoire-broadening, we may find it helpful to consider some hemisphere-related questions and patterns:

Is this a binary issue, or might it be a question of degree? *There are times when it is appropriate and helpful to switch from framing an issue as a Clear-cut yes/no to more a question of degree.*

Is the issue more about what is done, or the manner in which it is done? *The 'manner in which' can helpfully involve questions of process and pace – neither rushing decisions through, nor dragging them out indefinitely; being seen to have consulted, and reached a decision in a way that feels fair. It also involves how we relate to one another. Or again, there is whether we have a plan, and quite how we relate to the plan over time.*

Preserve and transform. *Is there a way of preserving what is most important to different groups of people, for instance, and combining them in a new, transformed proposal?*

To help flesh out these phrases, let's take an example, in an important area related to planning, and see how it could combine all three of these principles.

A desired endpoint – or sense of scale

If we are shaping some sort of development in the life of the church, it will frequently be helpful to attend to the likely scale of that development. Doing so can help engage our imaginations and direct us in beginning to address practicalities. As we have seen, the Church SLD uniformly recommends specifying a SMART objective: perhaps a certain number of new regular worshippers, within a particular timescale. This is very much a binary approach: there is likely to be clarity regarding whether or not it is met (and considerable effort may go into detailing definitions in order to minimize any ambiguity). There are, however, other ways of attending to the scale of the development. These involve preserving the positives, and exploring different questions of degree.

Instead of specifying a single number as the measurable objective, a second option would be to specify an indicative range: we hope there will be at least X, and possibly as many as Y. The third option goes further in the same direction, setting up not one but several different ranges. We might describe each of these as a possible scenario. Here there is further acknowledgement that we don't know in advance quite what will happen, but we want to be as prepared as possible for the issues likely to be relevant. A fourth option would be to rebalance our attention – giving careful consideration to what the fruit of our initiative might be, and what factors might be influential. Having probed and discussed this territory, we could then direct our primary energy towards discerning and planning our next steps, expecting to repeat the process in the light of what evolves.

Note that the option of a single-point destination, as indicated by a SMART objective, will tend to engage the narrow focus of the Clear-cut LH, construing the scenario as a task to complete. There will be situations in which that is entirely appropriate. In such a scenario, we will want to make sure that we remain centred in the RH, as discussed previously. The other options mentioned, however, will by their nature increasingly engage the RH, and its capacity to hold open multiple possibilities. Without losing sight of the need for appropriate action, this framing is likely to view the situation more relationally, and avoid the risk of seeing the people involved as a means to the end of meeting our objective. In each case, then, the aim has been to preserve what is good in the Clear-cut desire to engage with the potential scale of response. We have also, however, seen how that desire can be transformed. There can be contrast, interplay and mutual enhancement between channelling a proper desire for fruitfulness and wanting to avoid illusions of full control, or tipping into treating people as objects. Preserving what is good, but transforming how we frame it, will change the manner in which we engage – with each other, with any new development, with existing congregation members, and with potential new worshippers.

Motivation, intrinsic and extrinsic

Stepping away from a single-point focus can also be very helpful regarding our motivation. As we explored in Chapter 7, our motivation really matters. It matters ethically and theologically. It also makes a difference in our interactions. To understand this more, the concepts of intrinsic and extrinsic motivation are helpful. With intrinsic motivation, we engage in an activity because of the activity itself. With extrinsic motivation, our primary drive arises from something other than the activity – for instance, because we are being paid to do it, or because we want people to think well of us.

If my warm and welcoming interaction with a church newcomer is genuine, we can describe it as rising from intrinsic motivation. I'm interested in them; I want whatever is best for them; and I want to live in a way that shares God's blessing generously and open-handedly. If the context includes numerical objectives for church growth, however, things are different. Such a context is not uncommon. Indeed, as I write, the Church of England has named its desire to double the number of children and young people by 2030.[11] What an enquiring teenage newcomer may quickly come to suspect is that our motivation has switched to be primarily extrinsic. Rather than our friendliness being genuine, it is actually a means to an end. We want to meet our target; here is a teenager; if I behave towards them in a friendly way, this might help us meet our target. Michael Ramsey highlighted the issue in 1972: 'You will care about people for themselves, and be interested in them for themselves, and not only as potential confirmation candidates.'[12] A switch to extrinsic motivation transforms any relationship. What was I–thou becomes I–it. It's worth registering that this issue does not only apply to potential new members of church. Exaggerating for clarity, regular worshippers could come to feel that they were viewed primarily as potential contributors to church activities, in order to attract new worshippers, which would make the diocese pleased, which would sustain the funding ... It may not be impossible to stay centred in intrinsic motivation alongside the presence of SMART targets. Nevertheless, such objectives will at least complicate and skew motivation. Relying on them can seem rather like assuming that a dog will only venture into a wide open space if we throw a ball for it to fetch. Moreover, it can act to undermine the genuine intrinsic motivation that we all hope to bring. Our intrinsic motivation may indeed require sustained nurture and strengthening – in which case that is what we should give it.

One important strand in our growing in improvisation, then, is broadening our repertoire of possible responses. Having a broader repertoire is a good start. It will not, however, guarantee that we always choose well.

Growing in our improvisatory discernment

We will never run out of scope for learning when it comes to discerning how best to act. If our desire to learn and grow is genuine, one important dimension will be continuing to strengthen our discerning decision-making – both in the moment (in real-time improvisation), and in more phased situations.

Developed disciplines of reflective practice should form one crucial strand of how we invest in our growth in this area. This will helpfully include several different modes: reflection on our own; when possible, reflection with a skilled accompanier with sufficient distance from the situation; and reflection with others directly involved. Hearing the experience of others is invaluable – and itself requires discernment: what somebody else thinks should have happened, or what I think should have happened, must not be assumed to be the final answer. Nevertheless, understanding how a range of people experienced a meeting, development or event is invaluable material for reflection and digestion. Improvisation is not about the pursuit of perfection, or it would be experienced as an impossible tightrope of doom. Instead, an improvisatory approach seeks to nurture a culture in which experimentation can be welcomed, and 'failure' redefined. A bedrock of truthfulness and grace, with a willingness to learn and grow, can be transformative.

Questions can include: What went well? What were the key moments? Where was energy most engaged? What would it be good to understand better? What other options did we have? If we were doing it again, what might we do differently? What do we need to do now?

Roles of ministerial leadership often include challenging situations as we seek to discern what is best. In many contexts it can be difficult to know how to be generously receptive to each individual, and also enable decisions for the good of the whole. To facilitate some brief comment, let's imagine a scenario where we are trying to discern how to respond to someone's behaviour, request or proposal, which strikes us as problematic. Let me highlight three distinct strands that may be at play.

A first strand involves distinguishing between some broad categories. Might we be dealing with malicious intent, underdeveloped skill, poor judgement or a straightforward difference of opinion? Is there an over-inflated ego at play, or under-inflated (on our part or theirs)?

A second strand draws on questions of process. How can I (or we) best enable genuine depth of listening? Can we give space to hear both what is proposed and also the values and motivations behind it? What would be the most fitting process by which we can move to a decision? Ideally, those involved will know that they have been genuinely listened to and understood, even if a decision has not gone the way they would wish.[13] (And it is all too easy to assume, incorrectly, that if a decision has not gone our way, that means that we have not been listened to.)

A third strand relates to emotions. Might we need to expand our capacity to cope with the discomfort of others? Might we need to expand our capacity to cope with the disappointment of the decision not going our way? What is it that I am responsible for – and for what am I not responsible? (And perhaps, how realistic are my expectations that all my decisions will be excellent, and everybody will love them (and me)?) Holding and sharing an improvisatory perspective may help: we don't expect to know the right answers, but to do our best to find an ongoing good way forward. Not every decision will be the best one. Can we, together, be generously receptive to the learning that can arise, and discerningly incorporate it going forwards?

Nine nuggets

I offer next 'nine nuggets' – short phrases (each with brief commentary) that encapsulate different ways in which the essence of what we have covered might be applied and embedded within the ministry and leadership of the church.

1) *The purpose of a plan is to help us improvise well, together, with God*

Life is improvised. A well-constructed and skilfully held plan can be invaluable in communicating and coordinating as we seek to improvise together. Sometimes we will rightly follow our plan to the letter. At other times, some degree of variation will be right and proper – and having the plan in the first place can aid our discussion and discernment. In a culture that tends towards Clear-cut LH dominance, it can be very easy to slip into flipping this perspective, leading to something like: the purpose of our improvising is to help us implement our plans/complete the tasks/solve the problems. Moreover, once the priority becomes implementing our plans, improvisation is easily seen as something to avoid, rather than to embrace. Importantly, a plan is only one of the things that will help us improvise well together. Others include ongoing attentiveness (in multiple dimensions), relationship, depth of dialogue and engagement with all that is happening.

Having crystallized a plan, what happens next is important. We can sketch three main broad possibilities (exaggerating for clarity). The first possibility is that the narrow beam of our Clear-cut attention stays firmly locked on to the plan we have constructed. Our energy becomes substantially directed towards its accomplishment, largely to the exclusion of all other considerations. The second option sits at the other end of the spectrum. Having set out a plan, we then set it aside. We consider our task accomplished, and get on with the rest of life. The third possibility is different, with the plan acting to free up our attention. Here, the plan functions as a repository for our current best estimate of what will happen. Having clarified our present understanding of details and timing (to whatever degree appropriate), we can now set them down for the time being. Having done so, our attention is now free to be directed where it is most needed. This will include proper attentiveness both to what is in the plan and also to all that is arising around us, and lead to discerning responsiveness as needed. Having constructed a plan, we hold it as lightly or firmly as is appropriate and discern how best to incorporate its actions into the broader context. The third possibility is the one I recommend.

2) Be satisfied with 'sufficient'

For instance, what is a sufficient level of detail for our planning at this stage? Is this a sufficiently clear description of what we are aiming towards? (It's worth noting that, whereas the Clear-cut LH prefers the certainty of a watertight definition, a more indicative description will frequently suffice – and even be more helpful.[14])

Quite what counts as sufficient will normally be a matter of judgement. There is no algorithm or formula, and we should embrace the need to make a shared intuitive call, informed by the wisdom of experience, broad reason, relevant information and prayerfully imaginative consideration and dialogue.

What is sufficient will often take the form of a 'sweet spot', holding a creative tension between considerations. That sweet spot may need to move over time – for instance, at different stages of a development. But repeatedly being content with what is sufficient, what seems 'about right' at each stage, will generally lead to wise use of our energy.

3) Use shorthand as accurately and as consciously as possible

For reasons of conciseness, we may often find ourselves referring to groups or categories of people or of churches using 'shorthand' labels or headings (for example, regular worshipper, newcomer, group leader; thriving, healthy, small, struggling). We may also use short phrases to summarize complex processes – such as 'deliver' or 'implement' aspects of a plan. We will be wise to seek ever greater awareness regarding quite what shorthand we are using, what assumptions we may unconsciously be importing along with it, and what connotations it carries for others. Choosing our vocabulary well is a good start, and the practice of saying 'and I'm using shorthand here' can also be surprisingly helpful in raising awareness with others. It signifies that we know we're referring, at this point, to the map, not the reality.

4) Clarity can easily be mistaken for certainty

The LH prefers clarity, certainty and fixity. When these are not actually possible, it seeks a perspective on them – typically a simplified map of reality – which has the appearance of clarity, certainty and fixity. It is frequently the case that clarity is taken to imply certainty – but this is an illusion. We can have a very clear plan, based on what we expect is likely, and which seems convincing – but that tells us nothing about the unanticipated external factors that may lead in a different direction. A specific well-known illusion in this territory relates to statistical correlation. One factor may be strongly and clearly correlated with another – but causation may be totally different.

5) *What structure and atmosphere can best help life to flow?*

There is no point trying to push the river of life – but some ways of structuring our shared activity may help it flow, whereas others may get in the way. What sort of structure is most likely to be helpful in our context? Relatedly, from a different metaphorical angle, what sort of atmosphere will be conducive to life-giving improvisation? What might help enable such atmosphere – in terms of venue, timing, surroundings and the quality of presence that we each seek to bring to our discussing and relating?

For more substantial developments, this is as good a place as any to draw attention to a number of semi-structured approaches that can help churches review their current situation and discern next steps. Approaches broadly in tune with my emphases include Appreciative Inquiry,[15] Community Organizing;[16] Asset-based Community Development; and Partnership for Missional Church.[17]

This 'nugget' is one example of a more general principle – the importance of exploring what is acting as master in any given situation, and what is treated as a servant. In this case, are we using our church structures, or plans, to support and serve our participation in the life of God, or, conversely, are we treating church structures, or plans, as the things to be served?

6) *Use the language of 'strategy' and 'strategic' with care and clarity*

Discourse around strategy – what we might term 'strategy talk' – easily holds together a wide range of largely distinct dimensions. It may often be helpful to clarify which of these we do not intend, and which we do, not least because our listeners may assume otherwise. Here, for instance, are no less than seven distinct aspects, some or all of which may be present in any talk of strategy:

- Being strategic can simply mean a sense of 'standing back' to consider options, perhaps especially with a broader scale of time and/or geography in view. Done well, this can be a fruitful regular discipline (it is worth noting that the act of 'standing back' can easily tip us into 'I–it' relating, and away from 'I–thou').
- A 'strategy' can be an alternative term for a 'plan', with no extra connotations. The purpose of a strategy should be to help us improvise well, together, with God.
- A strategic approach can mean one that, because of timely action, and/or shared resources of some sort, brings genuine benefit, as perceived by all concerned.
- Strategy can easily carry connotations of centralization – in a benefice, diocese or nationally. Such connotations may or may not be accurate. Centralization is normally a question of degree. Moreover, any such centralization could consist of taking away autonomy, or of adding capacity. There is scope for false assumptions here, and thus for helpful clarification.
- Some strategies require or impose greater uniformity; for instance, across different churches – but again, this is not necessarily the case.
- Using the word 'strategy' can be assumed and used to add clout and kudos to what is being proposed. It can be a sort of synonym for 'good', 'strong' or 'carefully prepared'.
- Not unrelatedly, talking in terms of strategy can easily seem to give the impression that those who have crafted the strategy have thereby gained a greater degree of control over what will come to pass – and yet this is unlikely to be the case, for reasons discussed earlier.

Rather than using the language of strategy, if we were to talk of the 'approach' we plan to take, much of the rhetorical noise would be sidestepped, and we might thereby communicate more clearly, openly and inclusively. Doing so, however, would require letting go of the rhetorical attractiveness of strategy talk.[18]

7) Treat 'measurement and measures' carefully – and aim to cause no harm

Ministerial leadership roles properly include oversight of how various groups and activities are going. Some sense of scale of the activity, and of people's response, will often be a helpful strand within that discernment. Within our Western culture, it is easy to assume that greater effectiveness will arise from more detailed measurement. This can drive the pursuit of more 'precise' data, in the expectation that this will lead to more informed decision-making. In church contexts, this can occur at more than one level: national church institutions looking at dioceses; dioceses viewing churches and benefices; ministers surveying congregations.

All of this needs to be treated with great care – as the whole argument of this book has emphasized – for four main reasons. First, especially in a church context, what might seem to be more precise data may not be accurate or relevant. It will frequently not account for the deeper and more important aspects of Christian life, which are rarely countable. As McGilchrist points out, the roots of the word 'precise' point to the meaning: 'cut off early'. What appears to be a 'measure' may or may not be well correlated with what we should most fundamentally be seeking to discern. Calling something a 'measure' does not make it an accurate metric. Second, more data might lead to greater effectiveness if we were engineering a car, but we are not. As we explored in Chapter 6, drawing on the work of Snowden, the life of the church is not a 'clear' or 'complicated' domain, but rather gloriously 'complex', animate and alive. The punctuated processes of our intertwined stories under God are substantially shaped and formed by qualities of attentiveness, acts of kindness and receptiveness to *kairos* moments of the Spirit.

Third, most briefly, some 'measures' lend themselves to a degree of 'gaming', further skewing interpretation. Last, but by no means least, the activity of trying to measure is itself never neutral.[19] There are approaches, such as participative research, that deliberately aim to harness this fact in a positive direction. Nevertheless, what is intended as 'objective scrutiny' can too easily impact negatively, both on those being scrutinized, and on their relationships with those scrutinizing. We saw this clearly in Chapter 8, with our Ineson-inspired reflection on the experience of Jo, the very good vicar in receipt of grant funding. Similar dynamics can also apply between ministers and congregation members, or between dioceses and churches.

Repeated examination of a recently planted seed can easily stop it from germinating. Too much conscious attention can be actively destructive of some of the most precious gifts of life. Direct scrutiny can impede or injure friendship, spontaneity, love – and tender shoots of faith. Trying to render explicit what is substantially implicit may terminate it. As McGilchrist puts it, 'the best things in life hide from the full glare of focused attention'.[20]

8) *Is this tension one to be resolved, sidestepped, or constructively embraced?*

Each of these three options will sometimes be appropriate. Many of us default to assuming that resolution of tension will be appropriate – but it may be neither necessary nor helpful. As we have seen, holding a tension well can be both a necessary skill and a potent source of energy. Considerable experience in this area, focused on an American church context but substantially transferable, can be found in *Managing Polarities in Congregations* by Roy Oswald and Barry Johnson.[21]

Another way of approaching this question is to ask, in a particular situation: 'Do we need a binary (yes/no) answer, or is this more a question of degree?' For instance, when considering a possible new venture, options could include adjusting the frequency, considering a trial period, or addressing different components in different phases.

9) *Emulate the chaffinch*

The humble chaffinch with which the book began can helpfully act for us as an encapsulating symbolic reminder. We need both detailed focus on our own agenda, and also open, broad attentiveness to our full environment. A simple regular rhythm of the two is a good start. And the centre of gravity from which to improvise is the Holistic RH that remains more closely in touch with reality itself, rather than any simplified mapping.

Improvisation and fullness of life

Near the beginning of the chapter we made the link between fullness of vision and the form of attentiveness being advocated. At this point I want to make a similar link between healthy improvisation and fullness of life. The fullness of life that God gives is not something we can 'make happen'. Nevertheless, my suggestion is that the perspective we've been developing, seeking to participate ever more fully in the life and love of God, generates conditions in which we are more disposed to receive, enjoy and share the gift of such abundant living. Being centred in the relational and Holistic RH are important aspects of this, as are drawing on the gifts of the Clear-cut LH. Moreover, the pattern by which such fullness of life emerges over time will always be improvised, with all of the contrast, interplay and mutual enhancement that we have explored.

Having made this link, we turn now to consider how the ground we have covered helps us interpret and integrate various strands of church experience.

Sense-making and integration

In the first section of the book we gained an enriched understanding of the brain hemispheres, separately and together. In the later chapters, I have offered a vision of Christian life in which we are called to participate ever more deeply in the life and love of God. The shape of this participation is always improvised, and we have seen how improvisation itself not only models healthy hemisphere relating, but also – and more importantly – rings true to the life and example of Christ.

The approach and perspective I have been describing – improvised participation with others in God's life, centred in healthy hemisphere relating – enables us to make sense both of the Church SLD itself, and also of a range of responses to it. For example, let's revisit the 2007 diocesan Godly Leadership course I described in Chapter 1, and the three broad responses I witnessed in response to its Church SLD contents. How do those responses appear from the perspective we have since developed?

My experience of the 2007 Godly Leadership course

One group straightforwardly welcomed the Church SLD approach. It made sense to them as a promising means of moving parish life forwards. People in this group may well have been accurate in discerning that their local church life could do with greater harnessing of Clear-cut LH strengths, and that the Clear-cut LH is the particular specialism of the Church SLD. My sense is that the Church SLD seems like a 'bolt-on extra': a theologically neutral way to significantly increase effectiveness. Perhaps it seems like an outboard motor, which one could attach to a rowing boat, thereby considerably speeding trips across the water.

The 'opposite' group was comprised of people like 'Ben'. For them, the Church SLD simply hadn't connected to their understanding of the nature of faith, ministry or church life. The perspective we have developed helps us understand this response as well. People like Ben correctly discerned that the Church SLD is not theologically neutral. Moreover, its impact is all too easily negative. For, as we explored in Chapter 8, the

Church SLD approach tends to tip its practitioners too far into Clear-cut LH centring, undermining the likelihood of rich relationship with God and others. There is a qualitative difference. Adding an outboard motor doesn't just make your rowing a little faster.

It would be easy to describe the third group as situated between the other two, at a different point on a spectrum: seeing value in some of the Church SLD practices, even if the whole package was not convincing. A plausible interpretation is that they could see ways of strengthening LH involvement within their ministry, but intuited the need to stay centred in the Holistic RH.

However, this third response – or at least our developed understanding – is in fact actually fundamentally different, and not simply midway between the other two. In the terms of a boating analogy, it's not that I'm recommending we use the outboard motor some of the time, and row the rest of the time. Instead, let's recognize that the boat already has sails, and what is needed is our growth in awareness, skill and teamwork as we seek to navigate well together. Doing so involves making the most of what we've been given, improvising well in the context of our ever-changing surroundings. This is not a neutral extra bolted on to turbocharge performance, but about sharpening and developing skills and resources we already had, in an integrated, responsive, purposeful manner.

Other recent ministerial writing

This improvisatory, participative, hemisphere-congruent perspective can also help make sense of a range of recent ministerial writing that does not sit within the Church SLD. Such writing typically emphasizes one or more aspects of faith and ministry that are strongly linked to the Holistic RH. A range of such aspects have been chosen by different writers, as explicit or implicit alternatives to the Clear-cut strategic planning of the Church SLD. Sam Wells, for instance, has richly developed the concept and practice of 'being with' God and others, as theologically and missionally vital.[22] The priority Wells gives to attentiveness, presence, openness and relationship is strongly centred in the Holistic RH. Al Barrett and Ruth Harley, following some critique of (what I term) the Church SLD, frame their approach in terms of 'being interrupted'.[23] Although they do not focus on its vocabulary, their richly developed perspective carries all the hallmarks of improvisation, and is substantially congruent with a hemisphere-informed understanding. Mike Starkey describes his own engagement with Church SLD material, and his growing disenchantment with the constraining narrowness of the (Clear-cut) journey metaphor deployed.[24] Roberts and Sims highlight the life-giving importance and potential of narrative (again, centred in the RH) in the shaping of church life.[25] Michael Sadgrove majors on the richly integrated virtue of wisdom (requiring cooperative interplay between hemispheres).[26] David Runcorn diagnoses in the Church SLD a false sense of responsibility to 'secure the future' of the church, and prescribes ongoing transformation in our trust of God, and 'fear' of God (properly understood).[27] Once more, he critiques the mistaken sense of control offered by the Church SLD. The biblical emphasis he discerns on character and motivation require (in our terms) considerable RH centring.

A number of other writers, often without explicit critique of the Church SLD, hold some of its concerns alongside broader and more Holistic considerations. Examples include John Pritchard, Alan Bartlett and Emma Ineson.[28] Ineson, for instance, lists 'Four good reasons for counting and measuring things', followed by 'Four bad reasons for counting and measuring things', then helpfully proposes that theological counting must be held in the light of God's timing, and of God's grace.[29]

Given the Western cultural context in which the Clear-cut LH has held increasing sway, it is not surprising that something along the lines of the Church SLD has arisen. It is not surprising that many within the church have found it attractive and compelling, especially on initial acquaintance. Neither is it surprising that many have tested it and found it wanting. Moreover, the rich and varied complementary approaches I have summarized above (and there are of course others) all have in common a notable shift towards centring in the Holistic RH, and embracing a much more open, engaged and relational approach. Once more, such a response is not at all surprising, given the tendency of the Church SLD to tip into Clear-cut LH centring.

Integration

Our hemisphere-congruent improvised approach offers a perspective in which many different dimensions can be held together. Here we combine proper consideration of both doing and being, receiving and offering, initiative and responsiveness. Here we both seek the good, and hold lightly our current understanding of how the good can best be enabled. We both seek to play our own part, and also seek to welcome others into fulfilling their own roles. We seek neither to cling to control, nor to avoid taking action to influence for good.

Holding together multiple considerations, as others have done, is a good start, but the approach we have developed goes beyond a simple combination. The principles of both improvisation and healthy hemisphere-relating guide us in a holistic integration of multiple factors. This includes the principle of seeking a God-focused centring in the relational and Holistic RH. It includes the careful sifting and preservation of the gifts of LH analysis, and then their transformation, their discerning incorporation, as is fitting for this moment in God's ongoing story. It includes creating, tending and valuing the imaginative space in which to gather the insights of analysis, reason, experience, multiple perspectives and tradition. And it courageously trusts the guidance of the Holy Spirit in leading our informed intuition towards wise, creative and well-judged decisions and practices.

The word 'improvisation' is derived from the Latin for 'unforeseen'. An improvised approach highlights the fact that there are many areas in which we do not know and cannot know what will happen. Our predictions of what will happen, especially regarding the responses of others, can only be approximate at best. An improvised approach welcomes and integrates that fact, and draws our attention to what is needed as a consequence, including ongoing attentiveness, relationship, cooperation and trust, with God and with each other.

Improvising with God

God invites us ever deeper into shared participation in God's own life and love. This participation is responsive and improvised, never complete, always unfolding. It is not far-fetched to discern in God's own disposition towards humanity the vital facets of good improvisation. God offers us responsive attunement, in Christ and by the Holy Spirit. The generosity of God's receptiveness towards us knows no bounds. God finds discerning ways of incorporating the most unlikely people, and our most unlikely characteristics, into the ongoing story of God's life. And God seems to place remarkable trust – courageous trust – in our participation with God's mission of life and love.

The invitation of ministry, of mission and of church leadership, is so to improvise together with God that others, too, are offered a sign and foretaste of participation in the divine life. We are to shape our own improvising, and the improvising of those with whom we minister, such that the invitation and the call to join in with God is visible and tangible.

So we too are called to responsive attunement – to God, to our contexts, to all whom we encounter, within and beyond the church, and to our own realities. We are summoned to grow in the generosity of our receptivity, ever more open and eager to discover that which is gift. We are called to strengthen not only our discerning consideration, but also the wisdom and creativity of how we incorporate those gifts in the ongoing story. And we are invited to step forwards with courage, trusting unreservedly in the goodness and grace of God, and thus offering ourselves with the fullness of our ambiguities and abilities, and the totality of our hearts and minds.

As we let ourselves be drawn into ever deeper participation, with God and all creation, so the assumptions and blind spots of our discourses melt away. As we give ourselves to God and to others – with all of our heart, with the entirety of our minds, and from the depths of our souls – we find ourselves caught up in God's joyful dance of grace – the divine ceilidh, as it were. Moreover, this joyful dance is incorporated alongside the most wonderful meal with friends in the wedding feast of heaven and earth. Here there is union and integration, connection and relationship. Here structure is in service of life. Here God generously receives the ambiguous water of our human lives, and discerningly incorporates it into the wine of heaven. Here we find ourselves to be standing on no unstable iceberg, but on the solid ground of grace and truth. Indeed, through no accomplishment of our own, the solid ground on which we find ourselves to be standing turns out to be no less than the summit of the mountain of God.

Pure attention to the existence of the other

From the early pages of this book, we have repeatedly focused on a quality of relational attention, centred in God and in the Holistic RH. We encountered it in the meal with friends. We explored its foundational significance and impact in Chapter 2, along with its connection with personal knowing. We enriched our understanding of it in Chapter 4's exploration of the gifts of the right hemisphere. We examined its theological resonance in Chapter 7. Chapter 9's unpacking of the dispositions needed for life-giving improvisation revealed a remarkable overlap with the understanding we had developed. Such attention is not focused on the potential usefulness of the other, nor is it oriented towards scrutiny, judgement or categorization. Its centre of gravity, rather, is attentiveness to the other's state of being, to how they are. It is responsively attuned, and generously receptive. Its posture is of strong, flexible, poised attentiveness, of clarity and coding compassion. It does not avoid the truth, and is rooted in grace.

It is high time to articulate the fact that such quality of attention can best be described by the word *love*. McGilchrist quotes the French philosopher Louis Lavelle: 'Love is a pure attention to the existence of the other.' The Dominican theologian Timothy Radcliffe puts it powerfully: 'The first stage in loving someone ... is rejoicing that that person exists.' The theologian Paul Tillich emphasizes essentially the same concept: 'Love listens. It is its first task to listen.' Tillich leaves room for love to have other tasks. But the starting point, the foundation, is a similarly pure attention to the other. Erich Fromm, the German-American social psychologist and psychoanalyst, pointed out that most people approach 'the problem of love' in terms of how to appear lovable, and therefore try hard to appear successful and attractive.[30] The more important question is also more challenging: how can we increase our capacity to love. That is precisely the question we have been addressing, as we have deepened our understanding of fullness of vision.

As Chapter 2 made clear, and as experience confirms, if I can bring to my engagement with others an attentiveness centred in such love, it will make a difference not only to how they experience me, but also to how they experience themselves. They will ideally experience a welcome into the flowing dance of life together. Conversely, if my approach to them seems clinical and scrutinizing, they may well brace themselves in defence, experiencing, rather, the tightrope of doom. In Chapter 9 we registered the spaciousness of good improvisation, and how it can welcome forward the full personhood of all involved. In and through this experience, all involved can increasingly become more of the person they were created to be. Fullness of vision, therefore, offers a climate and a context conducive to fullness of life.

Loving into life

As we draw towards our conclusion, David Sims offers a phrase that I find powerfully apposite: *loving into life*. Some background will be helpful. Sims writes of how, as a then Head of a Business School, he was very surprised to find his understanding of organizations turned around by a chance encounter with a children's story, *The Velveteen Rabbit*.

In a nutshell, as a boy comes to love his toy velveteen rabbit more and more, so the rabbit gradually comes to life. Sims came across the story for the first time as an adult, one day on the radio on the way to work. By the time he reached his office, he was very surprised to find himself 'beginning to think about organizations as velveteen rabbits, coming to life when they were loved'.[31] Such a concept went right against theoretical ideas he had developed and held for decades. Nevertheless, the more he pondered the idea, the more it made sense of his experience in a wide range of organizational contexts.

This included shedding light on a variety of schools and businesses that flourished: 'some people were willing to love their organization, and the organization seemed somehow to come to life in response to that love'.[32] In contrast, he cites another organization that is never quite as good as it has the potential to be. 'The organization's biggest problem is that plenty of people are prepared to devote some time and energy to it, but no one loves it sufficiently for it to come to life.'[33]

If we imagine an infant child, the importance of 'loving them into life' should be very clear – not least because of the tragic consequences of failing to do so. It is a small step to think, for instance, of loving a family into life. Sims invites us to go a step further: in our context, to think of loving into life a church, or a church group.

As we have seen, love is necessarily centred in the Holistic RH, and also draws generously on the Clear-cut LH. If I am to contribute to loving a family, or a church, into life, I will love it enough to attend to helpful structures and processes, to life-giving decision-making and details. I will be anchored in compassion, and clear-sighted regarding all that will enable or constrain it. The Clear-cut components to the life of the church will always be treated as a trellis, supporting organic growth, or as a conduit – not trying to push the river of life, but letting it flow, helpfully channelled and unimpeded. Together, Clear-cut and Holistic can enable an atmosphere conducive to life and fitting for this context. The contrast, interplay and mutual enhancement between the Clear-cut and the Holistic will be part of what adds vitality to the whole.

The primary source of vitality, however, is God. It is God who loves each individual, and indeed the whole cosmos, into life. God's invitation to us is both to continue cooperating with being loved into life – by God and others – and also to participate in loving into life all whom we encounter.

One final insight from Sims is pertinent. Reflecting on why certain people feel and act with such loving commitment towards their organization, he discerns that this tends to happen 'if they see their own story and the organisation's story as intertwined'.[34] They are prepared to take the organization as part of their story, and to see themselves as part of its story. And so with God and the church. God invites us to discover more of how our own life is already intertwined with God's – the model and supreme invitation being the mutual intimacy of the Father with the Son by the Holy Spirit. God invites us to let our lives intertwine together more fully, within the church and beyond the church, integrating the Clear-cut and the Holistic in ways that bring health and blessing. And God draws us to appreciate and develop the intertwining of our life with other lives across time and space, participating ever more deeply in the life, love and ongoing story of God's engagement with the world. Such intertwining will often be partially planned and responsively improvised, with ambiguity and tension, intuitive discernment and imaginative depth, energized by contrast, interplay and mutual enhancement.

The fullness of vision that I have sought to describe in these pages leads to our receiving ever more fully the love of God, having our perception shaped in line with that love, and learning to attend to all around us in a manner which is itself increasingly that of love. Seeing with the eyes of love leads to acting with the heart and mind of love, in integrated initiative and response. We find ourselves both welcomed into the flowing dance of life, the meal and celebration of the divine wedding feast, and also privileged to be sharing that welcome with others. In all of this, God is the source, the creator, the sustainer. And as we discover ourselves, together, being loved into ever greater fullness of life, so we find ourselves living into ever greater fullness of a love beyond our imagining.

Questions for reflection

1 When setting out on a new venture, how much do you tend to want a clear endpoint in advance?
2 Which of the parts of this chapter struck you as particularly pertinent? What would be a good next step for you?
3 How do you tend to find the experience, when appropriate, of embracing tension, rather than seeking to resolve it?
4 David Sims offers the term 'loving into life'. Can you think of people who embody such an approach? To what extent would others say that you already love a group or church into life?
5 What has been most significant for you in reading this book?

Notes

1 John V. Taylor put it very well, more than 50 years ago: 'We have immeasurably extended our gift of sight, but not of insight. For that we have the same equipment as the eighth-century prophets. Potentially the same, but actually far poorer, for while we have been so busy extending one aspect of the knowing and telling self, we have allowed other aspects to atrophy. *We have built ourselves up into powerful transmitting stations, but as receiving sets we are feeble.*' John Vernon Taylor, 1992, *The Christlike God*, London: SCM Press, p. 69, emphasis added.

2 The moral philosopher Iris Murdoch wrote of the power of attention, describing it as 'accurate vision which, when this becomes appropriate, occasions action'. Iris Murdoch, 1970, *The Sovereignty of Good*, London: Routledge, p. 66, quoted in Andrew Louth, 1989, *Discerning the Mystery: An Essay on the Nature of Theology*, Oxford: Clarendon Press, p. 142.

3 David Ford, 2008, *Self and Salvation: Being Transformed*, Cambridge: Cambridge University Press, p. 21.

4 John Welwood, 2014, *Toward a Psychology of Awakening: Buddhism, Psychotherapy, and the Path of Personal and Spiritual Transformation*, Boston, MA: Shambhala Publications.

5 When I seek to describe this aspect of personal formation, I normally refer to it as psycho-spiritual growth, maturing or flourishing.

6 Joanna Collicutt, 2015, *The Psychology of Christian Character Formation*, London: SCM Press.

7 Such models can, of course, also be used unhelpfully: overly simplistically and/or to 'pigeonhole' people.

8 For an engaging and insightful exploration of the topic overall, I have found very helpful Douglas Stone and Sheila Heen, 2014, *Thanks for the Feedback: The Science and Art of Receiving Feedback Well*, London: Penguin.

9 It was my personal experience, as a recipient, of the power of both pastoral supervision and coaching that led me to train and gain accreditation in both disciplines.

10 See, for instance, Jo Whitehead, Sally Nash and Simon Sutcliffe, 2013, *Facilitation Skills for Ministry*, London: SPCK; Myrna Lewis with Jennifer Woodhull, 2018, *Inside the NO: Five Steps to Decisions That Last*, Deep Democracy USA; William Isaacs, 1999, *Dialogue: A Pioneering Approach to Communicating in Business and in Life*, New York: Doubleday.

11 See, for instance, https://www.churchofengland.org/about/vision-strategy/our-priorities, accessed 21.05.2025.

12 Michael Ramsey, 1985, *The Christian Priest Today*, London: SPCK, p. 23.

13 Lewis with Woodhull, *Inside the NO*.

14 The desire for a watertight definition is often linked to the deployment of a measurable objective.

15 Relevant resources include: Tim Slack and Fiona Thomas, 2017, *Appreciating Church: A Practical Appreciative Inquiry Resource for Church Communities*, Liverpool: Wordscapes; www.appreciating.church; www.aipractitioner.com, accessed 21.05.2025.

16 See, for instance, https://www.chelmsford.anglican.org/support-for-min isters/community-organising/what-is-community-organising, accessed 21.05.2025.

17 Patrick Keifert, 2006, *We Are Here Now: A New Missional Era, a Missional Journey of Spiritual Discovery*, Eagle, ID: Allelon Publishing.

18 See, further, Mats Alvesson and Hugh Willmott, 2001, *Making Sense of Management: A Critical Introduction*, London: Sage Publications, pp. 129–37.

19 As is the case with quantum mechanics, according to Heisenberg's Uncertainty Principle.

20 Iain McGilchrist, 2009, *The Master and His Emissary: The Divided Brain and the Making of the Western World*, New Haven, CT: Yale University Press, p. 181.

21 Roy M. Oswald and Barry Allan Johnson, 2010, *Managing Polarities in Congregations: Eight Keys for Thriving Faith Communities*, Herndon, VA: Alban Institute.

22 See, for instance, Samuel Wells, 2015, *A Nazareth Manifesto: Being with God*, Chichester: John Wiley & Sons Inc; 2018, *Incarnational Mission: Being with the World*, Norwich: Canterbury Press.

23 Al Barrett and Ruth Harley, 2020, *Being Interrupted: Reimagining the Church's Mission From the Outside, In*, London: SCM Press.

24 Mike Starkey, 2011, *Ministry Rediscovered: Shaping a Unique and Creative Church*, Abingdon: BRF.

25 Vaughan S. Roberts and David Sims, 2017, *Leading by Story: Rethinking Church Leadership*, London: SCM Press.

26 Michael Sadgrove, 2008, *Wisdom and Ministry: The Call to Leadership*, London: SPCK.

27 David Runcorn, 2011, *Fear and Trust: God-centred Leadership*, London: SPCK.

28 John Pritchard, 2007, *The Life and Work of a Priest*, London: SPCK; Alan Bartlett, 2019, *Vicar: Celebrating the Renewal of Parish Ministry*, London: SPCK; Emma Ineson, 2019, *Ambition: What Jesus Said about Power, Success and Counting Stuff*, London: SPCK.

29 Ineson, *Ambition*, pp. 53–89.

30 Erich Fromm, 1985, *The Art of Loving*, London: Mandala, p. 9.

31 David Sims, 2004, 'The Velveteen Rabbit and Passionate Feelings for Organizations', in Y. Gabriel (ed.), *Myths, Stories and Organizations: Pre-modern Narratives for our Times*, Oxford: Oxford University Press, pp. 209–22, p. 210.

32 Sims, 'The Velveteen Rabbit', p. 211.

33 Sims, 'The Velveteen Rabbit', p. 210.

34 Sims, 'The Velveteen Rabbit', p. 216.

Bibliography and Further Reading

Alvesson, Mats and Hugh Willmott, 2001, *Making Sense of Management: A Critical Introduction*, Reprint, London: Sage Publications.

Badenoch, Bonnie, see www.nurturingtheheart.com, accessed 21.05.2025.

Barrett, Al and Ruth Harley, 2020, *Being Interrupted: Reimagining the Church's Mission from the Outside, In*, London: SCM Press.

Bartlett, Alan, 2019, *Vicar: Celebrating the Renewal of Parish Ministry*, London: SPCK.

Bauckham, Richard, 2003, 'Reading Scripture as a coherent story', in E. F. Davis and R. B. Hays, eds, *The Art of Reading Scripture*, Grand Rapids, MI: William B. Eerdmans, pp. 38–53.

Beasley-Murray, Paul, 1995, *A Call to Excellence: An Essential Guide to Christian Leadership*, London: Hodder & Stoughton.

Begbie, Jeremy, 2000, *Theology, Music and Time*, Reprint, Cambridge Studies in Christian Doctrine 4, Cambridge: Cambridge University Press.

Bosch, David Jacobus, 1991, *Transforming Mission: Paradigm Shifts in Theology of Mission*, American Society of Missiology Series, no. 16, Maryknoll, NY: Orbis Books.

Bourgeault, Cynthia, 2008, *The Wisdom Jesus: Transforming Heart and Mind – A New Perspective on Christ and His Message*, Boston, MA: Shambhala Publications.

Buber, Martin, 2023, *I and Thou*, Walter Kaufmann (trans.), paperback reissue, New York: Free Press.

Buxton, Graham, 2016, *Dancing in the Dark: The Privilege of Participating in God's Ministry in the World*, rev. edn, Eugene, OR: Cascade Books.

Cherry, Stephen, 2012, *Beyond Busyness: Time Wisdom for Ministry*, 1st edn, Durham: Sacristy Press.

Cocksworth, Christopher, 2014, *Seeing Jesus and Being Seen by Him*, London: SPCK.

Collicutt, Joanna, 2015, *The Psychology of Christian Character Formation*, London: SCM Press.

Croft, Steven J. L., 2008, *Ministry in Three Dimensions: Ordination and Leadership in the Local Church*, new edn, London: Darton, Longman & Todd.

Damasio, Antonio R., 1994, *Descartes' Error: Emotion, Reason and the Human Brain*, New York: Penguin Books.

Davison, Andrew, 2019, *Participation in God: A Study in Christian Doctrine and Metaphysics*, Cambridge: Cambridge University Press.

Evans, Pippa, 2021, *Improv Your Life: An Improviser's Guide to Embracing Whatever Life Throws at You*, London: Hodder & Stoughton.
Fairclough, Norman, 2013, *Critical Discourse Analysis: The Critical Study of Language*, 2nd edn, London: Routledge.
Finney, John, 1989, *Understanding Leadership*, London: Darton, Longman & Todd.
Ford, David F., 2007, *Christian Wisdom: Desiring God and Learning in Love*, Cambridge Studies in Christian Doctrine 16, Cambridge: Cambridge University Press.
——, 2008, *Self and Salvation: Being Transformed*, Cambridge Studies in Christian Doctrine 1, Cambridge: Cambridge University Press.
——, 2014, *The Drama of Living: Becoming Wise in the Spirit*, Norwich: Canterbury Press.
——, 2021, *The Gospel of John: A Theological Commentary*, Grand Rapids, MI: Baker Academic.
Fromm, Erich, 1985, *The Art of Loving*, London: Mandala.
Garvey Berger, Jennifer, 2012, *Changing on the Job: Developing Leaders for a Complex World*, Stanford, CA: Stanford University Press.
Gibbs, Eddie, 1990, *I Believe in Church Growth*, London: Hodder & Stoughton.
Grint, Keith, 2005, *Leadership: Limits and Possibilities*, Management, Work and Organisations, Basingstoke: Palgrave Macmillan.
Hardy, Daniel W. and David Ford, 1985, *Praising and Knowing God*, 1st US edn, Philadelphia, PA: Westminster Press.
Hybels, Bill, 2002, *Courageous Leadership*, Grand Rapids, MI: Zondervan.
Ineson, Emma, 2019, *Ambition: What Jesus Said about Power, Success and Counting Stuff*, London: SPCK.
Ireland, Mark and Chew, Mike, 2009, *How to Do Mission Action Planning: A Vision-centred Approach*, 1st edn, London: SPCK.
——, 2016, *How to Do Mission Action Planning: Prayer, Process and Practice*, rev. and expanded 2nd edn, London: SPCK.
Isaacs, William, 1999, *Dialogue: A Pioneering Approach to Communicating in Business and in Life*, New York: Doubleday.
Jackson, Bob, 2002, *Hope for the Church: Contemporary Strategies for Growth*, Explorations, London: Church House Publishing.
——, 2005, *The Road to Growth: Towards a Thriving Church*, Explorations, London: Church House Publishing.
Kegan, Robert, 1997, *In Over Our Heads: The Mental Demands of Modern Life*, Cambridge, MA: Harvard University Press.
Keifert, Patrick R., 2006, *We Are Here Now: A New Missional Era, a Missional Journey of Spiritual Discovery*, Eagle, ID: Allelon Publishing.
Koyama, Kosuke, 2021, *Three Mile an Hour God*, London: SCM Press.
Kuhn, Thomas, 1962, *The Structure of Scientific Revolutions*, Chicago, IL: University of Chicago Press.
Lawrence, James, 2004, *Growing Leaders: Reflections on Leadership, Life and Jesus*, Oxford: BRF.
Lewis, Myrna with Jennifer Woodhull, 2018, *Inside the NO: Five Steps to Decisions That Last*, Deep Democracy USA.

Louth, Andrew, 1989, *Discerning the Mystery: An Essay on the Nature of Theology*, Oxford: Clarendon Press.
McFadyen, Alistair I., 1990, *The Call to Personhood: A Christian Theory of the Individual in Social Relationships*, Cambridge: Cambridge University Press.
McGavran, Donald, 1955, *The Bridges of God: A Study in the Strategy of Missions*, London: World Dominion Press.
McGilchrist, Iain, 2009, *The Master and His Emissary: The Divided Brain and the Making of the Western World*, New Haven, CT: Yale University Press.
———, 2021, *The Matter With Things*, London: Perspectiva Press.
Murdoch, Iris, 1970, *The Sovereignty of Good*, London: Routledge.
Oswald, Roy M. and Barry Allan Johnson, 2010, *Managing Polarities in Congregations: Eight Keys for Thriving Faith Communities*, Herndon, VA: Alban Institute.
Percy, Martyn, 1998, *Power and the Church: Ecclesiology in an Age of Transition*, Washington: Cassell.
Perry, John, 1983, *Christian Leadership*, London: Hodder & Stoughton.
Pickard, Stephen K., 2012, *Seeking the Church: An Introduction to Ecclesiology*, London: SCM Press.
Plyming, Philip, 2023, *Being Real*, London: SCM Press.
Pritchard, John, 2007, *The Life and Work of a Priest*, London: SPCK.
Pytches, David, 1998, *Leadership for New Life*, London: Hodder & Stoughton.
Ramsey, Michael, 1985, *The Christian Priest Today*, new rev. edn, London: SPCK.
Roberts, Vaughan S. and David Sims, 2017, *Leading by Story: Rethinking Church Leadership*, London: SCM Press.
Rosa, Hartmut, 2019, *Resonance: A Sociology of Our Relationship to the World*, trans. James C. Wagner, Cambridge, UK and Medford, MA: Polity Press.
———, trans. James C. Wagner, 2020, *The Uncontrollability of the World*, Cambridge, UK and Medford, MA: Polity Press.
Ross, Maggie, 2014, *Silence: A User's Guide: Volume 1: Process*, London: Darton, Longman & Todd.
———, 2011, *Writing the Icon of the Heart: In Silence Beholding*, Abingdon: BRF.
Runcorn, David, 2011, *Fear and Trust: God-centred Leadership*, London: SPCK.
Sadgrove, Michael, 2008, *Wisdom and Ministry: The Call to Leadership*, London: SPCK.
Slack, Tim and Fiona Thomas, 2017, *Appreciating Church: A Practical Appreciative Inquiry Resource for Church Communities*, Liverpool: Wordscapes.
Starkey, Mike, 2011, *Ministry Rediscovered: Shaping a Unique and Creative Church*, Abingdon: BRF.
Stone, Douglas and Sheila Heen, 2014, *Thanks for the Feedback: The Science and Art of Receiving Feedback Well*, London: Penguin.
Taylor, John Vernon, 1992, *The Christlike God*, London: SCM Press.
The Church as Communion report, https://www.anglicancommunion.org/media/105242/ARCIC_II_The_Church_as_Communion.pdf, accessed 21.05.2025.
Tillich, Paul, 1960, *Love, Power, and Justice: Ontological Analyses and Ethical Applications*, Oxford: Oxford University Press.

Wagner, C. Peter, 1976, *Your Church Can Grow: Seven Vital Signs of a Healthy Church*, Ventura, CA: Regal Books.
Wakefield, Gavin, 2006, *Conversion Today*, Cambridge: Grove Books.
Wells, Samuel, 2004, *Improvisation: The Drama of Christian Ethics*, London: SPCK.
———, 2015, *A Nazareth Manifesto: Being With God*, Chichester: John Wiley & Sons Inc.
———, 2017, *Incarnational Mission: Being with the World*, Norwich: Canterbury Press.
Welwood, John, 2014, *Toward a Psychology of Awakening: Buddhism, Psychotherapy, and the Path of Personal and Spiritual Transformation*, Boston, MA: Shambhala.
Western, Simon, 2008, *Leadership: A Critical Text*, Los Angeles, CA: Sage Publications.
White, Dominic, 2020, *How Do I Look? Theology in the Age of the Selfie*, London: SCM Press.
Whitehead, Jo, Sally Nash and Simon Sutcliffe, 2013, *Facilitation Skills for Ministry*, New York: SPCK.
Williams, Richard and Mark Tanner, 2004, *Developing Visionary Leadership*, Cambridge: Grove Books.
Williams, Rowan, 2018, *Being Human: Bodies, Minds, Persons*, London: SPCK.
Wink, Walter, 1992, *Engaging the Powers: Discernment and Resistance in a World of Domination*, Minneapolis, MN: Fortress Press.

Index

Ambition: What Jesus Said about Power, Success and Counting Stuff (Ineson) 119–22
animate systems 89
anomalies, and Church SLD 123–6
attention 20–2, 157–8, 176, 181–2
　dimensions and directions of 160–1
　and hemisphere relating 56–7
　and imagination 84–5
　and improvisation 138
　and Jesus 101
　and responsive attunement 149
Augustine, Saint 96
awareness, and improvisation 164

Barrett, Al 178
Bauckham, Richard 104
Begbie, Jeremy, *Theology, Music and Time* 131, 135, 136, 138, 139, 146–7, 148
Bible
　adultery 150–3
　Holistic RH response to God 95
　and improvisations 148
　life/ministry of Jesus 102
　nature of the Church 104
　simplified maps in 96

structure and plans 99
trust 103
truth and depth 99, 125
Bosch, David 104
Bourgeault, Cynthia 85
brain hemispheres 13–15, 17–19
　and Church SLD 109–17
　and theology 95–106
　see also Clear-cut LH; Holistic RH; interaction, hemisphere
breadth, and the Holistic RH 46
Buber, Martin 22

categories
　and the Holistic RH 48–9
　and simplified maps 33–4
ceilidh example 76–8
certainty 172–3
chaffinch cameo 1–2, 4–5, 176
　and McGilchrist's hemisphere hypothesis 21
change, and simplified mapping 35–8
Chew, Mike 112–13
　How To Do Mission Action Planning 110, 117, 122
Christian Priest Today, The (Ramsey) 109
Church, nature of the 104–5, 115–17
Church as Communion 104–5

Church Strategic Leadership
  Discourse (SLD) 6, 19, 109–17
  and the Godly Leadership
    Course 177–8
  ministerial writing on 178–9
  practice of Clear-cut 117–26
clear contexts/domains 88–9
Clear-cut LH 18, 21–2, 158,
    159–60, 163, 176
  and Church SLD 124, 126,
    177–8, 179
  and contexts 89
  and fact-focused knowing 24–5
  and imagination 84
  and improvisation 143–4, 145,
    147, 152, 167
  and the life of Jesus 101
  and love 183
  and structures 100
  and truth 98–9
  see also interaction, hemisphere;
    simplified maps
Clear-cut mode 4–5
communion, Church as 105
complex contexts 89, 90
complicated contexts/domains 89
connections, and Clear-cut LH
  38–9
consistency, and Clear-cut LH 39
constructedness, of simplified
  maps 32
contexts 88–9, 181
  and the Holistic RH 47
contrast 146–7, 167–8, 176–7,
  183–4
control
  and Church SLD 120, 121
  and Jesus 102
  and simplified mapping 35–8
culture 65–72, 127

Damasio, Antonio 45
Davis, Miles 137
depth 98
  and the Holistic RH 48, 159
desire 118, 150, 163
diagram, Western history 67
discerning incorporation 149–50,
  158, 180
discernment 169–70, 181
discourse (term) 90–2
dispositions of improvisation
  148–50, 158, 163
Drama Triangle, Karpman's 162

EEG recordings 15
emotions 170
  and the human face 49–50
Enlightenment 67, 70–1
epilepsy 14–15
extrinsic motivation 168–9

face, the human 49–50, 159
fact-focused knowing 24–5, 39
faithfulness 98
feedback 163
Feeney, Damian 117–18, 136,
  158
flexibility, and the Holistic RH
  46–7
flow 140–1, 173
flowing dance of life metaphor
  76–8
focus, and the Church SLD
  112–13
Ford, David 98, 100, 103, 159
foretaste, Church as 104, 105
Fromm, Erich 182

generous receptivity 135–6, 149,
  181

gifts/giving 135–6, 158
givens 136
God, improvisation with 180–1
Godly Leadership course 7–8, 177–8
good/bad hemispheres 55–6
grace 138, 153, 158
grace and truth 101, 105, 138, 148, 151, 158, 160, 181
Greece, Ancient 67, 68, 69
growing in fullness of vision 161–4

Hardy, Dan 100
Harley, Ruth 178
hemisphere interaction 55–6, 61–2, 73–8
  meal example 56–9
  preserve and transform 59–60
  skewed 62–6
  and Western history 66–73
hemispheres *see* brain hemispheres
Heraclitus 155n24
Holistic mode 5–6
Holistic RH 45–52, 159, 163
  aspects 46–51
  and Church SLD 112, 119, 123–4
  and improvisation 143, 144, 147, 149, 152, 176
  integration 180
  and love 183
  and McGilchrist 18, 21–2
  and MAP 119
  and the nature of the Church 105
  and personal knowing 23–4, 25
  and recent ministerial writing 178
  and simplified maps 33
  and theology 95–6
  and trust 103–4
  and truth 99
  see also hemisphere interaction
Holistic wisdom 62
How To Do Mission Action Planning (Chew and Ireland) 110, 112–13, 117, 122
human face, and emotions 49–50, 159

imagination 84–5, 159
  and Jesus 101
Improvisation: The Drama of Christian Ethics (Wells) 131
improvisation 131–2, 153–4, 164–70, 171, 176–7, 180
  and brain hemispheres 143–7
  dispositions of 148–50
  features 132–43
  forms of 142–3
  gifts and giving 135–6
  with God 180–1
  and Jesus 150–3
  and McGilchrist 143–7
  spaciousness 136–8
  and time 139
  timescales 141–2
  and tradition 147–8
  unfolding and flow 140–1
Industrial Revolution 67, 72
Ineson, Emma 179
  Ambition 119–22
instrument, Church as 104, 105
integration 179–80
  and the Holistic RH 47
interplay 146–7, 161, 167–8, 183–4
intrinsic motivation 168–9

intuition 86–7
Ireland, Mark, *How To Do Mission Action Planning* 110, 112–13, 117, 122
I-it/I-thou 22, 125, 168

Jesus
  and improvisation 150–3
  life and ministry 101–3
Johnstone, Keith 131, 135
journey metaphor 112

Karpman's Drama Triangle 162
knowing/knowledge 23, 26
  fact-focused 24–5
  personal knowing 23–4, 25

Lavelle, Louis 182
left handedness 28n8
limitations, simplified maps 41–2
Linear Logic 17
loving unto life 182–4

McFadyen, Alistair 137
McGilchrist, Iain 81–3, 175
  The Master and His Emissary 8–9, 18–19, 20, 21–2, 55, 73
  hemisphere interaction 66–73, 73–8
  The Matter With Things 19, 83–7
  biography 16
  and improvisation 131, 143–7
  primary question 17–19
  and simplified mapping 34, 35, 41, 73
manner in which *see* Holistic mode
maps, simplified *see* simplified maps

Master and His Emissary, The (McGilchrist) 8–9, 18–19, 20, 21–2, 55, 73
  hemisphere interaction 66–73, 73–8
Matter With Things, The (McGilchrist) 19, 83–7
meal example, hemisphere interaction 56–9, 143–4
measures/measurement 174–5, 179
Mission Action Planning 110–11, 113
  example of 117–18
models, and Clear-cut LH 38
Modern/Post-Modern worlds 67, 72
motivation 168–9, 170
mountain of achievement metaphor 74–5, 78
Murdoch, Iris 185n2
music 105
mutual enhancement 83, 146–7, 161, 167–8, 176, 183–4

narrative, and Holistic RH 51
nature of the Church 104–5, 115–17
neuroimaging 15
the new, and the Holistic RH 46
nine nuggets 170–6

optimism, and Church SLD 113–14
overaccepting 135–6, 136, 138, 149, 158

paired responsibility 118
personal knowing 23–4, 25
Pickard, Stephen 102

plans 99–100
  and improvisation 132–3, 143, 171
Plyming, Philip 107n7
positivity, and Church SLD 113–14
predictability 39
  and Church SLD 121–2
  and the Holistic RH 46–7
prediction 121–2
preserve and transform 57, 59–60, 61, 166, 168
punctuated processes 87–9
purposefulness, and simplified mapping 35–8

QALYs (Quality Adjusted Life Years) 39–40

Radcliffe, Timothy 182
Ramsey, Michael 168
  The Christian Priest Today 109
rationality 71
reason 71, 84–5
receptivity, generous 135–6, 149, 181
reflective practice 169
Reformation 67, 70
Renaissance 67, 68, 70
responsive attunement 149, 158, 181
Roberts, Vaughan S. 179
Roman Empire 67, 68, 69–70
Romanticism 67, 71
Rosa, Hartmut 89
Ross, Maggie 97
rule of life 97
Runcorn, David 179

Sadgrove, Michael 179

Salk, Jonas 86
scepticism, LH 62–3
self-awareness 35, 37, 118
self-presence 164–5
separation, and simplified maps 34
shorthand labels 172
sign, Church as 104, 105
simplified maps 30–1, 159, 162
  constructing 32–4
  examples and uses 31–2
  models/connections/consistency 38–40
  purpose/change/control 35–8
  relating to 35
  strengths/limitations/strategically reduced vision 41–2
  and theology 96–7
Sims, David 179, 182–4
SLD *see* Church Strategic Leadership Discourse (SLD)
SMART objectives 112–13, 114, 119, 167
Snowden, Dave 88–90, 126
Solzhenitsyn, Aleksandr 85
spaciousness 158, 182
  and improvisation 136–8
spiritual bypassing 163
Starkey, Mike 178–9
Strategic Development Funding 111
Strategic Leadership Discourse *see* Church Strategic Leadership Discourse (SLD)
strategically reduced vision 42
strategy/strategic, language 173–4
strengths, simplified maps 41
structure 99–100, 173
sufficient 172

symbols, and the Holistic RH 48

Taylor, John V. 185n1
Ten Commandments 96
tension 176
 and improvisation 144–6
theology, and the hemispheres 95–106
Theology, Music and Time (Begbie) 131, 135, 136, 138, 139, 146–7, 148
thought, flexibility of 46–7
Tillich, Paul 182
time 50–1, 88–9, 126
 and improvisation 139, 141–2
tradition, and improvisation 147–8
trust 102–4
 and improvisation 136–7, 165
 trusting courage 150
truth and grace 101, 105, 138, 148, 151, 158, 160, 181

unfolding 140–1

Velveteen Rabbit, The (Williams) 182–3
vocabulary 172

Wagner, Peter, *Your Church Can Grow* 109–10
Wakefield, Gavin 87–8
Wells, Samuel 147–8, 178
 Improvisation 131
Welwood, John 161–2
Western history 66–73
what is done *see* Clear-cut mode
Wink, Walter 107n11
wisdom, Holistic 62
Wordsworth, William 71
writing, ministerial 178–9

Your Church Can Grow (Wagner) 109–10

www.ingramcontent.com/pod-product-compliance
Lightning Source LLC
Chambersburg PA
CBHW021948290426
44108CB00012B/990